*The Ponte Vecchio*
COURTESY OF ALINARI

# The Man Who Saved Florence

DAVID TUTAEV

# *The Man Who Saved Florence*

COWARD-McCANN, Inc.
New York

FIRST AMERICAN EDITION 1967



*Library of Congress Catalog*
*Card Number: 67-28437*

PRINTED IN THE UNITED STATES OF AMERICA

# CONTENTS

To David, Christopher
and Mary

ACKNOWLEDGEMENTS

If the list of those persons to whom special thanks must be given is unconscionably long, it is because this book is the work of many hands and minds. They have been godparents and jurors combined, and it would be inexcusable on my part to dismiss them with the reminder that they are absolved from such service for the remainder of their lives, since they themselves may wish to pronounce their verdict on this book for whose errors and omissions they cannot be blamed. Everyone of them gave me much time in lengthy discussions, followed by lengthier correspondence, as well as provided me with documents, letters and diaries.

I owe an especial debt of gratitude to Professor Giorgio La Pira, until recently Mayor of Florence, for permission to quote his citation which appears as the Prologue; to Avv. Luigi Boniforti, sometime President of the Tuscan Liberation Committee whose tribute to the Consul provided the title to this book; to Dr Hanna Kiel, one of the Consul's closest friends, and to Dr Hans Wildt and Dr Erich Poppe who worked with him in the consulate in Florence, as well as to the Consul's private secretary Fräulein Maria Faltien.

Dr Riccardo Gizdulich, a member of the Tuscan Resistance, and one of the leading architects responsible for the reconstruction of the Ponte Santa Trinita, provided me with much valuable material. The Marchese Filippo Serlupi Crescenzi and Marchesa Serlupi who sheltered Bernard Berenson in their villa of Le Fontanelle at Careggi gave me a full account of Berenson's meeting with the Consul, as did Miss Nicky Mariano, Berenson's collaborator, who also gave me permission to quote from her diary.

My special thanks are due to Signor Jean Léon Steinhäuslin for the loan of his late father's private diary, photographs and other documents. Signora Maria Comberti and Avv. Gaetano

Casoni allowed me to quote from their diaries, for which I am most grateful.

Others whom I consulted were Mr F. W. Hartt, the Chairman of the Department of Art, University of Pennsylvania from whose book *Florentine Art Under Fire* (Princeton University Press, 1949) I have quoted; Dr Ugo Procacci, the Superintendent of Monuments of the Tuscan Provinces, as well as Professor Dr Ernst Heinitz, Rector of the Free University of Berlin, and Dr Ulrich Middeldorf, the director of the *Kunsthistorisches Institut* in Florence, all of whom helped me with much sage advice.

Among the members of the Tuscan Resistance on whose experiences I have drawn, I wish to express my warm thanks to Cav. Ferdinando Pretini who not only provided me with valuable personal papers, but relived some of the more gruelling episodes of the Resistance of which he was such an exemplary figure. Both Professor Carlo Frankovich, the director of the *Istituto Storico della Resistenza in Toscana* and Signor Enzo Enriques Agnoletti, Editor of *Il Ponte*, also gave useful advice and assistance in elucidating certain phases of the Resistance in which they were prominent members. Others who gave contributory evidence were Donna Beatrice Viganò, Miss Gladys Hutton, Miss Gladys M. Elliot, as well as Maestro Vittorio Gui, the founder of the *Maggio Musicale* and the Philharmonic Orchestra of Florence.

I am especially indebted to Dr Rudolf Rahn, the last wartime German Ambassador in Italy for his unfailing courtesy and help in answering the questionnaires with which he was assailed over many months. Two former German Ambassadors in London, Baron Hans von Herwarth and Baron Hasso von Etzdorf also provided valuable assistance. The Press Departments of the German and Italian Embassies in London greatly facilitated my visits to Italy and Germany. In particular, I wish to express my thanks to Signor M. de Mandato, the Italian Press Attaché and to Dr H. Scherer the German Press Attaché as well as his associates, Baron Rudolf von Pachelbel, Dr C. Huebener, Dr H. Schneppen, and Dr Tilemann Stelzenmüller; to the director of R.A.I.

in Florence and the senior reporter Dr Paolo Belucci, who helped me with numerous interviews in Florence.

General Sir Oliver Leese, K.C.B., C.B., C.B.E., D.S.O., the commander of the British Eighth Army whose XIII Corps liberated Florence in August 1944 gave me much useful information regarding the Battle for Florence, as did General Sir Terence Airey, K.C.M.G., C.B., C.B.E., chief of Intelligence at Allied Headquarters Italy, later Acting Deputy Supreme Commander. The inferences drawn from this material and such errors as may have appeared, belong to the author.

The chief librarians and their assistants at the Wiener Library, the Italian Institute, and the Royal Institute of International Affairs, Chatham House, proved to be invaluable guides and mentors on whose patience I lent heavily in borrowing books which became long overdue. I should like to acknowledge my appreciation for the help given by Mrs I. Wolff, the chief librarian, and Dr F. Hajek of the Wiener Library and to Mr Wilbur J. Nigh of the National Archives and Records Service in Washington, D.C.

I should like to express my thanks to Mrs Petronella Hoskyns-Abrahall for the preparation of the text; to Mrs Antonia Holland, Miss Angela Nessim and Miss Renata Hornstein, who worked on German and Italian documents, and particularly to Mr Henry Walton who was responsible for the draft of the Consul's correspondence. The largest debt of all belongs to Dr Eugen Haas and to Dr Klaus Heilmann both of whom helped to prepare material for this book, also to Miss Helen Belikov, my collaborator in the preparatory stages, who took the road to Florence and Fiesole in the voyage of discovery which culminated in this book.

The primary sources as indicated in the Foreword have been the unpublished letters and documents supplied to the author by Dr Gerhard Wolf and others, as well as recorded testimonies taken in Florence. Other bibliographical material will be found in the Notes. The author and publisher would like to thank the publishers of the listed works for permission to quote.

# FOREWORD

The subject of this study is a Dr Gerhard Wolf, a public servant of the Third Reich and a seeming Nazi who received the Freedom of the City of Florence for services to humanity performed at great personal risk during his incumbency as German Consul in Florence from 1940 to 1944. The concatenation of time, place and circumstance, joined to the somewhat startling fact that a member of Ribbentrop's Foreign Ministry should have received such a singular distinction, proved sufficiently irresistible for me to pursue a labour which has stretched over many years.

For the reader, who like myself only reads the author's preface when he has completed a book, some word of explanation about the author's intention and approach may not come amiss. Let me say at the outset that unbounded as I was by any ties of kinship or language, I knew the Germans only from the receiving end of a cannon, or in less apocryphal terms, at the receiving end of the V.1 and V.2 flying bombs. And the little I knew about them I did not like.

Florence itself was little more than a series of picture postcards sent by holidaying friends, supplemented by reading the Brownings and Landor. This amount of information was all the equipment I could bring to my task which began in the autumn of 1959 when my eye caught the following paragraph in Mary McCarthy's beautifully illustrated and sonorous book *The Stones of Florence*:

"The chief arm of the S.S. was a Florentine devil strangely named 'Carità', who acted as both informer and torturer; against the S.S., the chief defence was the German consul, who used his official position to save people who had been denounced. After the Liberation, the consul was given the freedom of the city, in recognition of the risky work he had done."

I took this challenging statement to the Wiener Library in London for verification, and was not altogether surprised that information about this German consul was scanty. The little that was known was contained in two press-cuttings from the German illustrated magazine *Der Tagesspiegel* (Numbers 22 and 23, 1955.), but the facts themselves were so moving that the chief librarian, Miss I. Wolff, who assisted me with the translations, was in tears by the time we had finished our labours. Sudden and unexpected goodness among one's former enemies is a paradox to which all of us, at one time or another, may be exposed. It is also something which must be survived.

In the late autumn of 1960, I journeyed to Florence where after some difficulty I tracked down the elusive Mayor of the city, Professor Giorgio La Pira, who told me: "I had the good fortune and happiness to know Consul Wolf, because he became a living symbol of human courage and fraternity to us here in Florence. In doing what he did, Consul Wolf rendered a great service to his country, that is to say to the real Germany (*la vera Germania*) and not Nazi Germany."

From the recordings which I brought back with me from Florence, I wrote and devised a radio programme, produced by John Tusa (B.B.C. Home Service, December 12th 1961). Much of the evidence gathered in these recordings has appeared in the text of this book although the opinions and conclusions which I reached can in no way be imputed to the British Broadcasting Corporation, whom I thank for permission to use this material.

Parallel with this research I began to look into the origins and development of the German Resistance which later appeared as a radio programme ("The Germans of the Resistance", B.B.C. Home Service, July 12th 1962), also produced by John Tusa to whom I owe an especial debt of thanks.

Although I had gathered many facts for the subject of this book, the idea that somewhere in the dark night of totalitarianism men not only watched and prayed, but acted against the dictates of their monstrous Government, still seemed a legend which every defeated people must re-create for itself if it is to discover its self-respect. I had read a score of memoires, apologias and all those attestations of good faith which streamed from the pens of the partially-innocent and the partially-guilty. Truth died a martyr to "good" Germans just as justice and mercy had died in the face of the "bad" ones. An outspoken young German journalist, Klaus Happrecht has put this more succinctly when he stated that, "After the war every journalist claimed to have written between the lines. Everybody who had not actively supported the Nazis, after 1945 found he had secretly opposed them. Omissions were inflated into deeds of heroic defiance. Nobody admitted to the sort of life ordinary folks live under totalitarian régimes."

The former German consul in Florence, I discovered at my first meeting with him in Munich 1961, where he had retired after serving as Consul-General in Pôrto Alegre in Brazil, made no attempt to exculpate himself: nor did he pretend that his omissions were cast in any heroic mould. He took no part in the numerous plots which existed to remove Hitler, nor was he involved in any grand scheme of national rejuvenation. He did, it is true, have tenuous but nevertheless real connections with some of the most active members of the German Resistance and he was kept fully informed in his "diplomatic backwater" of Florence of what was going on in Resistance circles. Like them, he was an opponent of the Government he had sworn to uphold, since he had made his ethical choice between treachery to despotism and loyalty to this undefinable *vera Germania* to which La Pira has referred. This and more will be found in the body of the book where the Consul's private letters and papers are frequently quoted. Source material unless otherwise annotated in the appendix is taken from these letters and from interviews with the Consul.

A word perhaps should be said about these letters and documents. The letters were essentially private, intended only for the eyes of his friend and protector Dr Rudolf Rahn, the last wartime German Ambassador in Italy. But since these letters may have been subjected to Gestapo scrutiny, they were sprinkled with protestations of "loyalty" and hopes for

Nazi Germany's victory. The Ambassador's answers, too, had this quota of "double thinking" which the specialist reader will recognise.

But it is on his actions rather than his words that the Consul's record in Florence must stand. And it is to these actions which I have devoted the closest research and documentation. As to the possible interpretation of the motives which led Dr Wolf to act as he did, I must leave the reader to make his own judgment, but the quality which I found most attractive in him and which finally endeared him to most Florentines, was that he possessed civic courage of a very high degree, the virtue of ordinary human decency which does not turn back on another man's need, but which requires patience, persistence and a deep regard for the human personality. Few people and fewer nations, least of all the Germans perhaps, have shown this quality to any high degree.

# The Man Who Saved Florence

# PROLOGUE

Your Excellency,

I have the honour of conveying to you, in the name of the Municipal Council of Florence, the following resolution, passed at its session of November 19th 1954:

the COUNCIL

bearing in mind the numerous recorded instances of meritorious actions carried out at constant risk to his own person by Dr Gerhard Wolf in his capacity of German Consul during the German Occupation of the city; and having agreed that such actions should receive a fitting tribute from the Community has

RESOLVED

that the Freedom of the City of Florence should be conferred on Dr Gerhard Wolf.

So now I have the honour of officially bestowing the Honorary Citizenship of the City of Florence upon Your Excellency.

Allow me to congratulate you most heartily and to make a few remarks suitable to the occasion.

Firstly, through the honour conferred on you, you have

become an integral part of this glorious and mysterious city which is itself one of the living centres of Christendom and civilisation. From now on you will be able to participate even more closely in this community of grace and culture, of art and beauty, peace and labour which constitute the external features of this city, a city considered by all peoples of the world as belonging to them also in some particular way, towards which they are drawn as to some ideal centre.

And secondly; Florence is not prodigal in conferring the Freedom of the City. It would not be difficult to enumerate the instances this honour has been bestowed, since such occasions require the commission of some act of conspicuous humanity, of cultural and historical significance.

In your case, Your Excellency, such acts of great spiritual and historical consequence have been fully demonstrated through your acts of incalculable courage, humanity, sense of brotherhood and Christian feeling, in one of the most tragic periods in the history of Florence, Italy and the world.

How shall I call to mind all that you did in those days of tribulation, Your Excellency? Shall I name all those whose deliverance is due to you, or describe the dramatic circumstances, happily resolved wherever possible, through your heroic intervention?

Certain pages can only be written by the hands of angels. These have been enscribed by angelic hands in the golden book in the City of God for all to read!

Through your efforts on behalf of the people of Florence, among them Florentines of Jewish origin, the most unjustly persecuted of all, you became part of the spirit and history of our city: by virtue of those actions you had already become an honorary citizen of Florence. The official bestowal of the Freedom of the City merely confirms what had already taken place in that period of Florence's history. Allow me to thank you once more for all that you have done. God Himself will render his thanks on the Great Day of Judgment. . . .

And, finally, Your Excellency, I come to the last reflection evoked by today's ceremony. I refer to the fellowship between nations and the significance of the City itself.

All men are brothers, children of one Heavenly Father, all peoples are of one inheritance. What is it that they all seek? Surely only that they should be left in peace, to continue their labours, to look after their families and to enjoy the fruits of liberty and culture.

Are they drawn to war with all its unspeakable horrors? You and, all who have experienced the untold terrors of the last war, know in our hearts the inestimable benefit of peace and concord.

We were created to love one another, to develop our spiritual and physical resources, to create a civilisation based on goodwill and fellowship.

We cannot be silent on such things today, Your Excellency, on an occasion which carries our thoughts back to the tragic and terrible events which we witnessed during the war.

Consider our cities, those mysterious cities whose very stones have been transmuted into Prayer and Beauty, where the habitations of man have become the House of God; these cities which in some sacramental sense God Himself helped to build.

Your Excellency, has anyone the right to eradicate these flourishing cities from the face of the earth? What generation can take it upon itself to squander this heritage of goodness and beauty accumulated through past ages for the benefit and enjoyment of mankind?

Such questions are bound to be on our lips and in our hearts at today's ceremony which has such depth of meaning for us. It is a true reminder to all peoples of the world to cherish their cities. Each city has its own particular atmosphere, its distinctive genius. Just as each of us has his own guardian angel, so each city has its own protector. No one has the right to bring violence and destruction upon them! Can one imagine what it would have meant to the history of civilisation if Florence had disappeared from the face of the earth?

Your Excellency, I have come to the end of my address. Allow me to share some part of your happiness and to thank you once more for all that you did for our City.

May I express the heartfelt hope that today's ceremony will have some symbolic significance, both as an affirmation of the genuine and profound desire for peace on the part of all mankind and as an augury of the advancement and prosperity of all the cities of men. May they flourish in virtue, in peace, at work and in freedom under the care and loving protection of the Heavenly Father.

Citation given by the then Major of Florence, Professor Giorgio La Pira in the Sala Clemente VII of the Palazzo Vecchio on March 25th 1955.

# 1

# Neither Their Side, Nor Ours

> Florence has a mission in the world: it does not belong to Italy alone, but to all nations—because of its pure beauty, a beauty which most nearly resembles the Beauty of God himself.
>
> GIORGIO LA PIRA

A few months after Benito Mussolini had dragged his reluctant countrymen into the war on June 10th 1940, the autumnal rains struck Florence with unaccustomed ferocity, swelling the turbulent waters of the Arno, which had risen ominously under the bellies of its seven bridges. Ammannati's slender, three-span construction—the Ponte Santa Trinita—seemed to float like a bird on the surface of the heaving waters, while its immediate upstream neighbour, the ancient, humpbacked Ponte Vecchio, creaked and groaned on its heavy Roman foundations.

In a city where history is a daily preoccupation, the rising of the waters was likened to the great flood of 1557 which had swept away the old wooden Trinity bridge (it had been carried away twice in the space of one hundred years), compelling Cosimo I, the Grand Duke of Tuscany, to put an end to its shifting insecurity. Cosimo then entrusted the handsome sculptor-architect Bartolommeo Ammannati with the task of creating a lovelier and more enduring structure.

Begun on April 3rd 1567, the new Ponte Santa Trinita was completed two and a half years later on September 15th 1569. The bridge so delighted and stung the imagination of the Florentines that one of the city's chroniclers was moved to declare that Ammannati's masterpiece was "beautiful, insubstantial and free in space . . .", a description which has never been bettered, despite all the eulogies which were subsequently heaped on the Ponte Santa Trinita.

Thus for almost four centuries, the bridge named after the Holy Trinity stood as a serene guardian of Florence's greatness and inviolability, proof against the erosion of time, the Arno's incessant buffeting, the horrors of war and the enemy's malevolence, protected by its beauty and the transcendental majesty of its name.

In the autumn of 1940, when the outcome of the war was still uncertain, the fate of the Ponte Santa Trinita like the fate of Dr Friedrich Kriegbaum, the director of the *Kunsthistorisches Institut* (the German Art Institute), in Florence who stood contemplating the bridge's ghostly image in the wind-ruffled waters, was obscured by the mists of time.

Ever since his appointment in 1935, Kriegbaum, a tall, dark-haired man of thirty-nine, with finely-proportioned, sardonic features, had left his small bachelor apartment adjoining the Palazzo Guadagni, which housed the Institute, at precisely eight o'clock each morning for his rendezvous with the Ponte Santa Trinita. He would stop occasionally to chat with Oreste, the Institute's caretaker, or to exchange jokes with the fruit and vegetable stall-holders on the Piazza Santo Spirito where his Institute was located.

Kriegbaum was a greatly-admired if eccentric character, whose obsession with the Ponte Santa Trinita—"our bridge"—provided much innocent amusement for the more down-to-earth working-class citizens on the left bank of the Arno, one of whom showed an instinctive grasp of the young professor's quality when he said: "He loved the Ponte Santa Trinita and understood her. He understood holiness."

Friedrich Kriegbaum had seen the Ponte Santa Trinita in all moods and weathers, bending its triple sickles over the placid Arno at night when the moon was "lamping Samminiato"—as Browning phrased it in his poem *One Word More*—or in the deep ochre of a summer sunset when the Lungarni on both sides of the river seemed on fire, and the bridge, like a heron, appeared poised to take flight from the Arno's muddy shallows.

Kriegbaum had long been troubled by the seeming disparity between Ammannati's other architectural creations in Florence, such as the courtyard of the Pitti Palace, or the Giugni Palace and the simpler, dramatic "expression of opposing forces brought to explosive tension" found in the Ponte Santa Trinita, as one expert, Dr Riccardo Gizdulich, has put it.

Like Gizdulich, Kriegbaum had observed that the lexical elements in Michelangelo's work, as shown, for example, in the vestibule of the Laurentian Library with its enormous staircase which dominates and pervades the entire space, were never developed for purely decorative reasons, but were used "with precise consistency to accent or repeat a fundamental idea: to balance the sway of opposing forces[1]".

This was particularly noticeable in the mysterious "catenary" arches of the bridge—so called because of the free-swinging loop caused by a suspended chain—whose shapes were "completely revolutionary in occidental architecture", as Dr Gizdulich affirmed. The paper-thin arcs, or at least two of them, came to a fine point, deliberately obscured by heavy scrolls, whose tension was further subdued by a finely perforated parapet without which the bridge would appear to rise into the air, breaking away from the heavy solid abutments!

This theme of "contrapuntal forces" was quite alien to Ammannati's temperament (his idealised portrait by Bronzino may perhaps give some indication of this) and lay outside his particular architectural lexicon.

It was this intuitive grasp on Kriegbaum's part which led him to draw attention to a letter which Giorgio Vasari, court painter and architect wrote to his patron Cosimo I on April 8th 1560. In this letter Vasari stated: "I have been with Michelangelo every day and examined the plans of the Ponte Santa Trinita, on which we deliberated at great length and which bear testimony to the spirit of his writings and drawings, based on the measurements which I brought him from the site. . . .[2]"

Kriegbaum that "illustrious and learned German" had been the first to draw attention to Vasari's letter from which he concluded that it was Michelangelo's genius which had inspired the elegiac Ammannati, his pupil, to respect the "spirit of his writings and drawings" in the final blueprint of the bridge, which was completed some three years after Michelangelo's death. This conclusion was subsequently confirmed by one of Florence's leading art historians Carlo Ludovico Ragghianti, a prominent and fearless member of the Resistance. But perhaps more strangely the haunting "catenary" curve was later discovered—as Mary McCarthy has pertinently observed "where no one had thought of looking for it, in the Medici Tombs, on the sarcophagi that support the figures of Night and Day, Twilight and Dawn. Thus, if this argument is correct (and it has been widely accepted), a detail of a work of sculpture, done for the glorification of a despotic line in their private chapel, was translated outdoors and became the property of the whole Florentine people[3]."

Three years after Kriegbaum's appointment as director of the German Art Institute, Hitler, together with Mussolini and their respective Foreign Ministers, Ciano and Ribbentrop, arrived for a breakneck half-day tour of Florence. This was on May 9th 1938.

The Führer had spent some miserable days in Rome trying to explain to the Duce his reasons for the forcible incorporation of Austria into the Reich, an exercise not altogether pleasing to the Italian dictator, since it brought German troops onto his northern frontier at the Brenner. Hitler had tried to soften the impact of his latest adventure, by declaring in a speech in Rome that "it is my unalterable will and my bequest to the German people that it shall regard the frontier of the Alps, raised by nature between us, both as forever inviolable[4]." The beauty of these sentiments was somewhat marred by the jeers which greeted the Führer's appearance on the newsreels where he was seen wearing a top-hat as he drove to the Opera House; there was also the frigid reception which awaited Hitler at the King's Palace where he was lodged. All in all, the Führer's Italian tour had not been a success. Only in Florence where he paused on his return journey to Berlin, was the gloom lifted.

"Florence," Ciano wrote in his diary, "welcomed the Führer with heart and head. It is a sensitive city, which understands everything. Hitler's speech on Saturday completely transformed the situation—even more perhaps than the declarations of respect for our frontiers, the Italians loved the lyrical impetus with which they were made[5]."

This euphoria was reflected in the preparations which had been made in Florence. Some of the city's streets had been specially widened, lamp-posts had been removed and pavements whitewashed along the route the two Caesars were to travel. Obedient claques organised by the local *Fascio* shouted themselves hoarse, although Anfuso (later the Duce's ambassador in Berlin) detected "un applauso ghibellino" in a city which had once been predominately Guelph.

Friedrich Kriegbaum, who had been appointed to act as Hitler's guide and interpreter, made every effort to interest him in the Ponte Santa Trinita, but the Führer walked briskly over the peerless bridge. He knew all about the Ponte Santa Trinita, he told Kriegbaum, yet he was far more taken by its crusty old neighbour, the Ponte Vecchio, which he promptly declared was his favourite bridge, although Kriegbaum pointed out as tactfully as he could that some of the Ponte Vecchio's most admired features had been completed as late as the 1860s. The Führer remained adamant: the Ponte Vecchio remained fixed in his retentive memory as his favourite bridge, with consequences which were to become apparent later.

There were other episodes connected with Hitler's first visit to Florence which Kriegbaum recounted to his friends. During a four hour tour of the Uffizi, the Duce, whose enthusiasm for the arts did not rival Hitler's, was heard to mutter as he trudged dispiritedly behind his guest—"Tutti questi quadri!" ("All these damned pictures!") Only when Hitler paused to admire a Titian painting depicting a group of Christian martyrs, did the Duce suddenly revive. For one chilling instant, Kriegbaum thought that Mussolini would remove the Titian from the gallery's wall and hand it over to the Führer! Happily, Kriegbaum managed to divert Hitler's attention to another painting[6].

On another occasion when Hitler was taken up to the heights of the Piazzale Michelangelo to view the spreading panorama of Florence—"he stood lost in deep feeling from which he found himself again with the ejaculation: 'At last I understand Feuerbach and Böcklin'[7]."

What he "understood" about these two nineteenth-century painters who had lived in Florence was far from clear, but it is known that he had recently paid 675,000 reichsmarks for Arnold Böcklin's "Italian Villa", an enormous sum for this second-rate Swiss-German master's work which he collected and stored in his art gallery at Linz.

All in all, Hitler enjoyed his half day in Florence. "The hours of joy he experienced on the Arno eclipsed his satisfaction in having been to Rome," he confessed to an Italian journalist[8]. Indeed, he was so overcome, that his eyes brimmed with tears as he bade the Duce farewell as they stood locked in fond embrace on the Central station. "Henceforth," he declared (according to Ciano), "no force will be able to separate us."

Florence, however, soon forgot about Hitler's first excursion and Kriegbaum returned to his peaceful researches into the origins of the Ponte Santa Trinita. Even Italy's precipitate entry into the war in the last phase of Hitler's victorious French campaign made little impact on the life of the city: coffee was still unrationed and one could ask for a cup of tea at Doneys, the fashionable café on the via Tornabuoni without being accused of "anglophile tendencies", in this most anglophile of all Italian cities.

True, the Palazzo Antinori which housed the British Institute and Consulate now stood shuttered and forlorn. The British colony which had numbered some two or three hundred had scattered, leaving only a handful of elderly women to maintain a dignified but inoffensive presence. There were also very few Germans about. A succession of dull, worthy German consuls occupied the ugly consulate on the south bank of the Arno, which they shared with the German Evangelical Mission.

The small German colony gravitated more naturally towards Kriegbaum's Art Institute at 9, Piazza Santo Spirito—"where free minds could meet, without being gagged or blindfolded", one of Kriegbaum's friends said later. Kriegbaum himself steered clear of his Nazi masters. He had repeatedly turned down offers of a professorship in the Reich. As an acknowledged authority on fifteenth- and sixteenth-century Florentine art and architecture, he was more concerned in maintaining the high tradition of German scholarship in the Art Institute, founded at the turn of the century by Wilhelm Bode, than in entering the madhouse of Nazi-controlled universities. He also openly befriended such "degenerate artists" as Eduard Bargheer and Rudolf Levy, as well as out-and-out opponents of the Nazi regime such as Rupprecht, the former Crown Prince of Bavaria, who had earned Hitler's lasting enmity.

Kriegbaum's only stipulation to the tall, grave, elderly Crown Prince, whom his followers addressed as "Your Majesty", was that he should refrain from signing the Visitors' Book at the Institute.

This proved to be an eminently sensible precaution. When Dr Bernard Rust, the Nazi Minister of Science, Education and Popular Culture came on a goodwill mission to Florence in August 1940, two months after Italy's entry into the war, he immediately demanded to see this Visitors' Book on his very first visit to the Art Institute.

Rust "who preached the Nazi gospel with the zeal of a Goebbels and the fuzziness of a Rosenberg[9]", having thumbed his way laboriously through this book, made the sour observation that most of the entries appeared to be either Jewish or foreign. Could Kriegbaum explain this phenomenon?

"But all art is international, Excellenz!" Kriegbaum is said to have riposted lightly. Then, as if to make amends for his unfortunate lapse, Kriegbaum proposed that Dr Rust should make an extensive tour of his institute. Rust, who did not know what was in store for him, assented graciously.

It was a particularly hot and suffocating August afternoon as Florence sweltered among her sheltering hills; the heat had even penetrated the foot-thick walls of the Palazzo Guadagni, but the institute itself was as silent as a pharaonic tomb. Kriegbaum had begged all "degenerate artists" and the Crown Prince, in particular, to absent themselves for the afternoon.

With maniac zeal Kriegbaum propelled Bernard Rust, the former schoolmaster and Gauleiter of Hanover from one room to another, filling his head with a wealth of useless information. Did the Minister know, for example, that the Palazzo was one of the best specimens of fifteenth-century Florentine architecture, supposedly built by Cronaca, or that it had once served as the private residence of Beppino Ricasoli, a former Italian Prime Minister when Florence served as the temporary capital of the Italian kingdom from 1865 to 1871?

Up and down the numerous "secret" stairs of the Institute, in and out of libraries and reading rooms, inspecting every nook and cranny went the unhappy Reichsminister, driven by the chattering director, until the sweat poured down in rivulets from his face. Rust begged Kriegbaum for a moment's rest, but he had barely seated himself in Kriegbaum's private office when the telephone rang. The Bishop of the Santo Spirito church across the Piazza had telephoned to say that he was waiting for the august Minister, so that he could show him round Brunelleschi's glorious edifice.

When Rust, demurred, murmuring plaintively that he had had enough culture to last him a lifetime, Kriegbaum told him of the "unfortunate misunderstanding" which might follow if he turned down this high church dignitary's invitation. The weary Culture Minister then gathered his remaining strength and sallied out to make a three-hour tour of the Santo Spirito church.

Accompanying Rust on this occasion was a youngish, slightly-built man, in his early forties, with clear blue eyes and sharply-cut features, dressed in a severe black uniform. Kriegbaum, despite his other accomplishments, was no connoisseur of Nazi Party uniforms. He eyed the forbidding uniform, wondering to himself: "Is he . . . S.S.?" The official, who was clothed in the regulation Foreign Office parade uniform designed by none other than Ribbentrop, was equally disconcerted by Kriegbaum's appearance. Kriegbaum had been lent a nondescript brown Party uniform in which to present himself before the Reichsminister. The Foreign Office man stared at Kriegbaum's ill-fitting uniform, asking himself: "Is he . . . S.A.?" (A Party man.)

The two men shifted uneasily from one foot to another, like two schoolboys, and then glanced surreptitiously at each other's faces. Somehow their faces did not correspond with the suspect uniforms. They burst out laughing simultaneously and went over to shake hands.

The man in the black Foreign Office uniform was a Dr Gerhard Wolf, a section head of the German Foreign Office's educational department, who had been sent to accompany Rust on his goodwill mission.

Three months later, in November 1940, Dr Wolf came as the new German consul to the city of Florence, "an unwanted partner, in an unwanted war", as he described himself. Not surprisingly, one of Kriegbaum's first invitations to the new consul was that he should accompany him on one of his morning visits to the Ponte Santa Trinita. As they approached the bridge from the via Maggio, the consul saw that the storm clouds which had gathered over Monte Oliveto had turned to magenta. The winter sun suddenly broke through the clouds, bathing the stark white purity of the bridge the colour of wine, tinged with gold.

Kriegbaum and the new consul stood contemplating the Ponte Santa Trinita for some moments in complete silence. Then Kriegbaum turned to him, saying with child-like gravity: "Who would destroy such beauty? Surely neither their side nor ours. . . ."

Yet the Ponte Santa Trinita was destroyed and then miraculously brought to life again. The story of the bridge, its death and resurrection, is also the story of the man whom they later called the Consul of Florence.

# 2

# Plato's Advice

> Seeing others without any law or order in them, he is happy enough if he may keep himself free from injustice and ill-doings in this life and then gladly go away with a good hope, calm and peaceful when the end comes.
>
> PLATO, *The Republic*

Gerhard Wolf was born in Dresden on August 12th 1896, the seventh and youngest child of a prosperous Protestant lawyer, Dr Eduard Wolf, a kindly, upright man devoted to his large family. When Gerhard's mother Martha Elise (née Bienert) died, he was eight years old; his upbringing fell to an elder sister, Gertraud, then nineteen, a woman of great charm and culture who had many friends in literary and artistic circles in Berlin and Dresden, among them, the gifted, restless poet Stefan George, who was to exert such an influence on Wolf's generation. But in 1914, Wolf was still too young to imbibe George's ambiguities, his pan-hellenic posturings or his open contempt for Christianity which he despised because of its Jewish foundations; nor was he lured by George's prophetic vision of a saviour who would lead Germany out of the dull technical age of Bismarckian democracy towards some undefined concept of national fraternity[1].

When the First World War broke out, the seventeen-year-old Dresdener, who was spending a carefree summer holiday on a friend's estate near Moscow, found himself an enemy in his host's country. During his easy-going internment—the regulations in Russia were very lax in those days—Wolf saw the first echelons of German and Austrian prisoners of war making their way down the endless, dusty Russian roads towards their camps in Siberia. Tragic accounts of hunger and typhoid which decimated those early victims of militarism, reached the impressionable youngster, relieved by stories of selfless devotion shown by the Swedish Red Cross worker Elsa Brändström. Not for nothing was this good woman called "The Angel of Siberia" by her sick and dying charges whose families she promised to succour on her return to their homeland—a promise she fully kept.

Elsa Brändström's example not only survived in Wolf's memory for many years, but left its mark on his psyche. According to one of his closest friends in Florence, Wolf himself had all the makings of an admirable "welfare worker": this opinion may provide some clue to his character and explain some of his actions later.

In May 1915, Wolf was allowed to make his way home to Dresden. The circuitous journey which took him through Rumania and Hungary lasted some six weeks. According to his personal file in the German Foreign Office, Wolf then joined the 17th Uhlan Regiment, with the rank of cornet. Rudolf Rahn, the last German wartime ambassador in Italy, whose lifelong friendship with Wolf began in 1921, said he reminded him of Rilke's cornet. "Like him, Gerhard Wolf loved the good and despised the mean and the tawdry," Dr Rahn stated. Like Rilke's cornet, too, Wolf showed a streak of quixotism: for example, he gave up the privilege of being a cavalry officer in the Uhlans and joined the foot-slogging infantry. ("I was sorry for my horse," Wolf explained.)

His military career took him as far afield as Latvia and the Balkans where he gained a number of distinctions, including the Iron Cross, First and Second Class. He was demobilised in 1919, when together with Rudolf Rahn, who joined him later, he resumed his interrupted studies first at Heidelberg, and then, at other famous German universities, studying under such eminent professors as Friedrich Gundolf, Edgar Sahn, Alfred Weber, Karl Jaspers and Heinrich Wölfflin.

Although Gundolf's merits as the leading contemporary

authority on Goethe may have sometimes been disputed, particularly by the Cambridge don Eliza Marian Butler[2], Gerhard Wolf always expressed his warmest admiration for the great Jewish scholar who first opened his mind to Goethe's values, his patrician calm and universalism, qualities which Wolf later discovered corresponded closely to the Florentine ideal. But it was the Heidelberg tradition of fierce personal loyalties and "democratic liberalism" which cemented Wolf's and Rahn's friendship.

After obtaining their degrees in the history of art and philosophy, the two friends studied in Paris and Geneva. In 1925, they separated: Wolf went for a few months to Cambridge to study English, while Rahn joined the information service of the League of Nations. On May 1st 1927, after passing the stiff entry examinations, Gerhard Wolf joined the German Foreign service, followed by Rudolf Rahn a year later.

A promising diplomatic career seemed to open before Gerhard Wolf when three weeks after joining the Foreign Ministry he was invited by Gustav Streseman, the German Foreign Minister, to accompany him to Baden Baden for talks with Georgi Chicherin, his Soviet opposite number. As both Chicherin and Streseman were sick men at this time, they took advantage of the curative waters at Baden, while ranging over the whole field of Soviet-German relations. Chicherin, it appeared, was much concerned in case the British might induce the Weimar Republic to break off relations with the Russians following the rupture in Anglo-Soviet relations occasioned by the celebrated "Arcos Raid"[3]. Wolf himself remembered little of the actual conversation between the Russian and German Foreign Ministers: the red-bearded Commissar for foreign affairs seemed more intent on airing his extensive knowledge of German literature than in talking politics, Wolf recalled later.

Wolf's own diplomatic career seemed likely to follow a normal course. But after serving some three years in Warsaw (1929–1933) as secretary of Legation, he was transferred to the Vatican where his friend and student colleague Dr Paul

Lips, the Swiss writer and philosopher, found him "in a state of great mental conflict and uncertainty". Hitler had come into power early in 1933, and Gerhard Wolf, like some of his colleagues, debated with himself whether to continue in the foreign service.

To resolve his dilemma, Wolf invited Monsignor Kaas, the former leader of the German Centre Party, who was living in the Vatican, to a private luncheon in his Rome apartment, at which Dr Lips was also present. This took place shortly before Easter in the Holy Year of 1934. Wolf asked Kaas quite openly what he should do. Kaas, whose *Zentrum* (Catholic) Party had voted in support of Hitler's "Enabling Act" in March 1933, which had "legalised" the dissolution of all opposition parties, including Kaas' own party, was probably a wiser, if sadder man for this experience. He certainly had no reason to feel any affection for the Nazis who had duped him so mercilessly. According to Dr Lips, Kaas advised his young host that "the best way of fighting the Nazis was to work with them.... A man of Wolf's pure and decent character would find opportunities to work for goodness and justice in his official capacity, even under this evil system.[4]" Similar Trojan Horse tactics had been advocated by the former Chancellor Bruening: he had privately warned German diplomats who had threatened to resign their posts that these would be promptly filled by ardent Nazis.

This argument had no overwhelming appeal for Gerhard Wolf. But he knew that the academic field to which he might have turned had also been filled by Nazi ideologues. Commerce also held little attraction for him, but "hope"—as Goethe said—"is the second soul of the unhappy". So Wolf temporised, argued with himself, with Lips, and with anyone who would listen to him, but finally decided to stay in the diplomatic service, hoping to find some way of resolving his personal dilemma.

Opportunities of opposition to the Nazi regime were not many. Despite the warnings which Wolf received from well-meaning German friends, he continued to invite such Jewish scholars as his former Heidelberg professor Edgar Salin and the poet Wolfskehl to his Rome apartment, a fact which was reported by a Nazi sympathiser who wrote to his superiors in Berlin that Gerhard Wolf was a "liberal democratic friend of the Jews". He also cultivated the friendship of so-called "non-Aryan" members of the diplomatic service, such as Hans von Herwarth, whose grandmother was Jewish. Herwarth, a post-war German Ambassador in London said that "of all my friends in the Foreign Office, Gerhard Wolf stood by my side, defended and protected me. . . .[5]"

But all this was "opposition" on a very minor scale. Indeed, it would be nothing short of disingenuous to inflate a few civilised courtesies between friends, a private kindness shown to a "non-Aryan", into some kind of heroic protest. Such manifestations existed in plenty. Like many of his countrymen, Gerhard Wolf only came gradually to a full realisation of the enormity of Nazi crimes, but unlike most of them, perhaps, he began seeking ways and means by which he could personally mitigate or frustrate those crimes.

It was only when Wolf was stationed in Paris in 1937 that he passed to direct action. He had learnt, in the course of his official duties, that a certain Johannes Ahlers, a German journalist and economics expert, had been summoned to Berlin on the pretext of salary discussions. Ahlers, who was suspected of "Communist leanings" was to have been arrested by the Gestapo the moment he reached Berlin. Following the warning he received from Gerhard Wolf, Ahlers left for Shanghai with his wife.

Oddly enough, a few days before he gave this warning to Ahlers, Gerhard Wolf had been invited by some friends to see a film in which the celebrated British actor Leslie Howard played the part of the languid daredevil "Scarlet Pimpernel". Wolf watched the film to the end without realising that Sir Percy Blakeney was a fictional character drawn from Baroness Orczy's imagination!

Thus Sir Percy joined Elsa Brändström as one of the formative influences on the young diplomat's impressionable mind: the real and the fictional had become inextricably mixed. In the spring of 1938, during the Munich Crisis, Wolf was again asked to make his formal application to join the Nazi Party. Refusal to comply, he was told, could mean his instant dismissal, or at best, his withdrawal from a foreign assignment: moreover, he might never again be sent abroad.

Wolf put in his application, but a few days later, he approached Jean Zay, the French Minister of Culture during an official reception, telling him that "if he wished to maintain peace between France and the National Socialist regime, he must incessantly stress over the radio, as well as in official speeches, that France would not hesitate to use force to curb the Nazis and not rely exclusively on treaties". Jean Zay who may have received this unexpected outburst from a German diplomat with some suspicion, made no reply.

Early in March 1939, Gerhard Wolf was formally enrolled in the Nazi Party (Party card number 7024445), one of the last German diplomats to receive this favour, although his wife Hilde whom he had married in 1933, refused to join the "Frauenschaft", the official Nazi Women's organisation, a fact which was noted on his personal file and which may have militated against Wolf's further promotion.

Shortly before the outbreak of the Second World War, Wolf found himself as a *Referent*, a section head of the Foreign Ministry's educational department. It was in this capacity that he accompanied Culture Minister Rust on his goodwill mission to Florence in August 1940. He had striven, as he himself recalls, without much apparent success to prevent foreign-based German Catholic and other denominational schools from passing under Party control: he was, by this time, on the verge of a nervous breakdown.

"After the unexpectedly speedy victory over France in June 1940," Wolf said later, "I lost all hope of exerting any sensible or moderating influence in Berlin. The victory mood of the Party had begun to permeate into the Foreign Office and had become unbearable. When I heard that the post of consul in Florence had become vacant, I felt justified in following Plato's advice that it is natural that a man should seek to escape from evil and tragic circumstances, and so to survive them."

Wolf's arrival in Florence as the new German consul on November 7th 1940 had been preceded by Hitler's second descent on the city about a week earlier. The Führer had arrived in Florence on October 28th, a few hours after Mussolini had launched his attack on Greece. A photograph printed in the *Völkischer Beobachter* (November 1st 1940) which showed Hitler and the Duce, standing with Ribbentrop and Ciano in the Sala Clemente VII of the Palazzo Vecchio, could hardly disguise the look of irritation in the Führer's eyes. The atmosphere between the two Axis leaders was electric despite Hitler's assurance of "full support in the operations" and his offer of a number of German parachute divisions for an attack on Crete. Hitler had every reason to feel displeased: Mussolini's pointless attack on the Greeks had frustrated his grander strategic designs in North Africa. "The ill-omened opening of that campaign encouraged the English to launch a successful offensive in Libya and, for the first time, made Franco hesitate..." Hitler wrote to Mussolini some years later[6].

Despite the undertone of bitterness which marred what proved to be his last visit to Florence, Hitler received a considerable consolation prize from the Duce. Florentines recalled seeing a huge military lorry trundling through their narrow streets bearing a twelve foot long canvas to the Central Station where the two brothers-in-arms were bidding each other farewell. Hitler had long coveted the famous triptych of "The Plague in Florence" painted by the nineteenth-century Viennese painter Makart in which numerous high-bosomed ladies were depicted in attitudes of distress during the visitation of the plague in Renaissance Florence. The Duce handed over his "present" with great panache at the moment of Hitler's departure and the Führer thanked him fulsomely for his gift.

Friedrich Kriegbaum who had absented himself from this unappetising charade—he had gone to visit Bernard Berenson at the latter's summer residence at Vallombrosa—discovered later that the Duce's "gift" had been confiscated from the Landau-Finlay family to whom the painting belonged, on instructions from Himmler's deputy Bormann! To cover up this barefaced theft, the painting was entered in the records of Hitler's art gallery in Linz as "a present from the Duce[7]".

Hitler who was evidently highly pleased with his capture of the Makart, played his part to the full in the comedy on Florence's Central Station. He even cracked a joke regretting that Makart's "ladies" could not be accommodated in his private compartment (because of the size of painting). The triptych was therefore consigned to the goods van attached to the Führer's armoured train taking him home to Berlin. Some years later, during one of his interminable breakfast conversations, he alluded to Makart, whose later works, he declared, were of little value "for by that time, he was a mentally sick man[8]".

By the time the new German consul Dr Gerhard Wolf had arrived in Florence, together with his wife Hilde and Veronika their five-year-old daughter, the city had forgotten all about the Führer's brief two-day visit. Hitler who had been upset by the Duce's ill-timed Greek adventure, had gone off to brood on a plan of greater folly: his attack on Russia. But these high and important matters did not concern the new Consul who had come to the peaceful "diplomatic backwater" of Florence to escape from tragic and evil circumstances. This escape proved largely illusionary, and Florence, that golden city, was a more severe testing ground than the witches' cauldron he had left behind him in Berlin. In the Consul's luggage was a treasured lithograph of Goethe.

3

# The Perfect Centre

> And he felt that here he was in one of the world's living centres, in the Piazza della Signoria. The sense of having arrived—of having reached the perfect centre of the human world: this he had.
>
> D. H. LAWRENCE, *Aaron's Rod*

The arrival of the new German Consul Dr Gerhard Wolf was noted briefly in the local Florentine papers, but passed largely unnoticed by readers who were regaled by the far more significant news of the battles outside of Mersa Matruh, and photographs of London's burning skyline.

The new Consul, having settled himself and his small family in the comfortable middle-class Hotel Minerva on the Piazza Santa Maria Novella, set out to inspect the consular premises at 20 via dei Bardi, across the Arno. Wolf was immediately struck by the gloomy sacerdotal atmosphere which pervaded the nineteenth-century "gothic" edifice which housed both his consulate and the German Evangelical Mission, whose Lutheran pastor occupied the top floor. The middle floor, consisting of four, white-washed rooms, was set aside for the Consulate.

The Consul's own private office, however, was pleasantly light and sunny, backing onto a garden with clumps of oleander bushes, which flowered magnificently in season. Adjoining his study was another office, occupied by the good-looking half-German, half-Italian Dr Hans Wildt (Wildt-Fusconi), and the somewhat myopic irrepressible Dresdener, Dr Erich Poppe, both of whom had lectured at Florence University and the Magisterium before joining the staff of the Consulate as interpreters. The Consul took an immediate liking to these two young assistants, and they seemed to approve of him, particularly after a trifling incident which seemed to place the Consul into some perspective.

Hans Wildt was the first to notice that the new Consul had removed the large obligatory photograph of Adolf Hitler from the wall facing his desk, substituting for it the Goethe lithograph: the scowling Führer was relegated to a dark wall behind the consul's desk. To Dr Wildt's innocent enquiry about this sea-change, the Consul answered without batting an eyelid: "But my dear Hans, surely our visitors should have the privilege and delight of gazing at the Führer? I reserve the Goethe strictly to myself!"

This playful explanation was lost on the Consul's next visitor, a dour schoolmaster, one Herr Rettig, who acted as the Party's "welfare officer" in Florence. This self-important political watchdog smiled sourly at the new Consul's eccentricity, but made no comment. Herr Rettig came into his own on such feastdays as Hitler's birthday every April 20th, when he ran up a large red and black swastika flag outside the Evangelical headquarters, "thus joining Luther and Adolf Hitler for one day", the Consul observed drily.

On such occasions the entire German colony was ordered to present itself at the "Brown House", or Party House, a shrine set aside in a large baroque apartment close to the consulate. Here they sang Party songs to the accompaniment of visiting German musicians, drank imported Munich beer, and less entertainingly perhaps, listened to interminable "victory" harangues delivered by Party orators.

It was on some such occasion as this that Herr Rettig approached the new Consul with what he called "an interesting suggestion". He began by commiserating with him on the cramped and unsuitable consular premises in the Evangelical Mission. Now that the British had left their spacious, elegant headquarters in the Palazzo Antinori, the local *Fascio*, with whom he had discussed the matter, had agreed that the German Consulate should take over the palazzo which was more becoming to the dignity of the Greater Reich.

The Consul thanked Herr Rettig for this initiative on his part, but said that his present premises were quite adequate for his purpose. When Rettig pressed him on this point, the Consul drew him aside, telling him in a conspiratorial whisper which he knew he would relish, that he had been sent by the Foreign Office to counteract the anglophile and americanophile tendencies among the Florentines—"at least in the cultural and social spheres". The blatant seizure of the Palazzo Antinori would not only strengthen such dangerous tendencies, but make the Reich into a laughing-stock, into the bargain. When Rettig tried to argue, the Consul informed him that both Kriegbaum and he had given instructions for the library and effects of the British Institute to be crated and placed under the protection of a neutral state (Switzerland). He asked Rettig not to meddle in matters which did not concern him.

Wittingly or unwittingly, the Consul had made his first enemy in Florence: he would make many more, but the few Florentines who heard of his encounter with Rettig, applauded the Consul's nice sense of protocol, and complimented Ribbentrop on his choice of so tactful a nominee.

There was little to disturb the serenity of Florence in the first three years of the Consul's tenure. Fortunately no enemy planes made any attempt to penetrate the city's defences which consisted of a few outdated anti-aircraft guns going back to the Abyssinian War. In the city itself a few half-hearted air-raid precautions were adopted: sandbags were laid at the foot of Giotto's delicate Campanile and around the giant Ammannati "Neptune" fountain on the Piazza della Signoria, that perfect centre of the human world, but the city's lights were left to blaze from dusk to dawn.

The knowledgeable assured each other that the R.A.F. would refrain from bombing Florence so long as the squadron which the Duce had lent Goering for his air attack on London kept away from the South Kensington museum area! Some relief was expressed when this squadron was hastily withdrawn from the Battle of Britain after eleven Italian planes were shot down over the Medway in November 1940.

In Florence itself there were very few Fascists about. "Most people wore the Party badge merely 'for protection'," according to the Consul, "and on official occasions many of them could be seen wearing their blackshirts somewhat shamefacedly. But on the whole we were left in peace. I had succeeded in persuading the Party authorities in Rome that if they wanted to create a positive attitude towards Germany, Florence should be considered as having a particularly distinguished, civilised atmosphere, which should be disturbed as little as possible by noisy and violent Party demonstrations[1]."

He himself went out of his way to create "a positive attitude towards Germany" by inviting some three hundred leading Florentines to a reception in honour of Furtwängler, who had come in January 1941 with the Berlin Philharmonic to give a series of Beethoven concerts. The Germans, the Consul was anxious to demonstrate, had a musical tradition outside the lugubrious *Horst Wessel*. Leading pianists, and musicians such as Giesiking, Backhaus, Kempff, Fischer and Erdmann, were welcomed by him, as well as the conductor von Karajan, who participated in the Maggio Musicale, the musical festival founded by the Consul's friend Maestro Vittorio Gui.

The Consul's predilection for the upper reaches of Florentine society, earned him a reputation for snobbery in narrow German and Italian Party circles, a charge which he made no effort to refute. He himself had been greatly taken by "the magic of the Florentine aristocracy" as he readily admits. "It is true that they live mainly in their great past", he said, later, "but they love and revere the past. When one meets them in their precious, and sometimes, dilapidated town palaces, or in their country villas, with their beautifully kept gardens, one rejoices in their tact, in the ease and friendliness of their social charm; in the simple elegance and beauty of their women."

Early in 1941 the Consul and his family had moved out of their hotel suite in the Minerva to the pleasant rural surroundings at San Domenico di Fiesole where he had rented a small villino known as Le Tre Pulzelle, from an American lady, a Mrs Denby. Two rather forlorn, weather-beaten stone maidens—the third had disappeared—gave the villa of the Three Maidens its name. It had been built in the early part of the fifteenth century by the ducal Medicis whose pawnbroker crest can still be seen embedded in the high portico. The villa had once served as a "riposo dei vescovi", a bishop's rest-house, conveniently situated near the Villa Medici which nestled in its avenue of tall cypresses, set on a steep incline, above Le Tre Pulzelle.

Le Tre Pulzelle made no pretence of grandeur, although the long terracotta-tiled terrace which jutted from the first floor, covered with vines and creepers, gave it a sense of elevation. The interior was small and compact, with long, pointed Gothic windows, with an air of cosiness, such as one finds in a Dutch painting, or indeed in a bishop's resthouse. A small staff included a cook, her gardener husband, and a chauffeur with a large, noisy family with whom Veronika, the Consul's small daughter played among the flapping household washing, in the unkempt but delightful garden.

The Consul had a great fondness for his rustic retreat. He would arrive at around seven each evening, often in a hired taxi, with his two associates, Hans Wildt and Erich Poppe, and closet himself with them in his study, away from the prying eyes and ears of less trusted members of the Consulate, or take drinks on the terrace with Kriegbaum or his friends, the Hamburg-born "degenerate artist" Eduard Bargheer, or Hans Purrmann, the eminent Bavarian painter, a friend of Matisse, who headed the "Villa Romana" school of painting. Rupprecht, the Bavarian Crown Prince was also a frequent visitor to Le Tre Pulzelle, as well as Dr Hanna Kiel, an expatriate German writer of anti-Nazi views, long resident in Florence. She recalls her first meeting with the Consul not long after his arrival in Florence.

She had apparently offended a wealthy German business man who recounted a particularly unsavoury story in her presence, boasting how he had turned away a Jewish acquaintance and his family from his door. Hanna Kiel promptly rounded on him, accusing him of cowardice. The outraged business man rushed off to lodge a complaint with the Consul, demanding that Dr Kiel should be sent back to Germany for her "unpatriotic remarks".

On the following evening Dr Kiel received an invitation to dine with the Consul and Dr Kriegbaum at Le Tre Pulzelle.

"I went off in great trepidation, hoping that Kriegbaum had somehow managed to smooth the way for me," Hanna Kiel stated. "When I arrived at around six o'clock, I found the Consul with Kriegbaum on the terrace, he immediately broke off his conversation, stretched out his hand and said: 'I have heard all about your misdeeds, Dr Kiel, and I thoroughly approve of them! You and I should be friends from now on!'"

Legends and anecdotes began to multiply around the new Consul. On his first visit to Kriegbaum's Institute, for example, he turned to one of the Director's more trusted assistants, saying in a loud whisper: "Now, perhaps, you'll be kind enough to tell me which of you here is the Party spy so that I don't say anything to upset him?"

On another occasion, during an official reception at Le Tre Pulzelle, he was approached by a sharp-tongued pro-Fascist *contessa* while he was engaged in conversation with Achille Malavasi, the chief censor, well known for his tepid enthusiasm for the Fascist regime.

"Why do you always seem to make friends with people who boast of their anti-Mussolini sentiments?" the Contessa demanded.

"But, Contessa, what else can I do?" the Consul replied. "Your Fascist friends are already on the right path. I must do my best to convert the others!"

But the Consul was not always tilting at contessas at official receptions. He could also give the impression of being "very reserved and glacial", as Signora Maria Comberti, who had returned to her native Florence after an absence of almost forty years in Germany, remarked. She had purchased a small, secluded villa, the Belvedere, on the outskirts of the old city walls below San Miniato, "with a grove of one hundred and seventy olive trees".

"I had my daughter with me, and my son served with the paratroops, so of course, I wanted and needed work, so I went to the German Consulate to offer my service as an interpreter. Dr Wolf, the Consul, was very reserved and glacial, and not half as friendly as I had expected, despite my references: I had been an interpreter at the Breslau Law Courts for eleven years. I wondered what had gone wrong." But she soon learnt the reasons for the Consul's caution: "I did not know, at this time (1942) that Dr Wolf's position was very difficult, and that he mistrusted someone like myself, who came from Germany, speaking German perfectly.... That same day, my friend, Erna von Hoesslin, told me that the Consul had a difficult time with spies sent to him from Germany.[2]"

But if the Consul was cautious in his dealings with the hospitable Italian Quaker Signora Comberti who in the months to come was to shelter Jews and Partisans in her villa, he showed a distinct partiality for the small colony of Englishwomen who still remained in Florence. These proud, self-reliant women, many of whom belonged to Anglo-Florentine families whose connections with the city stretched back over a hundred years, made up the congregation of the two Church of England churches of St Mark's and Holy Trinity. Miss M. Gladys Elliot whose grandfather came in 1884 with the Robert Stephenson Railway Company to build the first railway between Florence, Pisa and Leghorn for the Grand Duke of Tuscany, recalls that after General Wavell's victorious offensive in 1941 things began to worsen for the British colony, and the congregation in the two churches began to dwindle. By the spring of 1943, orders had come from Rome demanding the removal of all British and American subjects below the age of seventy. They were to be sent to the detention centre at Carpi, to await deportation to Germany.

Harassed Questura officials advised many of the "under aged" women to seek refuge with friends, or to retire for the duration of the war into the city's numerous private clinics, feigning illness. Miss Gladys Hutton, who was below the stipulated age of seventy at this time, found this expedient too expensive. After some hesitation, Miss Hutton went to the enemy Consul on the advice of her friend, the Swiss Red Cross delegate, M. Charles Steffen.

"The Consul received me extremely warmly," says Miss Hutton, "and listened to all I had to tell him. He then called in his assistant, Dr Wildt and asked him, 'Should we write a letter for this lady? Or will it get us into trouble?' At all events, he wrote a strong letter of recommendation on my behalf, saying that he knew me personally and would vouch for my correct behaviour." She adds with a grain of sly humour: "Of course, I did not tell him that I had contacts with the Resistance movement which was beginning to gather its forces at this time.[3]"

But the Consul was not only intent on playing the part of a Scarlet Pimpernel on behalf of a handful of distraught Englishwomen, some of whom came clutching their passports and birth-certificates to show they were over the stipulated age—"and no woman likes to admit being over seventy"—he was also involved in the wider aspects of the German Resistance, whose progress he followed from his "diplomatic backwater" in Florence. Two "routine" visits by General Hans Oster, the right-hand man of Admiral Canaris, and by Dr von Dohnanyi, were followed by the arrival of "Johnny" von Herwarth and General Koestring, a former General Military Attaché in Moscow, who came to outline some of the Resistance's plans and difficulties in trying to get rid of Hitler. "Not everyone could take an active part in the preparation of the Plot," said von Herwarth, "because we only needed a few people, but we knew that Wolf was on our side[4]."

Outwardly, however, the Consul maintained his air of calculated detachment. Miss Nicky Mariano, Berenson's secretary and collaborator who met him in the late summer of 1943 found that "Consul Wolf seemed to need turbulent times in which to show his real worth: in peaceful times, he appeared rather reserved, even lackadaisical . . .".

The turbulent times arrived with unexpected suddenness on July 25th 1943, when Mussolini was toppled from his pinnacle of power. The Consul was holidaying with Dr Kriegbaum, Hans Purrmann and Hanna Kiel in the woodlands of Vallombrosa, some twenty miles from Florence, when the news of the Duce's fall came over the radio. Searchlights probed the sky over Florence, and there was a sudden cacophony of anti-aircraft fire, although no enemy aircraft had made its appearance over the city. Kriegbaum who had a contempt for all air-raid precautions, observed: "Now the cowards will take to their funk holes! I'd rather be dead than see all I love destroyed!"

No one paid much attention to the German Art Institute director's prophetic words.

# 4

# *Salus Republicae*

And how can you be sure that I am not
Gulling the enemy?

FRIEDRICH VON SCHILLER,
*Wallenstein*

The German Embassy in the Villa Wolkonsky on the via Conte Rosso in Rome, resembled a tourist agency as six thousand German civilians clamoured to go home after the Duce's fall had been announced over the Italian radio-network at the late hour of 10.48 p.m. on July 25th 1943. The lovely old country palace (now the residence of the British Ambassador) was not large enough to accommodate the greatly augmented staff which now numbered close on a hundred persons. Special pavilions had been set up on the extensive grounds across whose lawns white peacocks strutted in sedate majesty. But now even these peacocks had gone berserk, pecking at the images reflected in the highly-polished surfaces of Embassy cars. Hitler, however, reacted in more predictable fashion to the dismissal and arrest of his friend and partner, by ordering his ambassador Hans Georg von Mackensen, the son of the famous World War I field-marshal, to seize the entire Italian Royal Family, together with Badoglio—an operation which lay outside the Ambassador's capacities, as S.S. Colonel Eugen Dollmann, Himmler's special representative in Italy, remarked[1].

The mood of universal rejoicing which greeted Mussolini's downfall was nowhere more evident than in Florence where a large crowd had gathered on the evening of July 25th on the Piazza Vittorio Emanuele. Here it formed itself into a long procession which moved slowly towards the Cathedral square, singing the ancient songs of the *Risorgimento*. The Consul who had left his friends to continue their holiday at Vallombrosa hastened back to the city where he witnessed the general rejoicing which greeted the Duce's downfall. Florence which had honoured Mussolini by making him her freeman in the early 'Twenties, now rose to shake off every trace of the Fascist incubus. Crowds roamed the streets, calling for a speedy end to the war, a large section of which approached the German Consulate on the Via dei Bardi.

The Consul who watched this demonstration from a window in his consulate, found that "the people of Florence can be very passionate, at times. And on such occasions they like to throw stones, but not always to good effect. My offices on the Via dei Bardi were situated in such a narrow street, that they could hardly have swung a cat. So they had little opportunity of throwing stones at me, or the Consulate, that night."

On the following morning Berenson's barber arrived "drunk with happiness" to inform his client that the gayest flags were hung out of the windows in token of gladness[2]. And there were persistent rumours that the Allies had landed at Livorno, Genoa, Venice and Trieste. The Consul himself recalled the mood of those days, some years later, when he stated that "the people of Florence were full of the premature hope that the fall of Mussolini meant the end of the war in Italy. Women tore up their ration books; and the few German soldiers who were about, were embraced by their Italian comrades, who assured them that the war was over for Germany also. In Florence some busts of Mussolini were pulled down (at the Cherubini Conservatory), and several of the most hated Fascists were beaten up, but nowhere did it lead to anything more than this. The Italian Government, the King and Marshal Badoglio have issued the not very credible declaration that Italy would continue fighting on Germany's side."

In the days that followed, the hated fasces were hacked out of walls and pediments, and the slogan "Credere, Obbedire, Combattere" defaced with whitewash. New slogans appeared in the streets as half a dozen political parties who had lain dormant prepared to go into action against the "royal dictatorship" of the King and Marshal Badoglio. The local Fascist headquarters were closed: a few Fascists who dared to appear with the hated insignia had their badges torn out of their lapels, and in working-class districts a number of them had castor oil poured down their gullets, in payment for past injuries. Reports from city hospitals showed that some thirty persons were treated for minor injuries. A few prisoners, too few for the mustering forces of the Resistance, were liberated from the Murate prison, among them, Carlo Ludovico Ragghianti, poet and art historian, who found himself at liberty on July 26th. But Communists and other left-wing opponents of Fascism were excluded from this timid amnesty. Nor were the severe disabilities imposed on the Jewish community lifted for fear of offending the Germans, although anti-semitic decrees were not enforced[3].

From the archiepiscopal palace near the Duomo came the announcement that the towering, austere Cardinal-Archbishop of Florence, the elderly Elia Dalla Costa, had thrown his support behind Badoglio, together with his brother-bishops of Naples, Milan and Bologna[4]. The courtly, gentle Count Alfonso Gaetani, the Prefect of Florence, also supported Badoglio, as did most of his officials. But the real ferment of the Resistance came from the University, which had long provided the spiritual nourishment of disaffection. The names of the historian Gaetano Salvemini, the Rosselli brothers, and the indomitable Piero Calamandrei, are but three in the galaxy of Florentine intellectuals who had conducted a relentless struggle against "the mystical languors and cynicism" of Fascism, but Salvemini had been driven into exile, and the Rossellis, who had been the guiding lights of the "Justice and Liberty" movement, had been brutally murdered by Mussolini's hatchetmen[5]. It was therefore left to Professor Calamandrei, an expert on constitutional law, to raise from the ashes of the dead past, a new and more formidable opposition party, the "Partito d'Azione", a grouping of liberals and socialists. Many of the Professor's closest collaborators such as Tristano

Codignola, Enzo Enriques Agnoletti, Carlo Francovich, Raffaele Ramat, and four others, had been imprisoned since June 1942.

From the cloisters of the ancient convent of San Marco had come a succession of obscure theological articles, penned by the soft-spoken, ascetic Professor Giorgio La Pira, a professor of Roman law, who together with his associates, the lawyer Adone Zoli (a future Prime Minister, 1957–1958) and Mario Augusto Martini, now formed the nucleus of the Christian-Democratic Party in Florence.

All the political parties seemed at this time anxious to bury their old hatreds and find unity of purpose and action in the bitter days to come. Their story can only be touched upon in these pages[6].

During Badoglio's "forty-five days", Florence found herself increasingly cold and hungry. Butter, which had been severely rationed, disappeared altogether and stocks of cooking oil and coal were depleted, but in the house of the notorious *squadrista* Amerigo Dumini on the Viale dei Colli, some two hundred bottles of beer and forty-five thousand razor blades, were discovered. Dumini who had been involved in the murder of venerable Socialist leader Matteotti was arrested with other leading Florentine fascists by the new authorities[7].

The fashionable, if elderly ladies who had once served at Court, continued to meet in the elegant, well-equipped hair-dressing salon on the via Tornabuoni, run by Signor (later Cavaliere) Ferdinando Pretini, to discuss the imminent end of the war under the hair-dryers. Some affirmed that Florence should proclaim her neutrality like the postage-stamp Republic of San Marino, and seek the protection of its emissary, the Minister to the Holy See, the charming *magnifico* the Marchese Filippo Serlupi Crescenzi, who flew the papal white and yellow flag over his villa Le Fontanelle at Careggi, near Florence. The tall, good-looking master-hairdresser, the son of a poor workman from Massalombarda, took these quips lightly. Like his patrons, he enjoyed the King's favour since he attended to the hair of the ladies of the Royal household whenever the King came to his summer residence at San Rossore.

On August 5th 1943, Dr Kriegbaum, the director of the German Art Institute, came to lunch at I Tatti, the lovely villa at Settignano, outside of Florence, where lived that greatest of all art connoisseurs, Bernard Berenson. "Such was the state of mind of us all that I did not have to guess what he was coming for," Berenson wrote in his diary[8]. "It was to procure my influence in favour of saving the German Institute of Art History from confiscation or even dispersal by the Allies. He was in touch with the German authorities, military as well as civil, an intimate friend of the German consul (of whom later), and it was clear that none of them expected to remain here many days. In fact a few weeks later all German residents were being advised, urged, and even forced to leave; and did leave."

The Consul, who had not as yet made Berenson's acquaintance, had received contradictory orders from Rome, telling him first to prepare to evacuate the entire German colony and then, final instructions to stay put and await developments. He had already sent his wife and young daughter to Switzerland as a safety precaution.

On August 30th, he received word that his Heidelberg student friend and Foreign Office colleague, Dr Rudolf Rahn, who had acted as civil administrator in Tunis, had arrived in Rome as Ambassador-designate and Minister-Plenipotentiary, replacing the retiring German Ambassador von Mackensen. Three days later on September 3rd, the Consul took train for Rome to upbraid his superior for what he regarded as an act of pure folly on Dr Rahn's part.

By the time the Consul had reached Rome the atmosphere of suspicion, charges and counter-charges had reached explosion point. Rahn who had seen the new Foreign Minister Raffaele Guariglia shortly after his arrival in Rome on August 30th, had told him that regardless of the Führer's personal feelings about the way that Mussolini had been treated (he had been sent into exile on the Isle of Maddalena), Hitler remained a realist who might countenance a "political" solution to Italy's problems, providing such a solution did not jeopardise Germany's strategic position. If on the other hand, Italy continued to fight by Germany's side, Hitler was ready to give him all the necessary support[9].

Guariglia who seems to have taken an instant dislike to Dr Rahn, whom he described as "half functionary, half soldier", refused to commit himself openly. He temporised and he lied, knowing full well that two of his and Badoglio's emissaries General Castellano and Lanza d'Ajeta, Ciano's former private secretary, were at that moment conducting secret armistice negotiations with the Allies in Lisbon. "It is certainly not a very good thing for a man of honour to admit that he has lied," Guariglia confessed later, but where the interests of the state were involved, he had no other choice. Salus Republicae suprema Lex...[10] Perhaps to quieten his own conscience, Guariglia records that Dr Rahn asked him to play down his association with the Nazis in the press and to stress his diplomatic function. A biography of Dr Rahn was distributed to the Italian newspapers to this effect[11].

Marshal Badoglio whom Rahn met in the afternoon of September 3rd was even more profuse than Guariglia in his protestations of loyalty. He asked the Ambassador-designate to do all he could to prevent German military authorities "from taking ill-considered or provocative action". Rahn promised to discuss the whole matter of Italo-German military co-operation with the chief of the General Staff, General Ambrosio, and the chief of the army staff, General Roatta, and "where necessary intervene on their behalf[12]". He also gave assurances that he would limit German intervention in purely Italian domestic matters.

Rahn's interview with Badoglio ended on a near-farcical note, when the ageing Marshal declared with pent-up emotion, "I am one of the three oldest surviving Marshals in Europe, Mackensen, Petain and myself.... The German Government's mistrust towards me is incomprehensible. I have given my word, and I shall stand by it." Three hours previously his Lisbon emissaries had concluded their secret agreement with the Allies! The axis partnership was dissolving in a sea of perfidy which Cataline himself might have envied.

The Consul himself arrived shortly after Rahn's interview with Badoglio. Rahn who may have sensed his old Heidelberg friend's disappointment at his readiness to serve as Hitler's emissary at this critical hour, proposed that they should take a stroll in the Villa Wolkonsky's gardens so as to escape from the microphones which Rahn suspected the Gestapo might have installed in his private office.

"After the first joy of meeting," Dr Rahn recalled later, "he began to reproach me in earnest: how could I accept the post of Ambassador-designate and Minister Plenipotentiary at the hands of Hitler who was about to lead Germany and the whole of Europe into the most frightful disaster? Here I contradicted him, not without passion. Surely he did not think that I would be so foolish as to consider my pathetic task here as a distinction? If we were to follow the inclinations of some members of the old Foreign Ministry, and withdraw cautiously from responsibility, then other less responsible hands would demolish whatever human or moral credit we still enjoyed abroad. It was up to us to prove to the world that there really did exist another Germany, distorted as this might have been by propagandist fiction."

Not dissimilar arguments had been put forward by Monsignor Kaas and ex-Chancellor Bruening, but the actual words which Rahn spoke to the Consul were more direct and simple. "I told Wolf—if I am not here, who will have the courage to do the job we must do? Who will find friends such as you to help me?" He also reminded the Consul that after having witnessed the horrors of Nazi occupation of Greece, he was determined to prevent their repetition in Italy.

"It was during my conversation (with Consul Wolf) that my direction and the nature of the task facing me in Italy became clear to me," Rahn wrote. "I would have to establish my position firmly from the very start. Ribbentrop, incidentally, had reacted quite reasonably and promised me his support, but I soon saw that I would have to act speedily and on my own responsibility if I wanted to forestall an economic collapse.[13]"

To help him assess the nature of the task before him, Rahn asked the Consul to sound out General Mario Roatta, the Italian chief of army staff. The meeting between the Consul and Roatta took place in the War Ministry on September 7th, a day before the official announcement of the Armistice, although Roatta later denied all knowledge of the secret talks which had been going on in Lisbon[14]. The German General Staff, who may have been better informed, had already given orders for all Italian army units to be disarmed, and German troops had begun to cross the Brenner in considerable force.

The Consul who had known Roatta from his legation days in Warsaw, when the Italian general had served as military attaché in the Polish capital, described him as a man of medium height "with dark, intelligent eyes". He had a great personal regard for Roatta, who unlike his superior, showed a considerable capacity for straight-dealing.

The two men conducted their interview in French, although the report which the Consul wrote subsequently was in German. Roatta began with a general appraisal of the internal situation in Italy. The collapse of Fascism was not the result of a plot as it was generally assumed in Germany, he told the Consul. The Fascist Party had simply committed suicide. The Army had been compelled to step in to prevent disorder, but the Germans had not understood this and had continued to harass the Italians "although it is not usual to kick a man when he is down or when he is sick, but to treat him gently". One could ask an Italian to do anything provided one asked politely, the General observed: "The forcible entry of armed troops over the Brenner Pass, without previous notification, has greatly shocked the Italians, but this shock has been overcome."

He then turned to the war situation, which he said, had deteriorated so rapidly because Germany had done nothing to prevent Mussolini's gamble in Greece. At a time when Britain was unprepared, America was still out of the war, and France defenceless "both Tunis and Gibraltar could have been taken, and the Mediterranean question solved, once for all". Now the situation had changed radically: "tomorrow, or the day after, the enemy can attempt a landing near Rome, and Italy will have to face the possible destruction of many of her cities from air-raids".

If Roatta had struck a chord with his mention of allied air-raids which might menace Italian cities, Florence among them, the Consul made no sign of agreement. He began to question Roatta on reports of military indiscipline among Italian troops, but the General begged him not to be deceived by outward appearances, which were frequently slovenly, he admitted. Nor should Italian soldiers' reluctance to return the military salute "be judged from a German point of view".

The Consul's report then touched on a more salient topic. The Allies, Roatta noted, had failed to reach any agreement with the Russians. They had hoped that both Germany and Russia would so exhaust themselves in their conflict that Britain could again play a decisive role in Europe, but Germany remained as the only real bulwark against Communism. Should any real danger of Communism arise, Roatta suggested that it "might then be necessary to wait for the right moment and to enlist Britain's aid in fighting it".

Having delivered this political bromide, which he knew would appeal to the Germans, Roatta explained his own reluctance to take up the post of Ambassador in Berlin. He felt that "as a serving officer he should continue to serve in the army in these difficult times".

The two men then parted, expressing their satisfaction at their frank conversation which they hoped to continue at a later date. They were not destined to meet again. The Consul returned to the Villa Wolkonsky to write his report.

At eleven o'clock on the following morning of the 8th, Dr Rahn had an audience with Victor Emmanuel who tried "to restrict the conversation to cordial and social matters". When pressed, the King reiterated Italy's determination to fight by Germany's side "with whom Italy is bound in life and death".

That same afternoon, the Consul took train back to

Florence. During the journey an American radio announced at 5.45 p.m. that an official Armistice had been signed between the Allies and Italy, although this was denied in Rome[15].

At seven o'clock Rudolf Rahn was summoned to the Palazzo Chigi where Guariglia announced to him, "I have to tell you that in view of the desperate military situation, Marshal Badoglio has been forced to ask for an armistice."

"This is treachery to a plighted word," Rahn replied, adding, "it will lie heavily on Italy's history."

"I do not think so," the Foreign Minister answered. "What we have done is for the good of the Italian people, and expresses their genuine desire."

Dr Rahn left the Foreign Minister's office, slamming the door heavily behind him[16]. Now that his diplomatic mission had failed to achieve any tangible results, it was left to Marshal Kesselring to inject a sombre sense of reality into the situation. A cloud of German parachutists descended near the capital which Kesselring threatened to rase to the ground with seven hundred bombers if Rome refused to surrender. The disorganised and dispirited Italian army melted away except for a few formations under the command of the King's son-in-law, Count Calvi di Bergolo. Three hundred and twenty civilians died in a futile attempt to stem the advance of the seasoned paratroopers, while the King and Badoglio slipped out of the capital on the morning of September 9th.

From the window of his office, hung with tapestries depicting the victories of Alexander of Macedon, Dr Rahn watched with growing consternation as paratroopers began to pitch their tents on the smooth lawns of the Villa Wolkonsky. Huge bonfires were lit. He saw a hungry paratrooper shoot one of the Embassy's fine white peacocks, which he proceeded to pluck before roasting it on a spit. Another soldier who had shot a deer in the Zoological gardens, was dragging its carcass over the lawn, preparing for a similar feast. Dr Rahn lifted the house-phone, demanding to speak to General Stahel, the new city commandant, who had made his headquarters in the Embassy.

When he remonstrated with the commandant on the

behaviour of his troops, Stahel shouted: "Now there is only one master in Rome, and that is I!"

"You will get that confirmed when you present yourself in my office," Dr Rahn replied.

Meanwhile the Consul reached Florence where he was met by Kriegbaum. The two of them then went to Le Tre Pulzelle to talk over the events in the capital. Neither of them, however, had heard the official announcement of the Armistice which Badoglio had announced at eight o'clock that evening over the radio. Shortly before midnight the Swiss Consul, Carlo Steinhäuslin, telephoned, offering his services. The Consul was extremely puzzled. "Haven't you heard about the Armistice?" Steinhäuslin enquired.

On the following morning, September 9th, the Consul received instructions to evacuate the entire German colony from Florence as well as the contents of the German Art Institute. On the next day, the German Ambassador to the Vatican, Ernst von Weizsäcker, whom he had known at the Foreign Ministry, telephoned to ask if German troops had made their appearance in Florence. On hearing that there was no sign of German troops, Weizsäcker suggested that the Consul and his staff should wait for the special diplomatic train which was due to arrive at any moment from Rome. The Consul then summoned a council of his friends. Kriegbaum, although he had no choice but to leave Florence with the Consul, said that he could not move the contents of his Institute at such short notice: Hanna Kiel, on the other hand, declared that she had left Germany "for good" and had no intention of returning there under any circumstances. Erich Poppe, who had gone off for a short seaside holiday, could not be contacted. Hans Wildt, whose wife and family were in Florence, agreed to accompany the Consul. It was therefore left for Hanna Kiel to lock up the Institute and hand over the Consul's private papers into the custody of the Swiss Consul. Signor Poggi, the Superintendent of the Florentine Art Galleries agreed to take the Institute under his protection, a service he had rendered the Institute in the First World War.

The next morning Hanna Kiel went to the Piazza Santo Spirito to help Kriegbaum with his packing, and to await the arrival of the Consul. He turned up a few moments later together with Dr Wildt. But they had barely entered Kriegbaum's study when they heard a menacing rattle of keys in the corridor. A junior employee, a fervent Nazi, had arrived to supervise their departure! Hanna Kiel promptly hid herself in a cupboard, where she waited until the Consul, Kriegbaum and the Nazi had left the building. She then locked up the Institute and took the Consul's private papers to Steinhäuslin.

When the Consul and his friends reached the Central Station, they were told that the diplomatic train from Rome had been diverted. They therefore decided to make their way to Bolzano. Erich Poppe who turned up shortly afterwards was greatly surprised to learn that he too would have to be evacuated.

When they finally reached Bolzano, the Consul and his friends alighted, telling the guard that "they had left some important suitcases at the station", a fictional excuse so as to skip the train, which proceeded to Munich without them. They then settled into a small hotel in Upper Bolzano to wait developments. It was then that the Consul began to have second thoughts about leaving the train at Bolzano. "Let's hope Herr Ribbentrop does not notice our absence when the train reaches Munich," he sighed. "Otherwise, I'll have to do a great deal of explaining."

On the night of the Consul's departure from Florence, Hanna Kiel saw the flash of searchlights from the window of her villa at San Domenico di Fiesole. She went to bed in the happy certainty that the Allies had landed and were marching to liberate Florence. She slept fitfully, her rest disturbed by the rumble of tanks coming over Monte Rinaldi.

"On the following morning I rose early, determined to watch the entry of Allied troops into Florence," she recalled. "As I walked through my garden, I saw tanks carrying white flags lumbering down the via Bolognese. I was certain that the Allies had arrived in Florence! Only when I reached the Piazza della Signoria, did I realise my mistake. I saw German troops standing around in shorts and khaki skirts, armed to the teeth, while their tanks moved solemnly around the city, like a procession from 'Aida', played in some provincial opera house! They were determined to impress the Florentines with a show of force, although, as a matter of fact, they had few tanks, and fewer soldiers. . . ."

# 5

# Fugitive from the Winning Side

> Always be ready to change sides with justice, that fugitive from the winning side.
>
> SIMONE WEIL, *La Pesanteur et la Grâce*

By mid-September 1943, the Germans were in full occupation of Florence, with their *Stadtkommandantur* firmly established on the Piazza San Marco. Despite the official declaration of war on Nazi Germany by Badoglio on September 12th, the Italian forces outside Florence, commanded by General Chiappi Armellini, surrendered to the advancing Germans. Others went off to join the small Partisan detachments in the mountainous area around the city. The unfortunate Armellini was dragged off to Germany for refusing to break his oath of allegiance to the King. A few desultory rounds of fire had been aimed at passing German aircraft, and a handful of soldiers had made an attempt to harry the troops advancing on the city, but hardly a shot was fired at the occupiers themselves, who now took their ease and pleasure among Florence's palaces and piazzas.

The Tuscan Liberation Committee, a part of the national Resistance movement, summoned Florentines to reject "the grotesque resurrection of Fascism", and urged German soldiers themselves to put an end to Hitler's insane war. North of the city, in the wooden districts of Pratolini on the Monte Morello, the Action Party and the Communists were mustering their first Partisan detachments while inside the city itself cells of Resisters were organising arms dumps, medical supplies, and escape routes for Allied prisoners of war.

The Occupation forces on their side tried to prevent the

situation from falling into utter chaos. The harassed young city commandant, a veteran of the Eastern Front with little experience of civil government, decided to recall the Consul who had left so precipitately on the orders of his government. But where was this Consul to be found?

Dr Kiel who turned up at the *kommandantur* to ask for some insulin for a sick Italian prisoner of war, was able to provide the commandant with this information. Kriegbaum had written to her from Upper Bolzano, giving her his and the Consul's hotel address. On September 19th, an urgent cablegram reached the Consul, countersigned by the commandant and the Prefect, appealing to him to return immediately to Florence. On the following day, without waiting for official instructions, the Consul and his three colleagues, came back to the city they had left barely eight days previously. The hour of recall was bitter indeed. Florence was no longer recognisable: a spirit of gloom and despair had settled on a city which had witnessed its own inglorious capitulation.

On the day following the Consul wrote to his friend, Dr Rahn: "I returned to Florence yesterday without waiting for a specific directive from the Ministry at the request of the local city commandant and the Prefecture". He described the confusion in the city, and the clamour of agitated visitors at the Consulate who had come to enquire about the fate of their relatives, army officers, soldiers and civilians who had been deported to Germany. The transport of these defeated men under appalling conditions, in cattle trucks, subjected to long periods of intense heat, without food or water, had embittered the population, the Consul wrote.

Another cause of resentment was the appointment of a notorious *squadrista*, the Blackshirt "General" Onorio Onori, as Federale[1] (Federal Secretary). "Generally speaking, there is considerable fear here of personal acts of vengeance exacted by individual Fascists." He wrote that an appeal for calm and unity made by local Fascists in Pisa had had a "reassuring effect", and that a similar appeal should be made in Florence. He ended his letter by telling Rudolf Rahn that he had taken temporary residence at the Hotel Excelsior, a luxury hotel owned by a Swiss family, which had been taken over by the German authorities.

The Ambassador answered his friend's letter promptly on September 23rd, telling him that in addition to his Ambassadorial rank, he had been appointed *Reichskommissar* or Plenipotentiary. "This should strengthen your position vis à vis the various civil and military authorities," Dr Rahn wrote, "because it will enable you to act with the authority of the Plenipotentiary of the Reich."

As to the arrest and deportation of Italian officers and men, this had been dictated by the harsh necessities of war so as to secure recruits for German war industries, and "besides, it is hardly our business to provide Herr Badoglio with troops for the British Army".

The more lenient the measures taken to secure these recruits "the better I like it", the Ambassador assured the Consul. Among the measures he proposed was the setting up of a special office for the recruitment of free labourers whose families would be maintained at the expense of the Prefecture. "Try to find Italians who will explain to the workers that they will find better conditions and security in Germany than in a place where military operations may make their working conditions more difficult sooner or later," he urged the Consul. As for the local Fascists who were causing the Consul so much concern, the Ambassador proposed a simple remedy. "If you do not approve of one of the Fascists in Florence, dismiss him and appoint a more suitable person, avoiding embarassing conflicts where possible—*aber Du wirst es nach dem Gestez der sanften Gewalt schon schaffen*—but you will manage this with the art (law) of gentle persuasion."

The Ambassador also told him in strictest confidence that the Duce would be arriving in Italy on September 27th to take up his seat of government in north Italy. "I shall try to remain mobile so as to clarify practical issues with you and other consuls in various localities." He himself hoped to visit Florence shortly "once the plane I have asked for has been placed at my disposal".

The Consul was greatly heartened by the Ambassador's

letter although he had no illusions about his powers to dismiss any fractious Fascist. "The most I could do was to complain," he has said, "or at times, obstruct. But these were purely passive powers.[2]"

The effective control in the city had rapidly passed out of the hands of the Prefect Count Gaetani, who had thrown his support to Badoglio and would shortly be dismissed and arrested, into the hands of the obnoxious Federal Secretary Onorio Onori, supported by the fire-eating Alessandro Pavolini, the Fascist Party Secretary, and Renato Ricci, the chief of the Black Militia. But the real power in the city resided in the small office in the *Kommandantur* where the S.S. and Gestapo had set up their post.

The Consul became aware of the Gestapo's presence a few days after his return to Florence, when he was asked for the whereabouts of one of Florence's most prominent residents, the famous Bernard Berenson. The Consul replied that as far as he knew Bernard Berenson "had gone to Portugal, via the Vatican", a story which he knew was untrue.

Eighteen months earlier, he and Kriegbaum had fobbed off one of Goering's "art buyers" who had descended on the city, making enquiries about Berenson and his famous collection of pictures. According to an entry in Berenson's diary[3], Kriegbaum had told him on his last visit to I Tatti that both he and the Consul had "frequently put their heads together as to how they could save I Tatti from depredation". The "art buyer" had heard of a villa belonging to an American which contained "valuable pictures and books", but Kriegbaum had managed to persuade him that "at I Tatti there were no paintings except of Catholic subjects, and no books of more than local interest". The art buyer left empty-handed. But shortly after the German occupation of the city, Berenson received hints "not only from the art Superintendent but from a friendly German, that we had better put books and pictures in safety".

Berenson does not identify this "friendly German", but the hint probably came from Kriegbaum himself, who together with the Consul had been to see the Art Superintendent,

Signor Poggi, shortly after their return to Florence. They not only discussed the future of I Tatti and its celebrated owner, but other matters connected with the protection of Florence's art treasures from Hitler's and Goering's "buyers".

One such individual, a certain Herr Sepp Angerer, had arrived claiming that he was Hitler's "personal art buyer". This fat, rather unprepossessing person who had been a former Berlin carpet-seller, appeared to have substantial reserves of cash with which to make his purchases for the Führer's private Linz collection. But first, Herr Sepp Angerer insisted on making his "art investigations".

The Consul, who had the dubious pleasure of accompanying Herr Sepp Angerer on one of these tours, noticed that he was greatly taken by the art collection belonging to Count Conti-Bonacossi, one of the leading art dealers and collectors in Florence. After gazing lovingly at one of the Count's pictures, he turned to him and said: "What a pity you're not a Jew!" As neither the Count Conti-Bonacossi nor the Consul could make sense of his remark, Herr Sepp Angerer drew a hairy finger across his throat, saying: "If you were a Jew, we would do just that! And all the paintings would be ours!"

This illustrative gesture must have alarmed the Consul, because he sent a message to Miss Nicky Mariano through her nephew, asking her to call as soon as possible at the Consulate. When she arrived the Consul told her, with some embarrassment, that while he would do all he could to protect I Tatti and its library and paintings, his task would be made considerably easier if Bernard Berenson was not there. Miss Mariano was happy to inform the Consul that Berenson was no longer at I Tatti, and the Consul appeared greatly relieved. "You have given me excellent news," he said. "I don't want to know anything more.[4]"

Berenson and Nicky Mariano had, in fact, left I Tatti on September 10th, shortly before the German occupation of the city. They had come to tea with the Serlupis in their villa, Le Fontanelle, and had been prevailed upon by their hosts to remain as guests for the next thirteen months!

To perfect Berenson's disguise, Marchesa Serlupi instructed

all her servants to address him as "the Baron". "We decided to give him a title, which was easy in Italy, and he was always known as Monsieur le Baron. Even after the war whenever he visited us, the servants addressed him as such," she stated[5].

Her husband, Marchese Serlupi, the Minister of San Marino to the Holy See, went further. He decided "with the help of a member of the Italian police who was living at I Tatti to reply to all enquiries that Berenson had gone to Portugal, and a few days later, the Italian radio announced this 'news'". To add to the German's confusion, Serlupi spread the rumour that Bernard Berenson was "the illegitimate son of a Russian Grand Duke" and, therefore, presumably an Aryan! The Consul solemnly reproduced this canard in an official aide memoire which he later wrote to the Ambassador.

Marchesa Serlupi and her servants had meanwhile taken a lorry and removed most of the valuable paintings from the walls of I Tatti and hung less valuable paintings in their place. She also removed paintings and books from Berenson's house in the Borgo San Jacopo which were hung at Le Fontanelle or stored in the nearby villa of Quarto which belonged to the Marchesa's mother-in-law, Baroness Ritter de Zahony.

On September 25th, while walking in the grounds of Le Fontanelle, at around noon, Berenson noticed a squadron of Allied planes forming a triangle over Florence. "It is my belief that the aviators were returning from a serious expedition and, without previous thought of doing so, happened to see a train passing along the edge of the town and thought it would be fun to pot it", he wrote in his diary, adding that "the result was a sad one.[6]"

Hanna Kiel also witnessed the R.A.F.'s first aerial attack on Florence. She was waiting for Kriegbaum to take her to a reunion luncheon which the Consul had arranged in a restaurant, and was whiling away the time arranging flowers in a vase.

Suddenly there was a loud shrill of sirens. She ran out onto her balcony in time to see the R.A.F. planes turn away at a sharp angle from the centre of the city. A stick of bombs fell in the direction of the Via del Ponte Rosso, aimed at the

Campo di Marte and military marshalling yards, sending up an enormous cloud of debris into the air.

The dust took a full half hour to settle before Dr Kiel could discern the familiar outline of the city. Mercifully none of the city's famous domes or towers had been damaged. She immediately ran to the telephone to contact the Consul, but the lines had been cut. An hour or so later, when communications had been restored, the Consul phoned to ask why neither she nor Kriegbaum had turned up for the luncheon.

"Haven't you heard about the air-raid?" she asked, ironically.

"Only the outskirts have been hit," the Consul reassured her. "Is there any sign of Kriegbaum?"

"No," answered Hanna Kiel. "If you'll send me a taxi, I'll go round all the city hospitals. Something dreadful may have happened to him."

"Nonsense. You're just imagining things!" the Consul joked. "You women, with your premonitions!"

A moment later, after he had put down the receiver, he was approached by a German Pioneer (Engineer Corps) officer who asked for his identity. The Consul satisfied the officer who handed him a visiting card, with the name of the Viennese art historian Leo Planiscig on it. On the card, a note had been hastily scribbled in pencil: "A bomb fell, and a German professor is lying under the ruins of my house. . . ."

The Consul, together with the officer and ten pioneers went to Planiscig's house on the outskirts of San Domenico di Fiesole, and saw them dig out the body of his friend, Friedrich Kriegbaum, from its ruins.

From accounts pieced together afterwards, it appeared that Kriegbaum had left his Institute shortly before noon, but instead of taking the usual tram which would have brought him to San Domenico in about half an hour, he had asked Oreste, the caretaker, to hail a passing taxi. It had been raining. The drive to San Domenico took ten minutes, and Kriegbaum had barely entered the Planiscigs' house before the raid started.

Leo Planiscig and the cook immediately hurried down to

the cellar, leaving Kriegbaum and Mrs Planiscig in the library. Kriegbaum made some joke about "people who run off to shelters the moment they hear an air-raid siren", and continued to sip vermouth, although Mrs Planiscig urged him to join her husband in the cellars.

At that moment, a bomb fell, burying Kriegbaum under a wall of books and debris. Mrs Planiscig was saved by a heavy table which had somehow fallen on top of her, breaking her arm.

It took several hours for the pioneers to extricate Kriegbaum's body from the ruins. "There was hardly a scratch on him," the Consul observed, sadly. "He looked as if he had fallen asleep...."

That evening a violent thunderstorm struck the city. The Arno rose by a few inches, while the bridge named after the Holy Trinity, whose secret Kriegbaum had unlocked, was illuminated by sudden flashes of lightning. The Consul and Hanna Kiel, Kriegbaum's closest friends, watched over his body which had been laid out in the Institute. Early next morning while drinking coffee with Dr Kiel, the Consul turned to her, saying: "Now the war has really begun...."

For the Consul, the war had begun with the loss of his friend, Friedrich Kriegbaum, whom Berenson himself described as "one of the most thoroughly humanized and cultured individuals of my acquaintance, gentle and tender, incapable of evil, and was doing nothing but good. He was one in a thousand, and if Germany had 75,000 like him she would be worth saving and cherishing[7]."

When Dr Rahn arrived on the next day, the Consul met him, and told him with tears in his eyes of his friend's death. "So instead of showing me round the city as I had hoped, the Consul and I went to Kriegbaum's funeral, where I delivered the last oration before his friends."

The air-raid which killed Kriegbaum and nine others, as well as wounding one hundred other persons, was considered a minor foray[8]. The fact that the R.A.F. had aimed at legitimate military targets led to the assumption that the Allies had given recognition, however, nebulous, to Florence's "open city" status, and on October 6th, the Consul wrote to Dr Rahn, at the Cardinal-Archbishop's suggestion, asking him to persuade Hitler to issue an official "open city" declaration although, as the Consul put it, "I am not quite sure what practical implications such a declaration would have. In any case, I should be grateful if you placed me in a position to give this important dignitary of the Church a reassuring statement." He had spoken to a General of Engineers the previous day "who viewed the situation in Florence not unfavourably". Apart from military considerations, the destruction of Florence would be an unmitigated disaster "from a purely propaganda point of view". This was language the Führer would understand.

In the same letter, the Consul drew the Ambassador's attention to the arrest of a number of clergymen in the south Tyrol, a district Hitler had annexed together with Venezia Giulia, shortly after the Duce's return to Italy. Everyone knew how much the clergy had done "in the difficult days after the First World War" when this area had been assigned to Italy. They had not only catalogued books, listed monuments, but had encouraged the teaching of German, and the printing of German religious books. "It would be regrettable," the Consul added, "if we were to make the same mistakes here as were made in Poland (*. . . die gleichen Fehler wie in Polen machen würden*)."

As far as his own parish was concerned, he was glad to report that the detested Onorio Onori was leaving the city. He was sorry that the weather had been so bad when Dr Rahn had last visited Florence and asked: "Could you not pass through Florence again?" The weather had improved, "brilliant October days, described by Baedeker" had succeeded the torrential rains. "I can't complain from lack of work," he added.

Two days later he explained the nature of this "work". He had been "suddenly informed by several old acquaintances in Florence that their closest relatives had been arrested and taken to prison". He had gone immediately to the Questura to find out who had given orders for these wholesale arrests. "I was told that the orders had been given by the newly-appointed Prefect and head of the Florentine Province."

A fanatical pro-Fascist Prefect had replaced the gentle Count Gaetani, who had been summarily dismissed from his post and arrested on October 1st, shortly after Mussolini's return to Italy. The Duce was determined to vent his spite not only on all of Badoglio's supporters but on everyone who had any connection, however remote, with the Royal Court.

On the morning of October 7th, when the Consul turned up at his office, he found his "usually silent and efficient" secretary Maria Faltien in a state of great agitation. The young Marchese Calabrini, she told him, had been waiting for him. As the Consul entered his private office, the Marchese threw himself on his knees. "They want to arrest my mother!" The elderly Marchesa Calabrini was a woman of seventy, who had been bedridden for many years with a bad heart.

The Consul immediately drove with the Marchese to the Palazzo Corsini and managed to dissuade the officials from making the arrest.

At lunchtime another urgent appeal reached him. The sister-in-law of the adjutant to the Crown Prince of Bavaria, had telephoned to say that the eighty-year-old Marchesa Beatrice Pandolfini had been arrested and taken to the women's prison of S. Verdiano.

The Consul who was beside himself with fury, rushed off with his two companions Dr Wildt and Dr Poppe to confront this "newly-appointed Prefect", a Dr Raffaele Manganiello, who, he learnt, had only recently been released from fortress imprisonment where he had been placed, together with other leading Fascists, by Badoglio.

When they arrived at the Prefectorial seat in the Palazzo Riccardi, they were immediately struck by the signs of occupancy of its new masters. Empty wine bottles and scraps of torn paper littered the place. They were shown into an anteroom where they were left for some time, before the new Prefect deigned to see them.

Finally, when they were led into the Prefect's study, they found a tall, hunched-up man, "with flattened, repulsive features", sitting behind a large, ornamented desk, surrounded by "types as sinister as himself", wearing black shirts, with revolvers strapped to their waists. "The scene reminded me of a Hollywood gangster film," the Consul said, later.

Dr Manganiello, the new Prefect, who continued to smoke without offering his guests a cigarette, waved them peremptorily to a seat and demanded their business.

"Why has the Marchesa Pandolfini been arrested?" the Consul demanded in his iciest, official tone. "And who authorised these arrests?"

The Prefect studied a file of papers on his desk, and after a moment's pause, answered: "I did."

"For what reason?"

"They offended against rationing regulations and uttered defamatory statements against the new republican government."

The Consul rose from his seat.

"Now kindly give me the *real* reason for their arrest," he exclaimed.

Manganiello seemed surprised. "The real reason should be obvious to you. Buffarini has ordered the arrest of all former courtiers and ladies-in-waiting of the Royal Household."

"But these persons relinquished their posts twenty or thirty years ago!" the Consul protested.

"They are to be held as hostages against the families of leading Fascists secured by Badoglio and the King in south Italy." Manganiello softened his tone. "Surely it is in the interests of both our countries...."

"It is in the interest of no one to arrest sick and elderly people," the Consul interrupted. "I should like a written order for their release."

Manganiello hesitated. Then a faint grin appeared over his unprepossessing, ugly features as he wrote out an order for the release of Marchesa Pandolfini and a suspension of sentence on Marchesa Calabrini. It was not worth arguing with the Consul of the Greater Reich over two old women.

"Benefits," said Machiavelli, "should be distilled by drops, that the relish may be greater."

The Consul took the release order from the Prefect's hand, drove to the S. Verdiano prison and obtained the release of the eighty-year-old Marchesa Pandolfini, whom he returned to her rejoicing family, as he told the Ambassador in his letter of October 8th. The arrest of these elderly Florentine aristocrats had greatly shocked the city. "Unlike other aristocrats elsewhere, the Florentine aristocracy has very close connections with the soil, and is generally popular with its tenants," he observed. "Persons who make defamatory statements should be punished, but I would strongly advise you to obtain a directive from the Duce prohibiting the arrest of aged, and often ailing persons, specially since the whole business smacks of private vengeance, carried out by subordinates."

The Consul had made a close investigation into the record of some of the Prefect's "subordinates" whom he described as "the scum of the Fascist Party (*Abschaums der fascistischen Partei*), who had come to the top as a result of recent events". The Consul had been provided with some startling information about the new Prefect's associates by obliging officials in the Questura. Most of this "scum" had served sentences of imprisonment for murder, bodily violence and theft. Such were the new rulers of Florence!

Despite his success over the two aged Marchesas, arrests continued unabated. The Consul therefore asked the city commandant Colonel von Kunowski to write to the Prefect, demanding to know the reason. Why, for example, had the seventy-four-year-old Admiral Notarbartolo, whose only "crime" was that he had served as the King's personal naval attaché in 1919, been arrested? Was the arrest of the aged Marchesa D'Ajeta and her husband due to the fact that their son had served as Ciano's private secretary[9]? Donna Magda Catalano Gonzaga, the wife of the celebrated admiral, a holder of the Iron Cross (First Class), who had spent the summer in Florence, had also been arrested: what were the charges against her?

Even more senseless was the arrest of the gentle Marchesa

Fiammetta Gondi, a prominent member of the Florentine Red Cross, a woman known for her good works among the poor of the Santa Croce working-class district. And more inexplicably, perhaps, why had the wife of a prominent pro-Fascist sculptor Antonio Maraini who was a "well-known anti-semite" and who because of her positive Fascist leanings "would be seriously endangered during an Anglo-American occupation" been arrested? Among others whom von Kunowski and the Consul mentioned was the Marchese Roberto Ginori-Venturi—"A trustworthy friend of Germany's, a supporter of Fascism, who is well acquainted with Marshal Goering."

"Not only have these arrests caused unrest and indignation among the Florentine population, but they have given rise to an entirely unjustified distrust of the German occupation forces who are made responsible for them," the city commandant concluded his letter to the Prefect. "For this reason I must insist strongly that I am notified of all intended political arrests, including the exact explanation of the reason for them, before such arrests are made. I also demand a careful examination and an early clarification of pending cases, as well as the prompt release of all persons whose arrest has been proved unjustified."

The casual name-dropping, the calculated suggestion that everyone was "a friend of Germany's", or "an ardent Fascist", or even "a well-known anti-semite", were all part of the game of deception which the Consul had to play with his own authorities, including the city commandant. Most of the persons for whom he interceded were later released[10]. "It was the least he could do—to save his friends!" someone remarked ungenerously. The Florentine *magnificos*, the admirals and retired courtiers and ladies-in-waiting were indeed the Consul's friends. But as the German occupation continued the Consul's circle of friends widened to include every kind and condition of men from lawyers and business men to railway workers.

In a letter written at that time to Dr Rahn, commiserating with him on a recent motor accident which had confined him to bed, the Consul went on to speculate on the future of Florence "if Tuscany should become a battlefield". He asked the Ambassador to remember that the Führer had often described Florence as his favourite city. "On his visit here, the Führer declared in the presence of various persons, that if unique structures such as the Ponte Santa Trinita, or the Ponte Vecchio, or one of the ancient palaces were destroyed, the loss would not only be Italy's, but the whole world's."

The Führer, of course, had said nothing of the sort. He had merely observed to Kriegbaum that the Ponte Vecchio was his "favourite bridge" but the Consul had transposed the Ponte Vecchio with the Ponte Santa Trinita. Or had he quite subconsciously put Kriegbaum's words into Hitler's mouth?

In the tormented months which lay ahead, the Consul would again and again refer to the bridge of the Holy Trinity, his insubstantial link with the recent past which had witnessed the death of his friend.

# 6

# The Cypresses

Know ye the land where the cypress and myrtle
Are emblems of deeds that are done in their clime;
Where the rage of the vulture, the love of the turtle,
Now melt into sorrow, now madden to crime?

LORD BYRON

Florence—after the shock of the first few weeks of German occupation—returned to a vestige of normality. Warm autumn days succeeded the rains. The Consul had moved from the Excelsior back to Le Tre Pulzelle at San Domenico di Fiesole, but the lovely little villa no longer seemed so warm and friendly. He missed his wife and daughter who were still in Switzerland. But recent events had brought a new extension to his personality which had seemed so often cold and remote.

His friend and neighbour Donna Beatrice Viganò, who belonged to a famous Anglo-Florentine family (her mother was a Miss Haskard, a Scot) came to ask him for a "document" to guarantee the inviolability of her cow and donkey. "At this time, a cow which gave milk, and a donkey with four healthy legs, were worth their weight in gold," she explained. She also asked the Consul to exempt her Austrian maid Annie from returning to the Reich. Annie was looking after the sick child of an Italian officer who was in hiding, and the Consul busied himself finding the right medicines for the child. By such small, but neighbourly gestures, was the Consul remembered at this time.

He was particularly pleased to report to the Ambassador

that the behaviour of the German occupation forces had been on the whole fairly exemplary. "The best propaganda has been the decent, polite and disciplined behaviour of German troops," he said. Iris Origo (Marchese Origo), the British-born author of many celebrated books about Italy, whose Villa Medici had been requisitioned by the Germans, also noted the "correct" behaviour of the Germans, although they were "so much hated that all the misdeeds which they have not as yet committed are attributed to them, as well as those which they have[1]". Another Englishwoman, Miss M. Gladys Elliot whose house was searched by the Germans, found them "cold, but polite".

But more serious privations were to follow in the wake of the occupation. The bread ration, as the Consul reported to Dr Rahn, had fallen to 200 grams daily. Signora Comberti, who had failed to secure a job at the German Consulate, noted in her diary that "bread had become one of the most treasured possessions".

Signora Comberti had gone to the *Kommandantur* to ask for some extra bread coupons for a doctor friend, and happened to ask a passing German soldier for the time. The soldier, a middle-aged reserve sergeant, saluted gallantly, pulled out his gold watch, and then promptly dropped it onto the asphalt where it lay shattered into fragments. Maria Comberti immediately offered to have the watch repaired—"but of course, he did not trust me. A person could live for a whole week on a gram of gold!" So she went home, found her late husband's gold watch and brought it to the sergeant as a pledge. A week later she returned with his mended watch. He was so delighted that he not only returned the pledge, but gave her a month's bread coupons into the bargain! She rushed off to a bakery and bought thirty 200 gram loaves, which she distributed to every passing beggar in the street. "I felt like Haroun al Raschid!" she wrote in her diary. "I can still feel the warmth of that new-baked bread on my hands. . . .[2]"

But individual acts of kindness were soon matched by depredations carried out by the hideous-sounding *Wehrmachts-erfassungskommando* IV which removed all stocks of gold and silver from the famous goldsmiths' shops lining the Ponte Vecchio and in other districts. Some hundred and twenty cases of theft and confiscation had occurred which required compensation, the Consul wrote[3]. The unfortunate jewellers had been forced to resort to the manufacture of cheap, imitation jewellery, and many of their craftsmen were out of work. "The fact that the local German jeweller, Fritz Scheurle, who acted as interpreter, directed the seizure of stocks belonging to his Florentine colleagues, because of his knowledge of local conditions and trade, had left a particularly unpleasant impression here."

Much of the growing unrest and disorder in Florence was due to the fact that the para-military *Carabinieri*, whose loyalties were undisguisedly monarchist, had been subject to various humiliations by the German armed forces. On October 11th, the Consul sent an urgent telegram, the first of many, over the military teletype, to the Ambassador, telling him: "Bloody clashes with Germans and arrests of Carabinieri are said to have occurred in Rome, because of the maladroit conduct of a General of the Carabinieri[4]. He had demanded a clear-cut decision from his officers for or against the Republican Party. In consequence, many Carabinieri both in Rome and in Florence have left their posts, and their co-operation which is urgently required for the maintenance of order, is jeopardised. Since the Carabinieri are so far the only authority with an excellent knowledge of the country and its people, there is great danger of anarchic conditions, especially in the countryside. Request immediate effective steps to be taken. These should consist in assuring the Carabinieri that their co-operation for the maintenance of order in the customary non-political form, is desired and appreciated."

On October 12th, he wrote again to Dr Rahn: "In my view we must absolutely make use of them for this purpose (maintenance of order), to relieve our own forces, just as you used the French police in Tunisia. Since, however, this force was established for the protection of the Royal Family it is traditionally strongly pro-royalist: this attitude must be considered if they are to serve us." There was no point in using the Carabinieri against the "bandits" (Partisans) as their employment against them was bound to fail and produce ill-will on both sides, he said. If the Carabinieri themselves are driven into the ranks of the Partisans, "they will take over the leadership of these gangs".

He himself was inclined to minimise the importance of these "gangs" if some way could be found of pacifying the population. "The Tuscans do not normally show inclination to form gangs, nor do they wish to fight," he wrote in his letter of October 12th. "Because of the not very cleverly worded proclamation which summoned all officers and men to report by a given date, many of them fled to the forests and mountains for fear of being shipped to Germany, or even to Russia. Here they join British and Serbian prisoners of war, and of necessity begin to form gangs." He was certain that they would surrender their arms and return to their homes "if they would be assured that they would be left alone. Otherwise they will not return, under any circumstances. If some of them are seized and shot, tremendous bitterness will be created, without producing any political or military advantage to us."

He also referred again to the arrests of the elderly Florentine aristocrats. These arrests had "evidently been initiated by Tamburini, the chief of the Italian police," he wrote. ". . . Is it not possible to put an end to this nonsense which is considered as naked terror by the population here?" he demanded.

Two days later he again wrote to the Ambassador after a chance meeting with General Mischi who had been appointed to head all the Carabinieri forces in Mussolini's Republic. Mischi had evidently been reluctant to discuss the "Rome incident", but he had been to see Mussolini and had urged the release of arrested Carabinieri officers and men, all of whom should have the opportunity to opt for service in North Italy. The Consul himself urged that "it would not be politically expedient to insist on a clear-cut decision for or against the monarchy. Such an attitude towards the arrested Carabinieri would be well received by others, and would be highly advantageous for their loyal co-operation with us."

He listed five separate incidents which had occurred in

Florence where German officers and men had raided Carabinieri barracks, disarmed some of the Carabinieri, forced others to put on civilian clothes, and had stolen arms, ammunition, furniture and office equipment. "It is quite certain that without the co-operation of this force so peculiar to Italy and so thoroughly tried, internal peace and order cannot be maintained in the long run," he ended his letter of October 14th.

But on October 15th the Consul was even in a more explosive mood, judging from a letter he sent to one of the city's army commanders, a Colonel Guse. He had just been visited by the Director of Artistic Monuments, Signor Poggi, and the Mayor of Fiesole, as well as other prominent citizens of the same town. They had told him that two German officers, staying at the Hotel Aurora in Fiesole, had demanded "that the ancient cypress trees of the Villa Medici should be cut down by 1 p.m. Failing this they would themselves have the trees cut down. The trees in question are hundreds of years old and are the property of an Italian citizen, the Marchese Origo. These trees are protected by State regulations, so that they may not even be touched by the owner, without the authorisation of the Florence administration of monuments."

The Consul sent the acting-director of the German Art Institute, Dr Siebenhüner to remonstrate against this act of vandalism—"the first incident of its kind to involve two German officers, who in order to obtain a better view from their hotel terrace, conceived the astonishing idea of cutting down the world-famous avenue of cypresses".

The two German captains, however, refused to countermand their order. The Villa Medici was "British property", they declared, and as such, they could cut down every cypress tree in the avenue! When Dr Siebenhüner protested, the two officers rounded on him and called him an "anglophile", telling him that "it was none of his business, nor mine, since he had referred to me", the Consul wrote. Dr Siebenhüner later reported that they had treated him in a manner not compatible with his honour as a German official, and demanded an apology.

The Consul then contacted Lieutenant-Colonel Schmidt of the Military Police, who arrived with a squad of his men at the Hotel Aurora, where they found the two oafs sprawled on deck chairs, sipping cold drinks. The Consul who turned up a few moments later repeated his arguments, explaining that although the property was owned by Marchese Origo, whose wife Iris was British, the villa and the cypresses were under State protection.

The two comic-opera captains then sprang up from their deck chairs and began railing at the Consul. He too was an "anglophile" and an "unworthy German"! While they "did all the fighting, he merely acted as a kind of watch dog!"

The Consul, who was an old soldier himself, knew how to deal with this insolence. He asked Colonel Guse to report the two captains to their commanding officer, who should explain to them that: "My position here is that of the German Consul and direct representative of the Plenipotentiary of the Reich in Italy. My present task is to assist German forces in every way, and to act as an intermediary between them and the Italian authorities, but at the same time to ensure that all unnecessary public unrest by private, arbitrary acts is avoided."

He ended his despatch in a more conciliatory tone: "I have reason to believe that the Italian owner of the hotel is behind the whole affair, and that he put the officers up to it. I have reported this suspicion to the Mayor of Fiesole."

The cypresses of the Villa Medici were preserved by the Consul for the enjoyment and recreation of countless tourists who still make their way up the slope leading past Le Tre Pulzelle to the villa where Lorenzo the Magnificent entertained his friends Poliziano and Pico della Mirandola.

A day and a night later, when the morning star had faded behind the dark green cypresses, a new and blacker star arose in the firmament above Florence. Now it was no longer a matter of saving a cow or a donkey, or even an avenue of ancient cypresses. Mario Carità had arrived, and was beginning to carve his eternal infamy on the minds and bodies of his victims.

# 7

# Carità

And to a part I come, where no light shines.

DANTE, *Inferno, Canto IV*

On October 15th 1943, while the Consul was remonstrating with the two German captains who seemed bent on chopping down the ancient cypresses of the Villa Medici at San Domenico di Fiesole, a certain Captain Mario Carità, the head of the *Ufficio Politico Investigativo*, of the 92nd Legion of the Republican Guard, together with a heavily armed posse of men, made a sudden foray against a small Partisan group holding out in the wooded area of the Monte Morello, north of the city.

After a brief exchange of shots in which two of his men were shot dead, Carità beat a hasty retreat, and never again showed his face in open combat with the Partisans. Instead, he decided to use subtler and more insinuating methods in dealing with the Resistance and its network of "commissions" which was spreading throughout the city.

The Consul who had received information from the head of the S.D. (Gestapo) post in Florence, Haupsturmführer Goebel, that "bandit" activities had suddenly intensified in the mountains around the city, wrote to the Ambassador on October 22nd 1942, telling him that "it would not be difficult for us to return most of the bandits to their normal occupations, if they received certain assurances from us that they would be free from molestation. Otherwise they will most certainly not return, and these gangs will even grow bigger if a number of factories in Florence are shut down, as planned."

He also contradicted the Ambassador's earlier dissertation on the need to prevent "Herr Badoglio" from securing men for the British army through mass recruitment of labourers to Germany. Among these, the Consul claimed, were "masses of people who were ready to place themselves at our disposal". Because of the close family ties which bound most Italians, immediate steps should be taken for them to communicate with their anxious families. "This 'cold terror of the soul' (*kalte Seelenterror*) was the best possible way for us to lose all the sympathies which we so badly need. If matters were handled more adroitly here from the start, it would have been easy to gain considerable sympathy."

He also pressed the Ambassador for an early reply to the Cardinal of Florence's appeal that Florence should be declared an Open City, before turning to what he called "a personal matter."

During the Ambassador's last visit to Florence, Dr Rahn had discussed the question of increasing the staff at the Consulate, but the Consul had firmly turned down his suggestion. He was anxious to preserve his small nucleus of trusted friends around him. His two vice-consuls, the university lecturers Dr Wildt and Dr Poppe, were "assisting me day and night in dealing with the vastly expanded work of the Consulate," he wrote. "Their thorough knowledge of the country, and command of the Italian language, as well as the high degree of trust established in us, make their help indispensable to me." They had been seconded to the Consulate only until the end of the month, when they expected to be called up, but the Consul urged the Ambassador to postpone this decision.

Something was clearly afoot which made it imperative for the Consul to retain the services of his two trusted stalwarts, his "private army", as he jokingly called them. This became apparent two days after Carità's unsuccessful attack on the Partisan detachment on the Monte Morello.

The harsh winds which fanned "the cold terror of the soul", now burst like a tornado over the city, as Captain Mario Carità erupted on the scene like an insane Minotaur to begin his wholesale repressions, tortures, ceaseless interrogations, all of which were accompanied with the most degrading brutality and humiliations.

The name of Mario Carità, an insult to any concept of charity, would deserve only the scantiest mention in these pages, but for the fact that his bloodsoaked career paralleled that of the Consul's for almost a year. A cursory examination of this thorough-going ruffian seems necessary therefore. The only charitable thing which could be said about Carità was that he was hopelessly insane. Some of his victims who endured unspeakable horrors at his hands, were convinced that he suffered from cancer of the brain, but the Consul considered that he was reasonably sane, as sane as anyone could be whose declared ambition (as Carità once told his mistress Milly)—was to become "the Himmler of Italy".

This too cannot explain the whole man. The few photographs which exist of Carità—he had a peasant's dread of the camera-lens—may provide some clue to his personality. Though he aspired to be another Himmler he bore little resemblance to that desiccated schoolmaster who rose to be the Policeman of Europe. Carità looked far more like the Duce: there was the same heavy jowl, frog-like mouth, with hooded eyelids covering his cold, lizard-green eyes, as well as the same arrogant, quasi-comic air of authority. A few decadent Florentine aristocrats who had reason to flatter him, described him as "a flaming archangel". Carità, however, showed less than angelic predilection for strong liquors and rich food, which he consumed in huge quantities before the eyes of his starving and bleeding prisoners. To food and violence, he joined his amatory interests, served not only by his revolting mistress Milly but numerous other female acquaintances as well. But his most abiding affection was reserved for his own skin: he invariably travelled in the safety and comfort of a requisitioned ambulance.

Little is known of this *condottiere's* antecedents beyond a few biographical gleanings. Despite his long residence in the city he was not a Florentine. He was born in Milan in 1904 according to an entry in a baptismal register which records this dismal event. His full name is given as Mario Carità del fu Gesú without identifying the name of his father. This omission may have left its mark on Carità's tender psyche, for his earliest years were spent in a private orphanage run by charitable, upper-class ladies. For this reason perhaps Carità always showed a marked aversion to charity and to aristocratic ladies whom he tried to humiliate in every possible way on his advent to power.

His education, in any case, was of the most elementary kind. By the age of fifteen he was to be found in the ranks of Luigi Freddi's bravoes in Lodi, a year or two before Mussolini's march on Rome. The actual date of Carità's arrival in Florence, however, is not known, but for some time before the war he worked with the Phillips electrical organisation from which he was dismissed for a number of unspecified irregularities. It was then that he opened his small radio repair shop on the via Panzani, which he ran with the help of his three sisters, supplementing his meagre income as a part-time police informer, reporting on customers who listened to the B.B.C.[1]

The war provided Carità with opportunity to pose as a battle-tried veteran. He returned unscathed from Mussolini's ill-fated Greek campaign, with the rank of centurion (captain) in a blackshirt legion, but lay low during Badoglio's "forty-five days" until his sudden emergence as the head of the sinister investigating office of the *Guardia Nazionale Repubblicana* shortly after the German occupation of the city.

He had been introduced to his masters by one Giovanni Castaldelli, a defrocked monk, who had no difficulty in advertising Carità's expertise and trustworthiness to the S.D. This alliance between the fascist centurion and the renegade monk provided Carità with some of his most respectable spies and informers: a tonsured pate seemed to exert an irresistible attraction for "the biting axe of Florence", who himself had been drawn into the wider ramifications of the S.D.

There were excellent reasons for this mutual attraction between "the flaming archangel" and the S.S. The S.D. post in Florence, unlike its sister organisation in Rome, was relatively small, run by a staff of some twelve "information" specialists, headed in the first few weeks by a Hauptsturmführer Goebel, and later by a "pale-faced, tight-lipped, better-educated version of Carità", S.S. Captain Alberti, a German from the Alto Adige.

To retain an impression of "neutrality", the gentlemanly cut-throats of the S.D. left the actual process of arrest, torture and interrogation in Carità's hands, while they themselves merely provided the necessary "information". This arrangement did not altogether satisfy Carità since it left all the opprobrium on his head, without any flattering recognition that he belonged to the S.S. Thus he frequently boasted, when he was in his cups, that he was "part" of the S.D., a boast which was readily believed by everyone, including the Consul, although Carità was never formally enrolled into that band.

But in the first few weeks of Occupation, Carità's name was unknown to anyone outside his own circle. The radio mechanic with the strong resemblance to Mussolini had, however, been liberally supplied with funds, an "office" of some one hundred men, which included a former variety actor, one Arrigo Masi, ten spies, six investigators, seven professional torturers, a personal cook, and a private guard of five, as well as an "assassins' squadron" led by Erno Manente, who operated directly under the S.D.[2] In addition, Carità also worked hand-in-glove with the new Prefect Manganiello and "the scum of the Fascist Party" which surrounded him.

On October 17th, two days after his frustrating encounter with the Partisans on Monte Morello, Carità diverted his attention to the hated Florentine aristocrats. This time he arrested Marchesa Maria Carolina Corsini, and her three daughters, one of whom was a child of fourteen, accusing them of "making derogatory remarks about the new government". The Corsinis who belonged to one of the most ancient families in Florence (they had given a Pope to the church, and a wife to Niccolò Machiavelli) appealed to the Consul, who managed to secure the immediate release of the fourteen-year-old girl. But Carità clung on obstinately to the Marchesa and her other two daughters, Andreola and Simonetta.

In a letter to Mollhausen, who headed the "rump Embassy" in Rome, after the removal of the German Embassy to Fasano, close to the rescued Mussolini's headquarters, the Consul wrote that the Marchesa Corsini was "a very talkative, hysterical woman, who says one thing one day, and denies it, the next. Everyone knows about this and laughs about it in Florence." In a further effort to mitigate the Marchesa's "crime", he added: "No one takes her seriously. She is of no political consequence." As to the further suggestion that the Corsinis were "pro-British" and "anti-German", the Consul affirmed that "both my wife and I know this is impossible. They have always had German tutors in their house, and consequently their three daughters speak German[3]."

In this same letter to Möllhausen the Consul asked him to enquire for the whereabouts of Count Alfonso Gaetani, the former Prefect of Florence who had been dismissed from his post and arrested on October 1st. Gaetani had thrown in his lot with Badoglio and had stayed at his post "only to prevent further bloodshed", the Consul assured Möllhausen. "If he has been arrested, please try to secure his release: Kappler (the head of the Gestapo in Rome) and S.S. Colonel Dollmann could help you with your enquiries[4]."

The Marchesa Corsini and her two daughters were released from Carità's clutches ten days later, but it took a platoon of armed soldiers sent by the city commandant at the Consul's insistence to release Signora Evelyn Firth-Scarampi, who had been arrested as a hostage, together with her maid and gardener. Her brother Aleremo had been arrested by Carità on October 21st, accused of gathering arms for the Resistance, but had managed to escape five days later.

Carità, although he was irked by the interference of the Consul, had plenty of scope for his activities. On October 21st, he had managed to lay his hands on the lawyer Luigi Boniforti, one of the leading members of the Action Party's arms commission. The tall, personable lawyer, who was seriously ill at the time, was subjected to a merciless beating by Carità, but steadfastly refused to name his comrades-in-arms. "I managed to send word to the Consul two days after my arrest," states Boniforti, "and he immediately sent Dr Hans Wildt to confront Carità. From that moment, the beatings were discontinued." Carità's ignorance of political matters was such that he could not even distinguish between the political parties in Florence! "He mistook my Action Party for Adone Zoli's Christian Democrats," says Boniforti. This "mistake" may well have saved Boniforti's life which continued to hang on the merest thread through many vicissitudes[5].

The wave of arrests and beatings continued unabated throughout late October and November, although the Consul was able to write to the Ambassador[6] that "most of the persons for whom I intervened have been released. On the other hand, numerous new arrests have been made, this time mainly among the middle-classes. Hauptsturmführer Goebel, with whom I discussed the matter before he left, told me that *there are currently eleven different authorities* who have the power to arrest in Florence, and that this nonsense should be stopped." The Consul added that there were rumours that the orders for these arrests had emanated from Pisa (the home town of Buffarini, the Minister of the Interior) because, so the story went, Buffarini himself had been arrested by Badoglio and was "now probably taking revenge on those who, in his opinion, did not intervene energetically enough on his own behalf".

After this side-swipe at Buffarini, came the Consul's first mention of Carità. He appealed to the Ambassador to ensure "that Italians arrested on the instructions of the local S.S. are not mistreated by the personnel belonging to the Italian Captain Carità, who has, himself, been taken over by the S.D.". With "eleven different authorities" making arrests in Florence, it was not difficult for the Consul to assume that Carità had been "taken over" by the S.D., a formality which hardly mattered, since the results were the same.

The seizure of five prominent members of the Resistance's military command by Carità early in November, was a blow from which the Partisans took many weeks to recover. Yet despite the wholesale tortures to which these men were subjected, Carità learnt nothing. New men took the place of the captives, and hatred for the invader and his Italian satraps intensified.

Most of the arrests ordered by the S.S., the Consul observed in his letter to Dr Rahn, were in connection with Partisan activities. "But some distinction should be drawn between so-called gangs here, and gangs found, for instance, in the Balkans. There, they comprise military groups whose main object is an active struggle against our forces. In Tuscany, however, so far as Italians are concerned, they consist of persons who have escaped into the countryside to avoid being conscripted and sent to Germany, or even Russia. Those of their friends and relatives who assist them with food, clothing and money are then arrested by the S.S." Although the arrest of active Resisters was "fully justified", the Consul added cautiously, some distinction should be made between them and their more passive supporters.

This plea to mitigate the indiscriminate savagery of "the uncontrollable Carità", as the new S.D. chief in Florence, S.S. Captain Alberti described his henchman to the Consul, must have gone largely unheeded, because the Consul again repeated his accusations against Carità in a letter he wrote in mid-November to the Ambassador[7]. There had been more complaints of mistreatment and brutality, he told the Ambassador. "I know the S.D. here is very short of men and therefore has to make use of these Italian volunteers who are supposed to be such dare-devils (*die tapferen Draufgänger*) but whose activities as amateur policemen merely spread disgust and dismay among the population." He would discuss the matter again with the S.D. but "a little pressure from above, however, would be quite useful".

Worse followed when the Consul received news of Carità's arrest of the fashionable hairdresser Ferdinando Pretini. Pretini was not only a master hairdresser of distinction, he was also an active member of the Action Party's clandestine "prisoner of war commission". By the end of October 1943, some forty-nine British, American, South African and Australian prisoners of war who had escaped from confinement had been brought to safety across Allied lines or into neutral Switzerland through the activities of the courageous "Penna" (Pretini's code name in the Resistance) and his friends[8].

Carità had already received full information about "Feather's" extramural activities from one of his well-placed spies, one Nello Nocentini, who accompanied an ambulance filled with escaping Allied prisoners of war. Another of Carità's informers, a Benedictine monk, Padre Ildefonso who had become particularly friendly with Pretini, was told to keep a close watch on the hairdressing salon at 33 via Tornabuoni where Pretini served his elegant clientele.

At around six o'clock on the evening of November 24th, Carità, together with his chief lieutenant, Pietro Koch, who had distinguished himself as a torturer in Rome, drove up in an ambulance to Pretini's salon which they entered with a large bodyguard of armed men. The ladies under the hair-dryers screamed as Carità ordered Pretini and his two assistants, both members of the Resistance, Dante Giovannoni and Clara Sospizio, to put up their hands.

Thrusting a heavy machine-pistol into Pretini's chest, Carità demanded to be told "everything—if you value your skin".

At that moment the telephone shrilled. Carità ordered one of his men to answer it. The caller was Padre Ildefonso. He was told to present himself at the salon immediately. A few moments later the gaunt monk entered, clutching two books under his arm. Carità promptly arrested his spy, whose identity he wished to keep hidden, and he was taken together with Pretini and his two assistants to the Villa Triste, the House of Sorrow, on the via Ugo Foscolo.

The scenes which followed belong more properly to pathological literature and can only be paraphrased here. They were fully described by Cavaliere Pretini in a lengthy testimony during the trial in Lucca which sat in judgment on the remnants of Carità's gang in 1952[9]. Professor Frankovich has, in the general context, described the "Kafkaesque atmosphere" which prevailed in Carità's hell-kitchen on the via Ugo Foscolo, where Padre Ildefonso played Neapolitan songs and Schubert's *Unfinished Symphony* on the piano to drown the cries of the tortured[10].

On this occasion, Padre Ildefonso was kept away from the piano. During the preliminary softening-up process, Koch demanded why Pretini had dared to intimidate the treacherous monk "with threatening looks". Pretini who had come to suspect Ildefonso at the moment of his staged "arrest", said nothing. Pretini was then thrown down a flight of steep stairs, taken to a small underground cellar where he was savagely set upon by two of Carità's gang.

"Speak, traitor!" they yelled at him. "You must speak and reveal everything! The fact that you've been brought here proves you're guilty!"

"But why are you hitting me?" asked Pretini. "Your Commander has not interrogated me yet."

"It will help you to tell the truth," one of his tormentors replied, striking him again. They then stripped him of all his valuables, his gold watch and gold pencil, but for some reason they did not touch his wallet. Then with a violent kick he was hurled onto a blood-soaked mattress. Looking round him in the small cell where he had been incarcerated, Pretini saw a number of other semi-conscious prisoners who had been similarly "prepared". He cautiously pulled out his wallet and began destroying all incriminating material, particularly a petrol coupon for fifty litres of petrol which had been intended for the Liberation Committee. He tore up and swallowed other documents from his wallet.

At around ten o'clock in the evening, Pretini was dragged upstairs to a large room where he found some thirty persons dressed in assorted S.S. and military uniforms, with a scattering of officials in civilian clothes. There was a momentary hush of expectancy as Pretini was pushed into the room. He immediately recognised his two assistants, one of whom, Dante Giovannoni was bleeding profusely from the mouth and left ear. He had evidently already been "interrogated". Padre Ildefonso was also present.

Carità himself sat behind a long table on which the remains

of a copious supper were littered, with a profusion of empty glasses and wine bottles. Carità and his guests were in high spirits, in anticipation of further entertainment.

"Well, have you decided to sing?" Carità demanded.

"Tell me what you want to know," Pretini answered.

This reply did not seem to satisfy Carità, who leapt up striking Pretini a full blow on the nape of the neck, below the left ear. Others joined in the fray. At a certain moment an Italian Air Force Lieutenant-Colonel Simini noticed that Pretini wore the badge of the crack "Alpini" regiment in which he had previously served. "Ah, you villain!" Simini roared. "You are also a member of the *Alpini*, are you?" He then redoubled his blows, stamping on Pretini's feet with his hobnailed boots until the latter's toes were reduced to a bloody mass.

Photographs of leading Resisters, most of whom were known to Pretini were then thrust under his eyes, but he refused to identify any of them. The beatings were then resumed with increased ferocity.

"This is nothing," Carità assured the gallant hairdresser. "Wait until you see what happens afterwards. . . ."

Carità motioned to two of his men who picked Pretini up by the arms and legs and hurled him headlong against a wall. Pretini almost lost consciousness. He heard someone say: "What shall we do with him now?"

"Let him be. He'll be shot presently," Carità exclaimed, irritably. Pretini himself thought his last moment had come. He was then bound to a chair and a mock execution followed as Carità fired two shots from his revolver across the nape of his neck. Pretini, who would have welcomed death as a merciful relief from his torments, still said nothing, enraging Carità further. Carità had promised his guests a display of his "infallible" methods and now he was let down through the obduracy of a hairdresser!

"Oh, what a hero!" he sneered, and then in a voice filled with menacing solicitude, he said: "Pretini . . . you must be thirsty."

Pretini's mouth was forced open and a jug filled with scalding hot water was poured down his throat. This torment was repeated at intervals during his first fourteen-hour interrogation. The master hairdresser was no longer recognisable when he was dragged on to a verandah to be displayed to his friends, many of whom were already in Carità's hands.

Perhaps the worst torment came when Padre Ildefonso approached Pretini to express his solicitude for the grievous harm he had suffered. For a moment the Benedictine monk may have even repented the Iscariot role he had played; on the other hand his solicitude may have been part of the hypocritical game of bluff which he continued under Carità's instruction.

A little later Pretini was dragged into a small side room where he was again tortured in full view of all the other arrestees. They were forced to watch this process as an example of what would happen to them if they refused to speak, but Pretini's courage fortified his friends who were amazed at his defiance.

Since physical methods had failed to make Pretini identify any of the Resisters, Carità resorted to other well-tried forms of "psychological" persuasion. When Pretini was removed to his cell, his twenty-five-year-old guard, a certain Corporal Lucarelli, told him that his wife and niece had been arrested and placed in a nearby cell. "Why not talk and give us the names of your friends?" Lucarelli suggested.

"I have nothing to say. Nothing," Pretini murmured.

A moment or two later two "detectives" entered his cell to announce that Pretini's wife and niece would be shot, after having confessed to Pretini's anti-fascist activities. The young corporal then sat down and wrote out a "confession" leaving Pretini sufficient space to add the names of his friends.

"Why not do what you have been told?" Lucarelli said. "What difference can it make to you if you betray your friends since you are going to be shot," he added, cynically.

When Pretini again refused to name his associates, Lucarelli drew his dagger and struck at Pretini's head piercing his left eardrum. That night and for ten successive days Pretini was subjected to every form of inhuman torture in Carità's repertoire until he was removed to a prison hospital. Apart from the hideous wounds he had suffered to his head and lumbar regions, Pretini lost twenty-one teeth.

When he had partially recuperated Pretini was again interrogated and judicially sentenced to death. He was kept in solitary confinement for almost seven months, waiting for the sentence to be carried out, but he was no longer subjected to torture. According to Pretini the Consul had made energetic protests to S.S. Captain Alberti and had been told by Alberti that "if you take an interest in the Pretini case, you'll end up like Pretini—and he will be shot![11]"

This account, however, is apocryphal. The Consul did, in fact, raise the Pretini case with the Ambassador some five months later when it was brought to his attention[12]. But both Carità and Alberti had taken great care not to bring their brutality into the open and the fact that the Consul was in frequent communication with the Ambassador in similar cases, may have saved Pretini further ill-treatment. In any case, Pretini himself managed to escape from one of the clinics where he was receiving treatment in June the following year.

Shortly after Pretini's arrest, however, the Consul did bump into Carità on a street corner in Florence. Carità was taking the air in the company of a Florentine business man who was acquainted with the Consul. The business man offered to introduce "the biting axe of Florence" to Dr Wolf. It was "an awkward moment", the Consul recalled. He had only recently intervened on behalf of the historian Professor Raffaele Ciampini, who had been arrested by Carità on November 6th 1943 and who had been released after much ill-treatment, due to the Consul's and Dr Wildt's protests[13]. The Consul smiled politely at the business man, then studied his adversary for a moment. With a contemptuous shrug of his shoulders he left the hand which Carità had stretched out to him and walked away briskly, without saying a word.

"Why are you trying to frustrate my work?" Carità shouted behind him. "Don't you want us to win the war?" But by this time, the Consul had turned the corner and disappeared.

# 8

# Berenson and Others

But happily human nature is centrifugal!

BERNARD BERENSON

The Consul may have received some inkling of the impending attack on the Jewish population of Florence some time towards the end of October 1943, when he went to spend a brief holiday with the Ambassador Rudolf Rahn and his family in Fasano, the small but fashionable watering-place on Lake Garda seven or eight miles away from Saló, where the newly-returned Duce had established his seat of government.

It would be tempting to speculate on the circumstances which confirmed the premonition which had been gathering in the Consul's mind for some time that the idiot masters of Naziland—as Berenson contemptuously called the Third Reich—would, after they had consolidated their hold over "Republican" Italy, waste their time and dwindling resources on settling the "racial issue". The Ambassador who was shortly leaving for Hitler's headquarters in Prussia to persuade him to make some declaration of his intentions towards Florence, may have provided the first clue to the anti-semitic measures being prepared by the S.S. and S.D. in Verona.

Although the conversations which the two friends had in the pleasant setting of the rose gardens in the Villa Bassetti, the Ambassador's residence in Fasano, have disappeared into the ether, the Consul's telegrams and reports give some indication of their scope. The Ambassador told the Consul that he was being deliberately kept in the dark by the S.D. on these proposed anti-semitic measures[1]. He had therefore decided to make a direct approach to Mussolini. He was aware that the Duce was being pressed on all sides to declare his attitude on the "Jewish Question[2]". Himmler had sent his personal physician and "race expert", Professor Karl Gebhard, to persuade the Duce to assent to the destruction of Italian Jewry who numbered less than one hundred thousand, although the total Jewish population in Italy had swollen through the influx of foreign Jews who had come to seek shelter in Italy. Giovanni Preziosi, a defrocked priest who had been excommunicated in 1914, was encouraged to make bitter attacks on the Jews over Munich Radio by the Germans. In these broadcasts Preziosi accused Mussolini and members of his government of being "lukewarm" to a radical solution, singling out such prominent personalities as Buffarini, the Minister of the Interior and even the firebrand Pavolini, the Fascist Party Secretary, for his attacks. He even dared to raise his voice against the official philosopher of Fascism, Professor Giovanni Gentile for his attempts to include the Jews in his programme of "national consolidation[3]".

It is not surprising therefore that when Dr Rahn asked Mussolini for his views on this vexed subject, the Duce was immediately suspicious of such "a leading question". Only when Dr Rahn expressed his own doubts on the wisdom of the contemplated anti-semitic drive which, he said, would meet "with the opposition of the Catholic Church and the population", did the Duce venture an opinion. "You are right, Comrade," he said. "There are two things a politician should never attack—women's fashions or men's religious beliefs[4]."

He also told Dr Rahn that Preziosi came to him to complain that the list of all Jewish residents in Republican Italy had mysteriously disappeared from Buffarini's Ministry of the Interior. The Ambassador may well have been heartened by this game of deception. He was, in any case, convinced that the "Jewish problem was not settled with any particular savagery during the period of my responsibility", largely because of Kesselring's and his delaying tactics. They were always explaining to Berlin that they did not have the required number of men nor the transport for such any wide-scale operation[5].

The Consul himself had few illusions as to what would

happen when the special S.S. *rollo-kommandos*—the so-called anti-Jewish detachments—descended on Florence. Shortly before leaving Fasano, he placed this aide memoire in the Ambassador's private safe. It was dated November 1st 1943:

"Should there be a round-up of Jews in Florence, I should like to draw attention to the fact that the eighty-four-year-old art historian Bernard Berenson, who enjoys world-wide reputation is a resident of the city.

"There is a current rumour, which I have no means of checking, that Berenson is the illegitimate son of a Russian Grand Duke, and is therefore an Aryan.

"Documents in the Foreign Ministry substantiate that Berenson, in his capacity as an American citizen, succeeded in preventing the removal of a great number of German works of art from Germany at the end of the last war."

What the Consul hoped to establish with this misleading aide memoire is not difficult to perceive. He had not only elevated Berenson to the patriarchal age of eighty-four, whereas he was seventy-eight at this time, but he now stated that Berenson resided in the city although he had previously told all and sundry, including the S.D., that Berenson had escaped to Portugal. Was this perhaps to provide a cover for himself should the S.D. locate Berenson in Florence after all? It will be recalled that Nicky Mariano had told the Consul that Berenson had left I Tatti, but she had not told him *where* he had gone. As to Berenson's undoubted services to "German works of art", real as these may have been, there is some genuine doubt whether the Allies seriously contemplated removing any of these "at the end of the last war". There had been much loose talk of seizing German works of art for reparations and Berenson may well have added a voice of protest to such a novel method of settling international accounts. To confuse matters further, the Consul deliberately reproduced the canard about Berenson's grand ducal antecedents which Marchese Serlupi had invented. But all this was little more than a paper barricade, a last ditch measure designed to bemuse and confuse Himmler's race experts, which may have delayed but not prevented the fate which would have awaited Berenson if he had fallen into the hands of the S.S.

The old gentleman himself seemed hardly aware of the danger which faced him as he sat in his *macchia de luxe*, his luxurious hiding place, as he called Le Fontanelle, where he enjoyed Marchese Serlupi's hospitality, surrounded by many of his precious books and paintings, while the yellow and white Papal flag flapped bravely over the villa, proclaiming the Marchese's "neutral" status as Minister of the Republic of San Marino to the Holy See.

Two days before the first round up of Jews began in Florence, Berenson made the following observation in his diary:

"It was said that the Fascist prefect, the moment he was installed, warned Jews to leave their homes and go into hiding. It is not easy to believe this, seeing that most reports make him out a blackguard. But happily, human nature is centrifugal![6]"

Unfortunately the Prefect's nature was far from "centrifugal" as the Consul had observed at his first meeting with the repulsive-looking physician Dr Manganiello. Rumours of the new Prefect's "humanity" quickly evaporated when he opened his *Ufficio Affari Ebraici* which became a veritable anti-chamber of death[7].

On November 6th special S.S. and Gestapo anti-Jewish commandos descended on Florence. They had deliberately chosen the Sabbath on which to attack the Jewish worshippers who had crowded into the synagogues. Many of these were taken straight from their places of worship to deportation trains waiting to remove them to Germany. The Consul who had returned from Fasano on the same day, immediately cabled the Ambassador, disregarding his warning not to send "open" telegrams over the military teletype.

"The rounding up of the Jewish population which began today, threatens to undo the satisfactory impression the conduct of German troops and my own efforts have had despite skilful enemy propaganda on the Florentine community," he cabled. "But now this impression is in danger of being

LAUX GESELLSCHAFTEN

Mussolini and Rudolf Rahn in Fasano

The Villa Triste
at 67 Via Bolognese

ERREGI

Commemorative plaque on the Villa Triste

ERREGI

NON PIU' VILLA TRISTE
SE IN QUESTE MURA
SPIRITI INNOCENTI E FRATERNI
ARMATI SOL DI COSCIENZA
IN FACCIA A SPIE TORTURATORI CARNEFICI
VOLLERO
PER RISCATTARE VERGOGNA
PER RESTITUIR DIGNITÀ
PER NON RIVELARE IL COMPAGNO
LANGUIRE SOFFRIRE MORIRE
NON TRADIRE

Mario Carità (center) with his favorite dog

Ferdinando Pretini

Bernard Berenson

COURTESY, GERHARD WOLF

Gustav Streseman in the center, with Dr. Wolf at right, c. 1927

Gebhard von Walther, Dr. Wolf, and Friedrich Kriegbaum

FOTO LOCCHI

Le Tre Pulzelle

The Villa Medici

ALINARI

# BILANCIO 1943

I generali di Roosevelt assicuravano nell'ottobre 1943: « Le Feste di Natale le passeremo a FIRENZE, per lo meno però a ROMA ».

Roosevelt stesso, alla sua partenza per la conferenza « dei tre » a Teheran, asseriva: « La guerra è VINTA DA TEMPO. Teheran rappresenta già una conferenza di pace ».

*Bluff! Gli anglo-americani si dissanguano negli ABRUZZI con la loro offensiva-lumaca malgrado l'impiego di pazzeschi quantitativi di uomini, materiali e munizioni!*

*Bluff! Nel comunicato su questa conferenza-fiasco si legge: « L'immensa macchina bellica germanica deve ANCORA ESSERE DISTRUTTA. » (Il signor Roosevelt dovrà ancora accorgersi di quali colpi decisivi essa è tuttora capace!)*

*

Churchill, in un suo discorso di fine giugno 1943, proclamava testualmente: « Nell'autunno 1943 i soldati dell'Impero britannico avranno raggiunto il BRENNERO ».

Nel Novembre 1943 Churchill annunziava: « I nostri incessanti attacchi aerei sulle città dell'Europa, specialmente quelle del-

*Bluff! In realtà questi debbono battersi, nell'Italia Meridionale, contro i patrioti italiani insofferenti del terrorismo d'occupazione. Nell'Italia Settentrionale invece, una nuova Italia sta preparandosi alla lotta contro i NEMICI DELL'EUROPA.*

*Bluff! Mai il fronte interno della Germania è stato più deciso di aiutare i*

A Fascist propaganda leaflet

German mines destroy the Ponte Santa Trinità during the night of August 3 and 4, 1944

COURTESY, RICCARDO GIZDULICH

The Ponte Santa Trinità in ruins

COURTESY, RICCARDO GIZDULICH

The bridge under reconstruction

FOTO BARSOTTI

ERREGI

Two views of the Ponte Santa Trinità as it looks today

FOTO LOCCHI

Professor La Pira handing Dr. Wolf the document of honorary citizenship of Florence

Closeup of the document

FOTO LOCCHI

Comune di Firenze

Deliberazione del Consiglio Comunale - Adunanza del [illegible] Nov. [illegible]

Il Consiglio

Tenute presenti le numerose documentate benemerenze acquisite dal

Dott Gerhard Wolf

durante la sua permanenza in Firenze, in qualità di Console tedesco, per le sue opere di bontà, compiute con rischio costante della persona, nel periodo dell'occupazione germanica della città;

Ritenuto pertanto doveroso riconoscere che a tanto merito, debba corrispondere un'attestazione di omaggio da parte del Comune;

Delibera

di conferire al Dott. Gerhard Wolf la cittadinanza onoraria di Firenze.

il Segretario Generale

Il Sindaco

reversed." Then followed this cryptic sentence: "Reference to the documents left by me in Fasano is not yet required." This code was sufficient to tell the Ambassador that Bernard Berenson was still safe from S.D. marauders.

On the following day, a Sunday, the Consul was invited to Le Fontanelle for lunch. He went, despite a severe bout of sciatica which had attacked him that morning, disregarding the doctor's orders to stay in bed for three days. Neither Berenson nor Nicky Mariano were present at this lunch since they had gone to the neighbouring villa, Quarto, to visit Baroness Ritter, the Marchesa Serlupi's mother, where some of Berenson's books had been stored. As he wrote in his diary the next day: "In that huge Noah's ark, haunted by the ghosts of the Demidoffs and Leuchtenbergs, of Thiers and of Princesse Mathilde, the Baroness has inserted a Louis XVI apartment which she, herself a Frenchwoman, occupies. It made me happy to pass some hours there in the midst of proportions, colours, chairs, tables, pictures, the most livable with, that have ever been seen.

"While we were at Quarto, about which there would be much more to say, our hosts here were lunching the German Consul. He has just returned from the north, where he had been with von Rahn, the last ambassador to the Quirinal, and brought back the news that Ciano was in custody, and certainly would be shot[8]."

The luncheon had indeed opened on this somewhat lugubrious note. The Consul expressed both his and the Ambassador's strong disapproval of the Duce's intention of settling accounts with his son-in-law, who had returned from Germany on October 28th and was now held together with four other leading Fascists in a prison near Verona. The Italians drew a line at shooting one's kin, the Consul observed, but Mussolini was under great pressure from the Germans and his neo-Fascists and would undoubtedly yield, although the Ambassador was trying to find some formula which might save Ciano, even at the last moment.

The Serlupis who exchanged glances over their long light wood table, where they managed to dine frugally but in some style despite wartime restrictions, wondered whether this was a suitable time to bring up the question of Berenson and of enlisting the Consul's help if the S.D. disregarded the extra-territoriality of Le Fontanelle. But the Consul if he noticed the air of tension around the table, continued his conversation.

He had been greatly alarmed, he said, at the orders he had received to remove the contents of the German Art Institute to Germany. Apart from the fact that the Italians might assume that the Germans were preparing to abandon the whole of Italy if they started moving out their institutes, the books and documents of the Art Institute might be seriously damaged in transit.

Marchese Serlupi immediately offered to store the contents of the Institute in one of the extra-territorial villas, if the Consul could obtain the agreement of his authorities.

"Would you like to meet Berenson?" Serlupi ventured.

"Is he here?" asked the Consul.

"We can take you where he is staying," said the Marchese. "He and Nicky Mariano are expecting us at Quarto."

Shortly after lunch the Consul accompanied by his hosts crossed the soft springy lawns of Le Fontanelle to the formal gardens of Baroness Ritter's villa, where Berenson and Miss Mariano were indeed waiting for him.

The Consul's memory of his first meeting with Berenson is somewhat fragmentary. He recalled a small, grave, bearded man stooping under a heavy blanket, which was constantly slipping off his shoulders, with whom he perambulated slowly around the gardens. According to Miss Mariano the Consul and Berenson talked mostly about German literature. They spoke of Goethe, Herder, the two Humboldts and finally about Friedrich Kriegbaum, whom they both had loved and whose untimely fate they had mourned. The Consul made no mention of the dangers facing Berenson. He left an hour or so later, fully convinced that Berenson was staying at the Quarto. "The Consul was a German, after all," Marchesa Serlupi admitted. "Only after we learned to trust him, did he learn the full truth."

The Consul himself, when he discovered it, was only too

happy about the deception. "If the S.D. had managed to get hold of Berenson everyone would have assumed that I had betrayed him!" he said in later years. He naturally made no allusion to his contact with Berenson in any official communication, and Berenson, too, omitted to make any mention of his meeting with the Consul in his diary, possibly because he did not wish to implicate him if his papers were seized by the Gestapo. Much later, when the tide of war was rapidly approaching Florence, he wrote him a most moving letter thanking him for the efforts he had made on his behalf[9]. But in his diary entry of November 8th, he merely quoted the Consul as saying to the Serlupis that some two hundred Polish and German Jews who had been found huddling in a Roman synagogue in Rome "had been carried to Naziland by the Gestapo".

Similar repressions had, as we have seen, taken place in Florence, but on November 8th, the day following his meeting with Berenson, the Consul wrote to the Ambassador that "the local action against the Jews terminated yesterday, until further notice". Many sick and elderly Jews had been transported and this had caused particular indignation in Florence "*since the racial issue directed against one section of the community is totally incomprehensible to them*".

Despite what the Consul had written, pointless and arbitary arrests still continued in Florence. "I think", he wrote, "it would be very useful if Colonel von Kunowski, the local military commandant and the local S.D. should be directed to supervise their Italian auxiliaries more carefully." The Consul expressed his hope that the Ambassador "will again visit Florence at an early date with General Toussaint[10], as intended. This will strengthen my position here considerably". Enclosed with this letter was a lengthy memorandum dealing with the proposed removal of the major part of the German Art Institute to Germany. He repeated Marchese Serlupi's offer to store these in one of his villas and told of the assurance given to Kriegbaum by Bernard Berenson, "the well-known art historian who has lived for many years in Italy", that he would preserve the Institute for Germany, in the event of an

Anglo-American occupation. Thus the despised Jew who, unknown to the S.S. and Gestapo, was being sheltered on their very doorstep became the putative defender of German interests in the city.

But Berenson was not the Consul's only concern. On November 12th, while Dr Rahn was away at Hitler's headquarters, the Consul wrote to him protesting at the ruffianly behaviour of the S.D. who had broken into an apartment belonging to the respected director of the Bargello, Professor Rossi, whose wife happened to be Jewish. Since he had failed to receive a satisfactory explanation from Obersturmführer Schmidt, the Consul had decided to investigate matters for himself.

When he turned up at Rossi's flat, he discovered that the front door had been broken down, but that everything else in the flat appeared to be undisturbed. The S.D. had been annoyed at not finding anyone at home so they fixed a notice on one of the walls warning everyone to stay out under penalty of death. The frightened porter told the Consul that he had been threatened with immediate execution if he did not report all callers to the local Gestapo office. The Professor's wife had sensibly left Florence.

Without wasting time on further enquiries, the Consul appealed to the Ambassador to send an immediate directive by telegram, allowing Professor Rossi to enter his flat unmolested. He also informed Rossi of the action he had taken, telling him that his wife should remain in hiding. If she was seized by the S.D. he would not be able to assist her, since "a German consul is not supposed to help Jews".

When new anti-semitic repressions broke out in Florence on November 27th and 28th Dr Wolf made no such clear definition of his consular duties. He immediately summoned Dr Ernst Heinitz, one of the Jewish representatives in the city, telling this half-German, half-Jewish lawyer that he strongly deprecated the atrocities committed against the Jews. He also offered to assist Heinitz in every possible way, but asked him not to advertise this fact "since by going against the Nazis' *Weltanschauung*, I not only risk losing my job, but even my life[11]". Because of his close contacts with the Questura and the regular visits he paid to the S.D. post, the Consul was able to discover the names of some of their intended victims. These names he would pass on to Dr Heinitz, together with the necessary travel documents. His main concern, the Consul said, was for the sick and aged, or for those whose eminence in some particular field made them a special target for Nazi oppression.

Not all of these efforts did, or could meet, with success, since circumstances varied with each individual. Rudolf Borchardt the well-known German-Jewish author, who belonged to the circle of friends of Hugo von Hofmannsthal and Alexander Schroder, was given a travel permit by the Consul, but he was arrested by the S.S. on his return to Lucca where he lived and died subsequently somewhere in the south Tyrol. Rudolf Levy, the delightful "decadent artist" whom Kriegbaum had befriended, was also warned to leave Florence by the Consul. Levy unfortunately broadcast this fact publicly in a cafe where he was overheard by some informer. He was arrested in his lodgings and died on his way to one of the extermination camps in Germany.

There were lighter moments, however, in the overshadowing darkness which engulfed the Jews in Florence. When Baroness Charlotte von Gebsattel (nee Friedman) received a travel permit to the Vatican for herself, her three children and her aged mother, the Consul asked her to convey his regards to a Mr Montgomery, the first secretary at the British Legation whom he had known during his stay in the Vatican (1933–1934). A few weeks later the Consul received a reciprocal message in the shape of a single *Camel* cigarette, which he smoked as a symbolic "pipe of peace", with great satisfaction.

Numerous accounts were circulating in Florence of the help given by the simple people of the city to their Jewish neighbours. The Consul's favourite story concerned a young Carabiniere who came to the flat of an elderly Jewish couple from Cologne. "I have orders to arrest you tomorrow," he said, "but of course I shan't do that. I shall hide you in my brother-in-law's flat instead."

The Church also played a notable part in these rescue operations. One of the most indefatigable and most courageous of all of Dr Heinitz's "secret" helpers was the frail-looking, stooping Monsignore Giacomo Meneghello, the secretary of the vice-cardinal Archbishop Florit. But since the Monsignore was in constant danger of being denounced by informers, he gave strict orders that no Jewish visitors should be admitted to his office. The names of these callers were registered and once he obtained further information about them from Dr Heinitz, he did everything he could to help them. He also turned to the German consul when he was in need of assistance. A sad, frayed bundle of testimonials, written on scraps of paper in Hebrew, Yiddish and Ladino written by Jewish women and children whom the Monsignore had assisted remains locked in his old-fashioned safe in the archepiscopal palace to this day[12].

Not surprisingly that magnificent prince of the church, Cardinal Elia Dalla Costa also took an uncompromising attitude to the "Jewish question" in his official dealings with the Germans. When the S.D. arrested some nuns whom they accused of sheltering Jewish women and children, he is reported to have donned his sacerdotal robes and gone out to confront their tormentors. The order to shelter these unfortunates, he told the S.D. had been given by him. He therefore invited the S.D. to release the nuns and to arrest him. He then added in his usual disconcerting way, that he regarded these Jews "merely as persecuted beings: as such it is my Christian duty to help and defend them". Should the day come when individual S.D. men found themselves in a similar predicament, he would not hesitate to defend them![13]

The Consul loved Dalla Costa's authentic charity, his disquietening goodness, and the Cardinal in a poignant moment, fifteen years after the war, spoke of Dr Wolf as "a precious memory[14]". The gentle sisters of the Little Company of Mary, whose convent at San Girolamo in Fiesole was threatened with confiscation by the German authorities, also had reason to speak well of the enemy consul who had managed to avert the requisition order[15].

But for the helpless Jewish population of Florence, help sometimes came from the strangest quarters. When the S.D. and Republican militia raided the Carmine Convent, a young Jewish woman of twenty was allowed to make her escape through an open window by one of the militiamen. Human nature, in this case, was "centrifugal", as Berenson had remarked, and the story would make a pleasing postscript to this far from comprehensive account of persecutions. But there is also another which concerns the Consul.

Shortly after the occupation of Florence by the Nazis, the well-known musical conductor of the Bayreuth Wagner Festival, Franz von Hoesslin, appeared at the Swiss Consulate to ask for an entry permit into Switzerland for his wife and himself. Erna von Hoesslin happened to be Jewish. The sympathetic Swiss consul Carlo Steinhauslin readily assented but told von Hoesslin that he would have to obtain an exit permit from the Germans. This seemed a hopeless undertaking, but Steinhauslin advised him to approach the German consul.

"I thereupon called on Consul Wolf and described the desperate situation facing my wife," von Hoesslin stated[16]. The Consul, much to von Hoesslin's surprise, immediately expressed his readiness to help him, although Erna von Hoesslin was no longer a German citizen, since all persons of Jewish origin had automatically lost their citizenship. After asking his trustworthy secretary Maria Faltien to fix Erna von Hoesslin's photo into her husband's passport, the Consul stamped and countersigned it. "Consul Wolf performed this dangerous act in utmost secrecy, knowing that he was under constant surveillance from other officials at the Consulate," von Hoesslin continued. The Consul also gave the von Hoesslins a letter of recommendation in which he wrote that "the well-known German conductor Franz von Hoesslin and his wife are travelling to Switzerland *under the special protection of the Führer and Reich's Chancellor.* All German military control posts are asked to give them the necessary help and protection."

The von Hoesslins crossed the Italo-Swiss border at Chiasso

under Hitler's special protection, making their way to Geneva where they contacted the German Consul-General von Nostitz, a close friend of the Consul's, to whom they revealed their secret. Von Nostitz replaced the old passport which had become invalid, asking von Hoesslin to destroy it. This von Hoesslin promised to do, "but foreseeing that I might perhaps render a valuable service to Consul Wolf by producing it one day, I did not keep my promise. The passport is still in my possession and is at the disposal of anyone who may wish to see it."

This intervention by the Consul was but a drop in the ocean of misery which overtook the Jewish population of Florence two hundred and forty-eight of whom perished either through shooting, deportation or in the ranks of the Resistance, but a bond of respect grew between Steinhäuslin and Dr Wolf. Their alliance was cemented when the German Ambassador, Dr Rudolf Rahn, set out on his mission to Hitler's headquarters in mid-November 1943 to make his plea on behalf of Florence, at the instance of his friend, Dr Wolf, whom the city was soon claiming as its own consul.

## 9

# Shop-window on the World

> The attack or bombardment of towns, villages, habitations or buildings, which are not defended, is prohibited.
>
> ARTICLE 25,
> HAGUE CONVENTION, 1899–1907

On November 10th 1943, Dr Rahn set out for Wolfschanze—"The Wolf's Lair"—Hitler's headquarters set deep in the forests of East Prussia, in order to persuade the Führer to declare his unequivocal attitude towards Florence. Neither Rahn nor the Consul had any illusions that this would be a formidable undertaking, since Hitler was still smarting from Badoglio's "treachery" and was in no mood to grant the Italians any favours. The defensive dispositions, in which Florence was included, had been decided as early as August 11th when the Royal Italian Government was still Germany's ally[1]. Florence was not only the pivot of a defence line which stretched from Pisa in the east to Rimini on the Adriatic, it was also the hub of a road and railway complex connecting Rome with the larger industrial centres of the north. Behind this "Arno Line" as it came to be known stretched the more formidable defences of the "Gothic Line" on which the Todt Organisation was expending many man-hours in setting up concrete gun-emplacements and other deep defence works.

The mild hammering which the R.A.F. had given the military railway and locomotive yards in Florence on September 25th 1943, was likely to be only a prelude to fiercer attacks which would follow any large-scale allied advance up the Italian peninsula. The road system, linking Florence with other major cities, would also be subjected to bombardment and the city itself would not be spared if it continued to house a large German garrison and staff quarters. Only a full-scale withdrawal from the city would convince the Allies that Hitler had any serious intention to spare this "jewel of Europe", as Hitler later designated Florence, but would he budge until he was forced to do so?

Both Kesselring and Rahn had managed to prevail on the Führer to maintain the "open city" character of Rome, which had been proclaimed by the hated Badoglio earlier in August. Troop movements had been restricted to a minimum and the seat of Government as well as the German Embassy had been moved to the north[2]. The Allies, however, had given no assurance that they would respect the capital's "open city" status. Was it likely therefore that they would hold parleys, however unofficial, to grant Florence such a status even if Hitler made an unilateral declaration of his intention to withdraw all defences from Florence?

Such imponderables must have exercised the Ambassador's mind as he sat in his private plane taking him to Hitler's headquarters. He had carefully rehearsed all the arguments he would put before Hitler to persuade him to declare Florence an "open city", but he knew that the idea must appear to originate from the great man himself. He would have to "manœuvre" the Führer, playing on his creative and artistic sensibilities, while deprecating his own.

Dr Rahn had, on the evidence of none other than his superior Ribbentrop, developed a special "psychological approach" in his dealings not only with the Italians, but the German High Command, Ribbentrop, and the Führer himself. Whenever he wished anyone "to agree to a certain measure, he would deliberately represent himself as worse than he was", Ribbentrop stated during his trial at Nuremberg[3]. "He would assume the position of a Jesuit, whose only consideration is the goal, and who does not care what means are used." The former Reich Foreign Minister went on to state: "I would like to mention that whenever Rahn felt that he had to use one of these immoral Jesuitic tricks, he would say to himself:

'I have to act as the advocatus diaboli—the devil's advocate.'"

When the "devil's advocate" stepped out of his plane on November 10th, he emerged in his full Ambassadorial uniform, to which he had added a revolver which he had strapped to his belt. But before "I was allowed to enter the *Führer bunker*, I was asked to surrender my side-arms," Rahn wrote later[4].

Having survived this touch of bathos, he was ushered into the Führer's presence. Hitler, who was alone, greeted his Ambassador perfunctorily since this was one of the many meetings which he had had with Dr Rahn in the irksome days following the Allied invasion of Italy. What Rahn told him was a skilful mixture of disappointments, carefully offset with military and political gleanings which Dr Rahn was able to gather as his "viceroy" in Italy[5]. The military situation in the south had stabilised. After the capture of Naples early in October, the Allies were now bogged down on the Winter Line where Kesselring hoped to keep them to delay their advance on Rome. But an advance in the spring might present certain dangers, especially to Florence which was still some two hundred and fifty miles away from the front line.

Recalling this meeting with Hitler, Dr Rahn remarked: "The conversation with the Führer was very interesting and something of a surprise. I made the first tactical move by telling him that although there was *every* military reason why Florence should be defended, the city was also '*eines der grossen historischen Schaufenster der Welt*' (one of the greatest historical shop-windows in the world), and that I needed it as a propaganda shop-window[6]".

The Führer who was probably as close a student as Ribbentrop of his Ambassador's "Jesuitic tricks", looked straight into his eyes, murmuring non-committally: "*Ja, die Stadt ist schön.*" ("Yes, the city is beautiful.")

The Ambassador then launched into one of his favourite historical anecdotes. He told Hitler how a young German lieutenant from Luneberg who served under the Venetian General Morosini had ordered his battery to fire at the sacred edifice of the Parthenon during the Venetian-Turkish War of 1687. The Turks had stored a large quantity of arms and gunpowder within the Parthenon's precincts, but a well-aimed shot from the young lieutenant's battery, situated on a nearby hillock, exploded the ammunition-dump, toppling a few of the columns and blackening part of the roof. The Parthenon may have been a legitimate military target, Dr Rahn observed, but the wave of horror which spread through the civilised world at this act of cultural parricide had branded the luckless Brunswicker from Luneberg for ever.

The parallel between this attack on the Parthenon and the possible destruction of Florence was not lost on Hitler. "Why do you go about it in such a roundabout way?" He asked irritably. "You don't have to. Florence is too beautiful a city to destroy. Do what you can to protect it: you have my permission and assistance."

The Ambassador was dumbfounded, but also "a little ashamed, I daresay" of his Jesuitical tricks. On November 12th, he left for Fasano by plane, as the sun was fading "on the last of the roses" which grew in heaped profusion on the stone walls of the Villa Bassetti, his official residence in Fasano. He hastily penned a letter to the Consul, giving him the glad tidings.

"Dear Gerhard," he wrote, "I have just returned from headquarters, where I have succeeded in obtaining permission from the Führer to declare Florence *an open city, unofficially*. The enemy is to be informed through the good offices of the Vatican of our *readiness to withdraw* staff and troops from Florence, if bombardment of the city can be avoided in this way, I have asked Herr von Weizsäcker to take this matter up with the Vatican. Sincere regards: excuse the hurry, hoping to see you soon. Always yours, Rudolf."

The Consul's first inclination on receiving this letter was "to embrace everyone in sight in the Consulate", but he resisted such premature rejoicing by underlining the two operative phrases—"an open city, unofficially" and "readiness to withdraw". What was the exact significance of that nebulous "unofficially" since the Germans were in *de facto* occupation of the city? Was that "unofficial" also? And more important, how would the Allies react to such an indefinite proposal? Had Hitler merely succeeded in turning the tables on the Ambassador by designating Florence "a propaganda shop-window", without budging an inch from the city itself?

The Consul decided to test Hitler's intentions immediately by writing to Ernst von Weizsäcker, his superior who had been Secretary of State at the Foreign Ministry and was now German Ambassador at the Vatican, protesting against a plan which had been mooted between Kesselring, the Central Administration of all Italian Art Collections and the Vatican to remove "the most valuable paintings in Florence, Turin, Venice and other cities" which were to be sent to Rome "to be protected against all enemy action under the auspices of the Vatican". This plan had received the approval of the British Minister accredited to the Vatican. "It seems to me that such a project is hardly feasible, if only because of transport difficulties and the danger of air attacks," the Consul wrote.

He had discussed, the Consul added, this projected removal of Florence's art treasures with the art superintendent Signor Poggi and the Marchese Serlupi. "I told the two gentlemen that Rahn had reported to the Führer, at my suggestion, on the protection and safety of Florence, during his recent visit to Germany. He had obtained consent that Florence should be considered *for all practical purposes, under verbal agreement*, an open city."

If this was so, the Consul argued, why should the art treasures be removed from Florence which was to be considered for all practical purposes an open city? A better plan was to ask the Pope to appeal to all warring governments not to remove "any cultural or scientific establishments in Italy"

Both gentlemen (Poggi and Serlupi) favoured this proposal. Marchese Serlupi wanted to write about it immediately to the nephew of the Pope who was a friend of his, "This is for your information." Moreover, Marchese Serlupi had offered to store the most valuable contents of the German Art Institute in one of his extra-territorial villas "if you could determine whether the Vatican would be prepared to extend the same protection to this purely scientific institute which it has already extended to the German Archeological Institute and the German Institute of Art in Rome".

The Consul ended his letter of November 12th to Weizsäcker, asking him to forgive him "for exceeding the competence of a German consul in Florence, as far as the first subject is concerned (the plan to remove the art treasures). But today when there is much talk about German and European culture, we witness the painful destruction of the greatest examples of that culture everywhere. It seems essential to me that everyone should do everything in his power to preserve for Europe all that can be preserved. I feel certain that you will agree with this view."

Ernst von Weizsäcker replied a week later, on November 19th. "As you know, this embassy, despite opposition from some quarters, shares the view that for technical reasons and as a matter of principle, it is undesirable to remove German scientific institutes from Italy. Many people in Berlin hold a different view: and here, too, our attitude is not generally understood in local Party circles. It would be very useful if Herr Rahn would again make his basic position clear on this subject. Unfortunately he is not often in Rome these days and *the matter does not lend itself to correspondence*. I shall therefore be interested to hear of his decision with regard to the Institute in Florence."

Weizsäcker also told the Consul that he had recently spoken with Monsignore Montini, the Under-Secretary of State at the Vatican (the present Pope Paul VI), who had expressed "the Vatican's willingness to use its good offices on behalf of local Institutes, in principle". The Vatican declined to act as "a protecting power", but would intervene with the Allies if and when such a step was required. But there was no urgency in this matter. "On the contrary," wrote Weizsäcker, "it would create an impression that we were about to abandon all of Italy, if such a step were undertaken." But that should not prevent Marchese Serlupi from informing the Vatican of his offer—"which I personally consider very useful".

The plan to move Florence's art treasures to Rome, together with art treasures in other cities, would be abandoned, in Weizsäcker's opinion. Von Tieschowitz, the chief of the army's art-protection service—"who is also known to you"—had arrived in Rome from Paris and had expressed his opposition "to all measures arising exclusively from panic". Weizsäcker went on: "As far as I know only the items in Latium are to be concentrated in Rome. Besides, on the very commendable initiative of Herr Rahn, *a personal order from the Führer has now been issued prohibiting the removal of any works of art from Italy*. Thus we may anticipate an appeal from the Vatican to all belligerents which corresponds with your suggestion, with some confidence."

"I hope I have replied carefully to your various enquiries: I shall be happy to be at your disposal in the future," Weizsäcker concluded.

Thus Weizsäcker ranged himself on the side of the Consul, Dr Rahn and von Tieschowitz, in opposition to the "local Party circles" headed in Rome by the limping, peripatetic Prinzing, the chief of all German cultural institutes in Italy. Prinzing, whose connection with the Gestapo was known to the Consul, supported the view of Professor Zimmerman, the Chairman of the Association for the Preservation of German Art Institutes in Berlin, who had called for the immediate repatriation of all German Institutes in Italy. It is hardly surprising, therefore, that Weizsäcker did not think the matter lent itself "to correspondence". At least it was gratifying that Dr Rahn had extracted "a personal order" from Hitler prohibiting the removal of works of art from Italy although this order like so many others was lost on the ardent S.S. "art protectors" who later streamed into Florence. The Consul had, however, clearly established in his own mind and in the mind of sympathetic officials such as Weizsäcker, that the issue of "art protection" and the removal of the German Art Institute from Florence, was inextricably bound with the fate of the "open city" status of Florence which hung so tremulously on the interpretation of the word "unofficially".

The Consul sent a copy of Dr Rahn's letter of November 12th to the Cardinal-Archbishop. He also went to consult with his colleague, the Swiss Consul, Carlo Steinhäuslin.

This fifty-one-year-old stockily-built banker, with large, wide-apart eyes and soft Tuscan accent, deserves more attention than he can receive in these pages, for his place in the history of his native city (he was a Florentine by birth) has a luminosity which the passage of years has not dimmed. A gentle, unassuming man of great natural finesse and intelligence, Steinhäuslin was the heir to the famous private bank which his father had founded. He managed to combine a rare skill in accountancy with his love for his native city and his loyalty to his own country Switzerland, whose Honorary Consul he had been since 1932. He carefully preserved an air of studied neutrality in his consulate which occupied part of his private bank premises in the Palazzo Sassetti, on the street of the same name, not far from the Palazzo Strozzi.

Carlo Steinhäuslin, however, was never "neutral" when it came to alleviating private and public distress. He used his considerable means and inexhaustible energy in the cause of the city he loved: he saw "the good in men before their weakness", a quality rare in a banker, and rarer still in the turgid diplomacy of his day. He also had a number of endearing eccentricities. As a symbol of faith and tranquillity he had hung a large reproduction of the famous Fra Angelico fresco of St Peter holding a monitory finger to his lips which may be found above the door of the sacristy of the San Marco, between two large windows of his study in the Palazzo Sassetti. Whenever his visitors or he himself became incautious, Steinhäuslin would point to the fresco, and then to his own lips. He also had the habit of pressing a cup of *Nescafé*—"our national drink"—on his visitors: a glowing ring stood on his desk on which to brew the hot water for the precious liquid (coffee had disappeared even from Florence's well-stocked black-market by 1943).

When the Consul came with the Ambassador's letter

shortly after November 12th, he told Steinhäuslin that the General of all administrative non-combatant forces had received instructions to declare Florence a *Sperrzone*, a forbidden zone, as a preliminary gesture in the open city negotiations. All superfluous military traffic was to be diverted outside the city's limits and only "under exceptional circumstances" would military personnel be able to enter Florence. That much had been achieved. "But it all sounds very well on paper," the Consul lamented. "It is quite another matter to put into practice. Technical difficulties are cropping up, mainly through the lack of administrative personnel, so these orders will not take effect for many months."

Steinhäuslin commiserated with the Consul's gloomy prediction. He also told him that there had been disquietening rumours that the German command—and here he pointed to the Fra Angelico reproduction—had stored ammunition in the subterranean cellars of Florence's famous churches and even in the cities hospitals and orphanages.

The Prefect, with the Cardinal's support, was planning to create a "neutral" commission to investigate these rumours, Steinhäuslin said. He himself would be willing to serve on such a body, if its neutrality could be guaranteed and if he received the necessary permission from his government.

And there the rumours, like the promised open city negotiations, rested for many months, while the Vatican made approaches to the Allies for their reaction to Hitler's "unofficial" declaration. The Resistance, not surprisingly, regarded this declaration as a ruse whose main object was to hamper its own activities inside the city. The only "open city" the Germans would be likely to respect was one from which they had been forcibly ejected, the Resistance claimed.

To lend substance to this argument, three young men fired point blank at a Lieutenant-Colonel Gobbi of the National Republican Guard, killing him on the doorstep of his house in the evening of December 1st 1943, a few weeks before Florence's first and last Christmas under German occupation. The consequences were immediate. The Prefect and Carita, who had a not unnatural fear for their own skins, summoned a special tribunal which passed sentence of execution on ten hostages, among them five prominent members of the Resistance's military committee who had been handed over by Carità to the German authorities earlier in November. But since neither the German city commandant nor the S.D. wished to embroil themselves in such "minor" domestic matters, they refused to surrender the five Resistance men to Carità's vengeance.

On the following morning five anarchists and communists, veterans of the Spanish Civil War, were dragged from their cells, where they had languished for many years, to the Cascine shooting range. In this delightful park where Shelley composed his *Ode to the West Wind*, an unedifying drama was enacted as the brother of the deceased Gobbi railed at the five innocent victims, who he said "should be grateful that they died in the light of day and were not shot down at dead of night like my brother, while going about his business...[7]".

Having delivered this tirade, the demented man stepped back into the execution squad and fired at the five men who sang the *Internationale*, united in death as they had never been in life, in tragic defiance of their executioners.

The Consul, who had just returned from Fasano where he had been to confer with the Ambassador, wrote protesting against this slaughter of innocent men. No effort had been made to discover the real culprits of Gobbi's murder, either deliberately or because of indifference or the inability of the local police, he told Dr Rahn. He intended to admonish the Prefect, the local General of the Carabinieri and the Questura, telling them that such slackness on their part would lead to further outbreaks of violence and "result in the use of stronger German police forces, which would hardly be compatible with Italian prestige". The idea of frightening these worthies with the S.D. whom he also blamed, however obliquely, for this slackness, had a piquancy of its own. He asked the Ambassador to convey his sentiments to the Italian Government[8].

But at least both the Communist and non-Communist Resistance had refrained from striking at any German soldier or officer whom they found within the confines of the open city; and the Consul was all the more gratified when the Cardinal-Archbishop appealed on December 5th to all Florentines to desist from further acts of violence and to behave "with humanity and respect to all German soldiers and commanders", and especially to avoid killings of "a private or treacherous nature".

The Cardinal's invocation in which he referred to the Sixth Commandment was promptly challenged in the clandestine *La Libertà*[9] by Enzo Enriques Agnoletti, a Resister of great courage, charm and authority, who said that His Eminence had given the impression of condemning "the killing of one man, while condoning the slaughter of five men by the authorities, or the so-called authorities". No word of protest had fallen from Dalla Costa's lips at the brutalities of the S.D. and their Italian supernumaries. Through his silence the Cardinal had become "the moral accomplice" of these monsters. This was stern stuff indeed, but the Cardinal refused to rise to the bait.

On the following day, December 6th, the Consul had a less consequential matter to attend to, or so it appeared. A certain Major Beck, a liaison officer on the staff of General Becht, requested an urgent interview with the Consul. He arrived one hour and a half late for the appointment, without offering any apology or explanation. Instead, he told the Consul that he had been sent ahead to find accommodation for his general and had happily lighted on the Villa Sparta at San Domenico di Fiesole.

The Consul who had taken an instant dislike to the young quartermaster major, told him that delightful as the villa undoubtedly was, it was the private property of Helen, the Queen Mother of Rumania, "a country allied to Germany". A no-entry sign had been posted outside the gates by the city commandant, whose orders had to be obeyed explicitly.

"I only obey the orders of the chief of the O.K.W. (High Command), General-Fieldmarshal Keitel," Major Beck retorted grandly. "Besides, the lady should be honoured that a German General and his staff wish to lodge at her villa."

"But shouldn't you at least obtain an invitation from the 'lady'?" the Consul asked caustically.

"That is my precise intention," said Beck. He saluted stiffly and went off.

The Consul would have forgotten all about this trifling affair, if he had not received a visit next day from the distinguished-looking Count Giuseppe di Montezemolo, who told him that the Villa Sparta had been left in his care during the absence of the Queen Mother from Florence. Major Beck had turned up at the neighbouring Villa della Cisterna where he tried to cajole the Queen Mother's sister Irene, Duchess of Aosta, to allow him to occupy the Villa Sparta. The Duchess referred the insolent young major to the Rumanian Embassy in Rome.

The matter did not rest there, however. Major Beck telephoned the Consul the next day to say that he had "arranged everything with the Rumanians". When the Consul checked on this information, he discovered that Beck had told him a downright lie. Thoroughly irritated by now at the Major's antics, the Consul reached the Ambassador at Fasano and appealed to him to get Kesselring to bring the young man to his senses. "The stubborn behaviour on the part of a German officer has done us no credit with the Rumanians," he fulminated.

Major Beck was brought back to his senses. He was told to find other accommodation for General Becht who was expected in the "open city" of Florence on January 15th. But why had Beck been so anxious to gain entry into the Villa Sparta? Count Montezemolo, who had been left in charge of the villa, was in point of fact no ordinary caretaker: he was the leader of the pro-Monarchist Partito Azzuro, the Blue Party, "the moving spirit" behind the Resistance in Rome, as Kesselring described him[10]. Before Montezemolo's arrest in January and his tragic death with other victims of the Ardeatine Cave massacre, he was reputed to have more than thirty hiding places! The Villa Sparta may have been one such hiding place, and Major Beck may have been an intelligence officer, although the Consul could scarcely credit him with any intelligence. In any case, the sequel which followed close on the Villa Sparta affair, may throw some light on this odd occurrence.

The S.D. had begun to show more than a passing interest in the few "Royals" who still remained in Florence and who for one reason or another, had not left to join their relatives in "the King's Italy". Four days after his talk with the egregious Major Beck, the Consul received an urgent request to visit the Duchess of Aosta at the Villa della Cisterna.

The Duchess, a Greek princess, was married to Aimone, Duke of Spoleto, the "uncrowned King of Croatia" who had succeeded to the Aosta title on the death of his brother, Amedeo, in Eritrea in 1942. Since she was about to have a child she had been unable to follow her husband, a naval officer, when he made his escape in his yacht to southern Italy in late September[11]. She had remained in Florence, together with the Dowager Duchess Anna, a Princess of the House of Orleans. Despite her family's reputed anglophobia because of the alleged ill-treatment of Duke Amedeo at the hands of the British during his captivity in Eritrea, there was great concern for her safety, and the safety of Duchess Irene and her infant son. This may explain the urgent summons which the Consul received on December 10th to visit the Duchess Irene, who had been fully informed of his efforts to safeguard her sister's Villa Sparta. She now turned to him in an even more serious predicament. The Duchess began the conversation by telling the Consul of a strange visit which she had recently received from Professor Karl Gebhard, the well-known orthopædist of the Holenlychen Hospital, who was also a Lieutenant-General in the S.S.[12] This sinister individual who stood close to Himmler, tried to impress her with his intimate knowledge of the Italian political scene. He told her "that there was little satisfaction in Germany with the new Fascist Government. Mussolini seemed disinterested in political developments, although he was now hale and hearty (*frisch und munter*). Pavolini and other members of the Government, were all more or less Communists and were of little use."

Having established Himmler's dislike for Pavolini's egalitarianism and the so-called Verona programme of extended nationalisation and "worker-participation", Gebhard suddenly expressed his regrets at the Duke of Aosta's absence—"otherwise, instead of liberating Mussolini, reliance could have been placed on *apparently* trustworthy members of the Royal family".

The Duchess must have held her breath at this open invitation to her husband whom a former fascist party secretary had described as a "frondeur sick with ambition[13]" to set himself up in opposition to the ruling House, but being a woman of some intelligence she said nothing. Gebhard then went on to express his contempt for Marshal Graziani's new army which, he said, was nothing more than "a private army". The most able general, in German opinion was the King's son-in-law, Count Calvi di Bergolo, "whom the present government apparently seeks to assassinate, but who is under S.S. protection".

The Duchess's credibility must have been strained to breaking-point, since Calvi di Bergolo had refused to collaborate with the Germans and had been taken forcibly together with many of his officers to Germany. The orthopædist now began back-tracking gently. It was true, he said, that Princess Mafalda (the king's second daughter) had been arrested because she had sent her children to the Vatican and had made preparations to flee herself, and that Philip, Prince of Hesse, her husband, had been arrested for homosexual practices, but the S.S. was most anxious to place the Duchess of Aosta under its special protection since she had made no attempt to flee, and because she was the sister of the Queen Mother of allied Rumania. Gebhard was not certain whether the S.S. were prepared to extend similar "protection" to Anna, the dowager Duchess of Aosta. The Duchess Irene promptly came to her sister-in-law's defence, reminding the orthopædist that after September 8th, German papers had referred to the late Duke of Aosta as an exemplary Italian officer, who might have influenced the course of events, had he lived.

To calm the Duchess, Gebhard explained that the Duce's

government was preparing to arrest all persons related to the Italian Royal family and that was why the S.S. was interested in her fate. The interview concluded on this touching note, but on the next afternoon Gebhard again turned up at the Villa della Cisterna, bringing with him the Head of the Gestapo in Italy, General Wilhelm Harster, whose good manners greatly impressed the Duchess until Harster asked her pointedly what she proposed to do in the event of an Allied advance upon Florence. She told him calmly that she would go to Stresa, but Harster immediately objected. Italian circles might persuade her to move to Switzerland, he explained. Instead, he proposed to place a plane at her disposal in which she would be taken to Germany!

The Duchess who must have been thoroughly disturbed by now, said with all the dignity she could command, that since she had become an Italian by marriage, she wished to remain in Florence "under all circumstances" or at the worst to go to her sister-in-law's estate between Turin and Como. General Harster did not press the point. He agreed to discuss the matter further with her two adjutants in Verona early in the following week. The Duchess then asked permission for her staff to retain their side arms, and appealed to Harster to provide her with an S.S. guard "to protect her silver and personal belongings". Harster readily agreed to this ingenuous request.

The Duchess then told the Consul that although she had been "agreeably impressed by the politeness" of her two visitors, she subsequently learned from members of her household staff that while both she and they were engaged in conversation, certain members of their entourage had taken extensive photographs of the Villa della Cisterna. This had caused her "certain misgivings", as it might well have done!

The Consul reported the Duchess of Aosta's conversation with the two highly-placed S.S. and Gestapo men, hoping to warn the Ambassador of the attempts being made to divide the remaining members of the Italian Royal house, and failing this, to place them under their unholy "protection". But to no avail: in the following year the Duchess together with her small son, the Dowager Duchess Anna and her daughters, were removed to a secret destination in Germany. Unlike the unfortunate Mafalda who perished in an allied air-raid on Buchenwald, they survived the rigours of S.S. "protection[14]", but the villa Cisterna was reduced to a heap of rubble in the fighting which followed the Liberation of the city.

On the Sunday following the Consul's conversation with the Duchess, Elia Dalla Costa, the Cardinal Archbishop of Florence delivered a sermon in the Annunziata, in which he said that the chief dangers for contemporary society today were nationalism, racism, and tribalism. "The church was only half full and the congregation consisted for the most part of the lower classes, some of the men in uniform," according to the entry in Bernard Berenson's diary of December 13th. The Cardinal's congregation "seem to have listened with grins and even laughter, and whether it was of approval or of jeering, my informant could not say."

The Consul, however, had a far clearer picture of the situation in Florence. In his December 14th report on the internal situation and attitude of the population he wrote that "the basic difficulty facing all German propaganda in the Tuscan provinces is that the entire population is tired of war. This feeling is reinforced by the conviction that the war is irretrievably lost for Italy. The progressive disintegration of Fascism (exemplified by the prosecution of the war, corruption, etc.) which war events had accelerated, has deeply disappointed the population and has destroyed all confidence in the Fascist system. A growing anti-German attitude springs from the conviction that without German support Fascism would have collapsed long ago. The proper conduct of German forces—with a few isolated exceptions—brought about considerable improvement in the public attitude towards Germany during the first weeks of occupation. This considerable success has, however, again been jeopardised by the arbitrary regime of terror of the new Fascist rulers, from whom the decent elements of the old Fascism had almost entirely disassociated themselves."

The Consul warned that "the arrest of largely innocent

persons" and the brutal ill-treatment which was meted out to them would ultimately lead to an explosive situation "which may also endanger the lives of German troops". But because of the social and economic character of the city there was "no danger of Communism in the Tuscan provinces". The influence of the Catholic Church was sufficiently powerful to prevent the spread of Communism, he stated, and added: "It is therefore regrettable that the lawyer Adone Zoli who is one of the most respected proponents of these efforts, has been kept in prison, together with his two sons, for many weeks by the Security Service. The investigation of his alleged offences is making no progress whatsoever."

The Consul went on to belittle the danger of Partisan activity which he said "is seriously over-rated here by the authorities responsible for combating them. In Tuscany, these so-called 'gangs' consist mainly of persons who wished to escape the uncertain fate which awaited them through compulsory recruitment and deportation to Germany, and even to Russia." He proposed that such compulsory recruitment should be stopped and that voluntary labourers should be given the opportunity "to send money regularly to their families in Italy and to communicate with them".

Trade and industrial activity had been hampered not only by the removal of plants and machinery but by "the demagogic and planless interference of the Fascist authorities which resulted in sudden wage increases, and the forced distribution of bonuses to workers, etc.". The danger of inflation had also become acute. Wages of manual workers and white-collar operatives no longer bore any relation to each other. A postman or a train conductor earned only 700 lire a month as compared with the 1,800–2,000 lire earned by an armaments worker. The Prefect himself received 3,000 lire a month—"the danger of inflation should be obvious," the Consul added, with a nice touch of malice. Olive oil production was down to half of the previous year's harvest, the Consul noted, due to lack of farm labour and the shortages of fertilisers. "The situation will become critical in February–March of next year." There was a shortage of fresh fruit in Florence "since there are no oranges or nuts from the south, with which people used to supplement their diet here", and the farmers of Tuscany were already "preparing to hide their produce next year" from voracious State officials.

Having painted this gloomy picture of four months of Nazi occupation, the Consul went on to complain of the poor quality of German news broadcasts which alternated with "pop" music designed to appeal to the armed forces, "but in the interest of German politico-cultural activities, operas and chamber music should also be put out on the air". An Italian radio station, under an Italian director, should be re-established "otherwise Italian listeners will switch to British broadcasts, where dance music alternates with the news". Very few persons bothered to listen to German broadcasts in Italian, while German broadcasts to Britain "are popular because they are lively and amusing".

The public was bored with the Fascist press and radio, despite the efforts made by the new editor of Florence's leading daily *La Nazione*, to inject some life into this newspaper. The Consul had met the mercurial Mirko Giobbi. He had found that his views "coincided with his, that after three and a half years of war, actions rather than words, were the best form of propaganda".

The enterprising and hard-hitting editor had already been cautioned by Pavolini, the Fascist Party secretary "because of certain critical remarks" which Giobbi had made in his newspaper and "two other new and stimulating periodicals have already been banned". But now Giobbi offered to publish "true stories of Italian military assistance to the German forces, as well as accounts of German efforts to protect Italian works of art, but such reports have to be thoroughly authenticated to see whether they accord with the facts", the Consul added. He ended his December report with an appeal for 10,000 lire for unspecified "propaganda purposes[15]".

Christmas came, a cheerless Christmas with cuts in the food rations. A feeling of gloom and despair had fastened on the city. It was also a lonely Christmas for the Consul, cut off from his wife and daughter who were still in Switzerland.

Hanna Kiel, one of the Consul's closest friends, was spending part of Christmas in a small trattoria near the famous stone quarries of Maiano, whose *pietra serena* had decorated most of Florence's public buildings. But in the winter of 1943, the deep stone galleries cut in the pink and grey rock, provided hiding places for escaping P.O.W.'s, deserters and conscripts fleeing from Graziani's "private army". The innkeeper, who suspected that Dr Kiel was in trouble with the German or the Fascist authorities, offered to hide her in one of the quarries, and his lovely daughter "with the face of a Boticelli", confided that her husband had taken to the *macchia*.

Christmas Day passed tranquilly for Hanna in these rural surroundings, but on the following day, Carità sent a posse of his men to arrest the innkeeper, who was accused of harbouring Partisans. The innkeeper's young daughter was so terrorised by Carità's gangsters that she suffered a severe miscarriage from which she died subsequently.

Hanna Kiel appealed to the Consul who managed to obtain the release of the hapless innkeeper, who returned, together with his son-in-law, in time for his daughter's funeral, a sad, pointless death brought about by Carità's thugs who had removed all medical supplies from her village. But in Florence itself new rumours had begun circulating that Carità had been removed from his post, because even the S.D. had sickened of his brutalities. These rumours only came to an end in the following year when it was officially announced that Carità had been promoted to the rank of major.

The Consul, however, was not on the face of it so fortunate. The Ambassador had put in a recommendation for promotion, which had been favourably considered by the deputy-head of the Personnel Department in the Foreign Ministry, but no official confirmation came through. The Party nucleus in the Ministry had blocked all hope of promotion. The Consul was greatly relieved: he had no desire to be promoted out of his post in Florence and to return to the cauldron in Berlin from which he had escaped to the "diplomatic backwater" of Florence three years earlier.

Cold, blustery weather, succeeded by clear bright days and

bitterly cold nights, ended the old year of 1943. The Allies bogged down on the Winter Line before Cassino, 200 miles to the south, had made no attempt to repeat their bombing raid of September 25th, but they would surely return with the improved weather. The Consul who had spent New Year's eve with the Swiss Consul, had left the Palazzo Sassetti early, and had made his way, as he had done so often towards the Ponte Santa Trinita.

As the old year divided from the new, he recalled Kriegbaum's words: "Who would destroy such beauty? Neither their side, nor ours...." And then, out of the caverns of memory, came this line from one of Stefan George's poems: *Auf stiller stadt lag fern ein blutiger streif....* "Above the silent town a streak of blood[16]". The Consul returned late to Le Tre Pulzelle. He had been walking most of the night.

# 10

# Your Majesty

Aye—this state-craft! Oh, how I curse it.

FRIEDRICH VON SCHILLER, *Wallenstein*

Eight months stood between the opening of 1944 and the Liberation of Florence. As the tension gradually built up, the portrait of the Consul which had been vague and indeterminate up to now, began to stand out in stronger colours. His dreamy, rather discursive character had hardened under the weight of growing responsibilities. He revealed an unexpected streak of argumentativeness, especially in his dealings with the local office Gestapo. There was also a tendency towards recklessness against which Ambassador Rahn had to warn him on a number of occasions.

Whatever the ultimate evaluation of Dr Rahn's role in Italy, there is no doubt that the loyalty and protectiveness which he showed his friend in Florence played an important part in guaranteeing the latter's immunity from the constant pressure and surveillance to which he was subjected by S.S. Captain Alberti and the more powerful but remote head of the Gestapo in Verona, S.S. General Harster. Rahn, with his easy access to Hitler and his network of friendly alliances inside the Foreign Office, together with his capacity to deliver the unpalatable truth, had carved a well nigh impregnable position for himself. That much the Consul knew. He was also aware that he could, with a certain degree of circumspection, play off the Wehrmacht against the Gestapo with calculated appeals to the "honour of the German Army" where the ancient traditions still lingered despite heavy infiltration by the Nazis. But the Consul's room for manœuvre narrowed as the front approached Florence. If Florence was to be saved from destruction much would depend not only on the action of Allied generals, but on the attitude of the German command in Italy. Fortunately relations between the German commander-in-chief Marshal Kesselring and Ambassador Rahn were excellent, and the Consul could confidently hope that the city he loved would be spared the ultimate horror of a useless defence which would reduce it and its immovable treasures to a heap of rubble. The art of diplomacy, the Consul knew, was to make the probable impossible, and it is in this context that his despatches, letters and reports should be read. These were not written for posterity, and still less with any intention of exonerating himself from the toll of murders, rapines and thefts which were to become an almost daily occurrence in Florence, but to provide the Ambassador with a mirror of reality in which to see his own policies and those of his government; but even here, the "Heil Hitlers" and other obligatory formulas of unswerving loyalty, made their own commentary. The Ambassador who was adept at reading between the lines grew increasingly to respect the Consul's opinions and predictions, most of which had an uncomfortable way of coming true. But it was the city itself that embraced the man and nurtured his goodness, gave him its pain as its lasting treasure, and its hope of salvation as his constant companion.

The year 1944 opened with predictable cold weather. Berenson's first diary entry for the year tells us it began with a "radiant icy day with gemlike details in landscape as in the backgrounds of the Van Eycks, Roger Van der Weyden, and their followers. Out of the wind, it is warm yet invigorating." Signora Comberti, whom we have already met, discovered moths and was "terribly upset" when she was rummaging through some old clothes in the attic where "two Partisan officers had spent some nights, bringing their radio set with them". Another of Signora Comberti's diary entries reads: "Went to Careggi: gave 300 grams of blood, got plenty of additional ration cards". These extra rations evidently came in useful when a Miss Clench, an Englishwoman, married a Dutch painter. Signora Comberti gave a party for them in her villa.

Clearly social life had not been entirely extinguished, despite the German occupation of Florence. According to an earlier entry in her diary, Signora Comberti had been invited to take tea with the Franchettis. "Kronpriz Rupprecht von Bayern was there, too. A fine old man, very good-looking, in a light grey suit. He was NOT introduced to us. I became aware of his identity when he left and our hostess curtsied to him, calling the old gentleman, *Eure Majestät*—Your Majesty."

But later in January, the Bavarian Crown Prince ceased taking tea with the Franchettis. He had been warned by the Consul that he had been placed under surveillance by the Gestapo. Rupprecht secluded himself thereafter with his eldest son Prince Heinrich in his large apartment opposite the German Consulate on the via dei Bardi.

On January 8th, the Consul had received a "strictly confidential" ruling from the First Secretary of the German Embassy in Fasano, Bock (who was acting as *chargé d'affaires* during Dr Rahn's absence from the Embassy), reaffirming an even stricter order which had been issued previously, withdrawing all consular privileges from the Crown Prince and his family. Ever since 1923 when Rupprecht had refused to participate in Hitler's and Ludendorff's madcap scheme of uniting Bavaria and Austria into some kind of "South German Catholic State" under the Wittelsbachs, Hitler had raged at the Crown Prince, who he declared in a fit of pique, was "a traitor because of his business[1]".

The Crown Prince had been allowed to settle in Italy where he had been invited by his relative the Italian King in 1938. But when Rupprecht asked permission to return to Germany at the outbreak of the Second World War, Hitler maliciously turned down his request. Later when Rupprecht's son Prince Heinrich presented himself at the frontier asking to volunteer for the German Army, he was turned back on three separate occasions. A testimonial to this effect was given to him by the German Military Attache, at the Consul's prompting, so that Heinrich would not be considered a deserter at the end of the war.

"The former Crown Prince is now more than seventy years old, and next to General-Fieldmarshal von Mackensen, is the last surviving General-Fieldmarshal of the First World War," the Consul wrote in answer to Bock's memorandum. "Since a Fieldmarshal can never be fully retired, but always enjoys the right to an adjutant, he had been assigned the former Bavarian Captain Baron Fraunberg, who lives in Florence, as his adjutant." But, he added, although Rupprecht had been allowed to draw up to 2,500 DM from funds remaining in Germany each month, "these payments have ceased since last October, so that the former Crown Prince and his family are again in serious difficulties".

The Consul had already written to Weizsäcker when the latter was Secretary of State at the Foreign Office, complaining of the treatment meted out to the Bavarian Royal Family. "In that letter I pointed out the impossibility of the situation and remarked that such an attitude created a very bad impression in Italian circles," the Consul told Bock. "Meanwhile, I have learned confidentially from the S.D. (Gestapo) here, that they have been instructed to prevent the Crown Prince from going to Switzerland or to the Vatican. Since he has no money, cannot stay with relatives in Switzerland and does not have permission to return to Germany, I would be grateful if I could be told what he should do in the event of an Allied advance on Florence.[2]" Not surprisingly neither Bock nor the Gestapo gave the Consul any firm instructions.

On the same day as he was writing to Bock about the Crown Prince, the Consul despatched an urgent appeal from the Cardinal-Archbishop on behalf of Zenone Benini, a former under-secretary of Albanian affairs who had served as Minister of Works in two of Mussolini's administrations. Although Benini had not been present at the fateful meeting of the Grand Council in July 1943 which had voted against the Duce, he was detained together with Ciano and six other "traitors" in a prison near Verona. Benini had "So far, not been interrogated," the Consul informed Dr Rahn. "His wife and children anxiously await his return. One word from you to the Italian authorities could obtain his release.[3]"

The Ambassador's efforts on behalf of Benini were far more successful than his attempts to save Ciano's life. Dr Rahn had flown specially to Hitler's headquarters on January 8th to obtain his consent to a plan by which German intelligence would kidnap Ciano, allowing him to escape to Switzerland[4]. The only assurance the Ambassador could get was a promise "not to interfere with the Duce's decision either in a positive or negative way". Hitler himself was quite certain that Mussolini would not execute his own son-in-law. As a further concession, Dr Rahn asked that the Duce's wildcat daughter Edda Ciano should be treated "courteously and correctly[5]". She, at least, was allowed to make good her escape to Switzerland, carrying with her part of her husband's diaries which she hoped to trade for his life.

Edda Ciano's dramatic if futile attempts to save her husband's life have been fully if not always accurately documented, but the Consul's part in the curious machinations which followed Ciano's execution on January 11th, deserves some mention. On February 1st, he wrote to the Ambassador appealing on behalf of Marchese Emilio Pucci whom he described as a "brave, twenty-eight-year-old Air Force lieutenant, the recipient of the Iron Cross", who had been arrested by the S.S. on January 9th, when he tried to follow Edda Ciano to Switzerland. "Edda Ciano had drawn Pucci into her circle: at least, that is what Pucci's relatives think," the Consul confided to the Ambassador, after he had received a visit from the young man's father.

Pucci had, in fact, been instrumental in helping Edda Ciano to get to Switzerland, as well as assisting her in secreting part of her husband's diaries. Some six of these earlier records, out of a total of sixteen volumes, had been handed to the Gestapo as a token of goodwill[6], but a large part of the remainder were taken out by Edda Ciano, secured to a belt under her skirt, to Switzerland. The Duce, curiously enough, sided with the gallant young Air Force lieutenant. He had protested to S.S. General Wolff about Pucci's arrest, but without any success, he told his private secretary Dolfin. "Pucci is a brave officer, who sank 85,000 tons of enemy shipping and whose behaviour towards my daughter showed that there were still Italians who will not betray their friendship in time of trouble," Dolfin reports Mussolini as saying. He also discounted all rumours that Pucci was Edda Ciano's lover. Pucci's action was the "disinterested act of a gentleman and that was the cause of his misfortune.... Pucci has always been a loyal friend to my daughter and nothing else.[7]"

Despite the Duce's intervention Pucci was brutally interrogated by the Gestapo, who injured his skull in several places. The Consul, who knew nothing of his involvement with Edda Ciano's escape to Switzerland and still less about her husband's diaries, telephoned the Embassy at Fasano on numerous occasions, as his letter to one of the secretaries, a Dr Gumpert, dated March 27th 1944, indicates[8]. Later in the year Pucci was released and allowed to join Edda Ciano with the ostensible purpose of persuading her not to publish the famous diaries[9].

But the Pucci affair was overshadowed by the events which followed closely on Ciano's execution. On January 30th the Consul reported to Dr Rahn that "four bomb attacks were made in Florence, directed at German military establishments and the offices of the Republican *Fascio*". The young "gappisti" who had little reason to mourn Ciano, celebrated his execution nevertheless by blowing a hole in the Fascist headquarters on the via dei Servi on January 15th, following this up with a bomb attack on the Hotel Excelsior where the S.D. and high military officers had their quarters that same evening.

Despite a certain relaxation of tension "because of the elimination of some neo-Fascist elements", new outrages had been reported from smaller Tuscan towns around Florence. An elderly university professor "who had always been known as an anti-fascist, but who enjoyed great popularity" had been arrested in Lucca. As a result, "the leader of the local

Fascio (Maestro Fusi) was recently shot dead at Borgo San Lorenzo, near Florence, and today, a large Fascist rally in the Teatro della Pergola was interrupted by a bomb attack". An infernal machine had exploded during this meeting called to commemorate the growing list of Fascism's "martyrs", killing and wounding a number of persons.

Both the Prefect and S.S. Captain Alberti believed that these attacks had been organised not by any "large scale organisation", but "by small groups, who may be backed by enemy agents". Cleverly worded and well-laid out illegal newspapers "showed that the opposition is not based on an unified Communist front, but that the groups are sharply divided among themselves", the Consul's report continued. The Partisan danger "has grown somewhat during the past month", although "the reassuring announcement which I had proposed in my December 14th report, brought a number of these fugitives back to their regular place of work".

Others, however, had stayed behind in the mountains and were preparing for more determined resistance. "In addition to attacks made on German military vehicles, increased 'banden' activity was noted in the border area between Romagna and Tuscany, as well as north of Arezzo and Siena and in the mountains of Falterona. The somewhat optimistic Prefect of Florence thinks that the police forces at his disposal are adequate to maintain order because of the generally pacific attitude of the population", the Consul informed the Ambassador.

The somewhat optimistic Prefect had managed to drive back some 1,800 striking workmen at the Pignone Iron Foundry, after a strike lasting two and a half hours which had broken out late in January. But this was only a prelude to the vast wave of strikes which would paralyse the economic life of the city in March.

The level of the Italian radio had also improved, the Consul told Dr Rahn, but broadcasts about Italians living in German internment camps should also be encouraged, if only to provide news for their anxious relatives in all parts of Italy; the time had also come for "art historians to write articles and small brochures about the destruction of some of the most treasured monuments of occidental art in Italy, a destruction which was senseless from a military point of view", the Consul urged. "The fewer propaganda slogans, the better. . . ."

On January 19th, despite the representations which the Consul had made to Weizsäcker and Prinzing, in which he was loyally supported by the newly-appointed director of the Institute, Dr Ludwig Heydenreich[10], he received final orders to remove the contents of that establishment to Germany. Both the Consul and Heydenreich insisted that the crates with the Institute's effects should receive a military escort and top priority transport on the heavily-taxed Italian and German railway systems, taking them to the salt-mines at Kochendorf near Heilbronn-on-the-Neckar and Miltenberg-on-the-Main.

The removal of the German Art Institute, the Consul knew, boded ill for the flagging open city negotiations which had hung like a rag to the mast of Hitler's avowed intentions. On January 22nd, the Consul received word from the Cardinal-Archbishop that the British Embassy at the Vatican had asked the Cardinal Secretary of State, whether the German Government was planning to make an official announcement via the Vatican. This unequivocal request was made at a time when the Allies had carried the beaches at Anzio and were clearly in no mood to argue about "unofficial" declarations, but Weizsäcker, the German Ambassador at the Vatican obviously had orders to hold fast to the letter of Hitler's declaration. All he could provide, the Consul stated, was "an official declaration of the unofficial declaration and then only verbally and not in writing[11]".

The day before the heaviest bombardment on the world-famous monastery of Cassino, the Vatican's official newspaper *L'Osservatore Romano* reminded the belligerents that "a similar responsibility lies on those who destroy and those who provoke[12]". This warning went unheeded as Allied gunfire and air attacks reduced the ancient abbey to ruins, despite German disclaimers of "provocation".

The propaganda barrage put out by both sides was equally

deafening: the Germans insisted that they had no defenders *inside* the abbey and the Allies claimed that the defence works *outside* the abbey must be attacked if their progress on Rome was not to be impeded. The Consul himself took no side in these arguments. He reported on February 1st that "the appearance of Florence has become more and more military in recent weeks". The appointment of General Unruh, a noted disciplinarian, as the German garrison commander should be used to investigate "the claims of numerous staff and military establishments who have made their quarters in Florence, *of all places*". General Unruh should be told "of the Führer's personal order that Florence was an open city". The Consul had deliberately dropped the word "unofficial" from his vocabulary.

A few days later, on February 4th, he repeated that "the clearance of troops from Florence is making no progress whatsoever, since the responsible authorities seem incapable of mastering the technical difficulties". The reason for this had been explained to the Consul by an expert whom he had consulted. The Commanding General (Unruh), the Transport General and the Special Assignments General Haase, did not take their orders from one another, but were all subordinate to Kesselring.

The Consul did not waste his time arguing with this assortment of brasshats: he decided to visit the Commander-in-Chief himself at his headquarters in Monsummano. Between February and May 1944 (according to the Consul's secretary Maria Faltien) he visited Kesselring on four different occasions, travelling over hazardous roads and temporary bridges, mostly at night to avoid air attacks.

The proposals which the Consul brought Kesselring were extremely simple: a special reinforcement of some sixty to eighty military policemen should close all approaches to Florence with large diversionary signs: a traffic control point should be established *outside* the city, to prevent lengthy stopovers inside Florence: all passes of military personnel should be carefully scrutinised and all unauthorised persons should be removed.

Kesselring agreed with all these provisions. In his memoirs he maintained that "Florence, with its unique art treasures, was declared an open city as early as February 1944,[13]" but in actual fact, his instructions only took effect some three weeks after the fall of Rome in mid-June 1944. He did, however, remark to the Consul and to many others that "he never realised what it was like to fight in a museum, until he came to Italy". He certainly gave the Consul and the Ambassador every assurance that he would respect the open city status of the city, but despite these assurances, rumours of Florence's impending fate hung like a black cloud over the city.

Iris Origo noted in her diary on February 5th: "The oddest story circulating in Florence is that a meeting took place in the Grand Hotel a few days ago between the German military and civil authorities to discuss, in cold blood, whether or not the city (when the time comes to retreat) shall be sacked. The Consul and other civilian officials were said to be against the looting, the soldiers in favour.[14]"

Apart from the fact that the Consul had already been elevated in popular imagination to the status of the city's defender, the story had little substance. A meeting had been arranged late in January between the Consul, the Ambassador, the military command in the city, and S.S. General Karl Wolff, but it had been postponed because of an air attack on the city's peripheries. The S.S. General also "had to postpone his long-planned visit to Florence", the Consul wrote to the Ambassador, but Dr Rahn's presence at subsequent meetings with the generals "has been most valuable in strengthening my position here with the military".

He asked the Ambassador as tactfully as he could to clarify Hitler's Army Order 15, which gave the local military commander full responsibility for "the conduct of the war, and in all administrative matters". An addendum should be inserted into this order, stating that "in all localities where there is a representative of the Plenipotentiary of the Reich (i.e., the Consul himself), his approval is required in the following circumstances: in all measures not directly concerned with the conduct of the war, that is in all political, economic and administrative matters, and in all military and security matters, in as far as they have political consequences."

The military, he explained, for all their good intentions, had little understanding of the mood and temperament of Italians, although "they frequently do more for Italians than may be expected of them: i.e., they assist in moving baggage, help with transport, etc. But this is done without any understanding of Italian mentality and in a manner which achieves a contrary effect on public opinion." He had in mind a recent episode where a number of hospitals in Florence had had to evacuate their patients to make way for German war wounded. The "gruffness" with which these measures were conducted, had given the impression "that the patients had been ruthlessly removed". Better liaison with the civil authorities would have explained the reason for the evacuation. The representative of the Reich Plenipotentiary, on the other hand, "if he is to assess and influence political developments in his area. accurately and properly, should be consulted in advance of such moves".

The Consul was asking, in effect, that all political and security matters should be brought to his attention, so that he could warn all those against whom these measures were directed! There is no recorded answer to his request and he was left to tussle as best he could with the military commanders. A note of asperity and impatience had begun to creep into the Consul's own correspondence. On February 4th he had learnt with great alarm, he told Dr Rahn, "that the compulsory recruitment of Italian workers to Germany is to begin around the middle of this month in Florence. I cannot fail to caution you most earnestly against any ill-considered step in this delicate matter." He hastened to add: "I myself would insist on the ruthless execution of even the harshest measures in the pursuit of the war, if this action were likely to have its hoped-for effect."

He then launched into a lengthy argument saying that the Germans could have counted on a large number of voluntary workers if they had succeeded in convincing them that the families they left behind in Italy would receive regular monetary transfers. "I have asked for this repeatedly in my oral and written reports," he chided the Ambassador. "This opportunity has now passed. Italians have lost all faith in their own victory and—since the enemy has almost reached Rome and the Russians are making constant inroads—they have lost confidence in German arms. There is no point in deceiving oneself if one is to weigh the situation carefully and act sensibly." Workers would resist being separated from their families, since such separation might last for years. They were also frightened of Allied attacks on German factories. Those who absconded would join the Partisans in droves and stab German soldiers in the back. "Sympathy strikes will break out throughout all northern cities to express solidarity with their fellow-workers who have been 'carted off' to Germany." The few thousand workmen whom "we shall ultimately succeed in taking to Germany—in place of the desired million—will either work badly or commit acts of sabotage". To hold down the rebellion which such measures encouraged "we shall need more German soldiers than we can hope to secure in Italian workers. And all this is quite apart from the very effective propaganda material which we are handing over to the enemy."

The Consul was sure the Ambassador understood the issues involved, but he nevertheless considered it his duty "to indicate how things really stood, so that you may not be driven by purely military or economic considerations and thus fail to deal with this difficult problem".

To make doubly sure, the Consul sent a copy of his letter to a Dr Haack, an official in the R.U.K., the German Arms Commission which was trying to attract "free" Italian labour into German war industries. "If you share my views, which are based on an accurate assessment of Italian attitudes," the Consul told Haack confidently, "I should be grateful if you would influence your superior in this direction also." The Consul was deliberately playing-off General Leyers, the head of the R.U.K. in Italy, against Fritz Sauckel, the slave-labour overlord of Europe, who had demanded "the desired one million" Italian workers.

With or without the Consul's prompting, the Ambassador had done his best to resist Sauckel's exorbitant demands Sauckel managed to acquire barely a quarter of his desired million[15].

To mitigate Sauckel's raids on Italian manpower, Dr Rahn arranged to despatch some 530,000 parcels, containing food, clothes, medicaments and tobacco, each of five kilos, to Italian internees and slave-labourers in Germany. With the help of the Italian and International Red Cross three hundred and fifty-eight railway wagons went trundling to Germany on their errand of mercy. Meanwhile the Sauckel man-hunts continued with unabated ferocity, reaching Florence in mid-March and not mid-February, as the Consul had been incorrectly advised.

On February 12th, another matter engaged the Consul. He had been visited by the newly-appointed Rector of Florence University and the Pro-Rector who had come to complain of the arrest of the eighty-two-year-old Jewish university professor Riccardo Dalla Volta, who was half blind. The professor had been arrested by the S.D. together with his son and daughter and taken to Camp Carpi near Modena. "Dalla Volta is one of Italy's leading economists and a pioneer in the field of Fascist ideology in political science," the Consul told the Ambassador with barely disguised irony. "For many years he was dean of the faculty of political science in Florence. The Rector and Senate of the University unanimously appealed on his behalf." The Consul added an ironic "Heil Hitler!" in a fit of fury to his letter, but this did not help to save the unfortunate professor, nor his children.

That same night, the Consul penned a personal letter to Dr Rahn, telling him that "a sudden and unexpected opportunity enabled me to sit up in the middle of the night to acquaint you with some of the thoughts which have occupied me lately". The unexpected arrival in Florence of his friend, the army Major Gericke, who volunteered to take the Consul's reflections serenely to Fasano, made it possible for the Consul to write frankly to the Ambassador.

"Sympathies for Britain and America which were due to

personal connections and for other reasons and which played a certain political role in Florence for many years," had declined considerably in recent months, he assured Dr Rahn. "While naïve persons among all sections of the community had anticipated great benefits from an Anglo-American occupation not so long ago, they now showed a marked change of attitude. News from south Italy, combined with accounts of barbarous air-raids on some of the most beautiful cities—which can no longer be justified from a military point of view—has given rise to deep mistrust of Anglo-American intentions." Then came this tormented explanation of Florence's unabated hope of liberation: "The only reason why, in spite of all this, many Tuscans still hope for Anglo-American occupation, is the certainty that this would finally liberate them from Fascism. I have been told by many people that the correct and proper conduct of German troops had convinced them that a German occupation was easier to bear than an Anglo-American occupation. They say that if they prefer an Anglo-American occupation, it is because it would free them decisively from this hateful Fascism which is propped up by Germans." The Consul had certainly found an ingenious argument to convince the Ambassador, but his purpose became clear in the next sentence. The neo-Fascists, he said, were principally engaged in wreaking vengeance on their opponents, or in casting round for new opportunities to commit treason. "Under these circumstances, I feel it is my duty to point out once again, that the elimination of the neo-Fascist regime would make our position considerably easier. Its replacement by experts, without political records, whose reputation is flawless, could greatly facilitate your task in Italy. I ask you to give the most earnest consideration to this matter, which may be of decisive importance to the outcome of the war," the Consul wrote, without telling Dr Rahn where he could lay hands on such "experts".

He then turned to his own parish. Rumours had been circulating in Florence "that the elderly ladies-in-waiting (whom the Consul had rescued earlier) are about to be re-arrested, and that Captain Carità—whom rumour had already 'arrested'—has begun his arrests and tortures again last Monday. The day before yesterday, an elderly, respected lawyer, was killed in his office, because he had allegedly neglected to give the raised-arm salute to a passing Fascist detachment!"

The rumour of Carità's "arrest" was exploded on February 24th, when an official communiqué was issued elevating the detested captain of the Black Militia to the rank of major for his initiative and perspicacity in conducting his "successful and tempestuous" operations against "criminal and anti-nationalist elements". The communiqué offered Carità, whose girth had increased with his rank, its "Vivissimi rallegramenti", its heartiest congratulations[16].

A new reign of terror opened as the neo-Fascists strove to consolidate their hold over Florence. From an elegant apartment house in the suburbs came the cry of the tormented as Carità and the S.S. plied their fiendish operations. The mask of "civility and culture" with which such apologists as the philosopher Giovanni Gentile and "idealistic rebels" such as Mirko Giobbi, the editor of *La Nazione*, had covered the face of Fascism, decayed into a death-mask in the charnel House of Sorrow, on the via Bolognese. Signora Comberti noted in her diary: "To the Kommandatur, because they had again arrested Carlo. . . ." Once again, Carlo, Signora Comberti's son, had been caught listening to the B.B.C. And then this line, which brought a chill to the heart: "The Villa Triste on the via Bolognese. . . ."

# 11

# The House of Sorrow

> No longer shall it be known as the House of Sorrow, for within these walls, innocent and fraternal spirits, protected only with their conscience, faced by spies, torturers and executioners, in order to eradicate this shame and to maintain their honour and save their comrades, chose to languish, to suffer and to die, but not betray.
> 8.9.43–11.8.44
>
> Plaque on the wall of 67, via Bolognese, Florence

Ten minutes bus ride from the heart of the city, rising on an incline from the Piazza della Liberta, at the intersection of the via Bolognese and the via del Pellegrino, stands a sedate, five-story luxury apartment house, built of greyish marble and yellow sandstone. This was the Villa Triste—the House of Sorrow—the last, and perhaps the most terrible of all the villas and apartments which went by that dolorous name, inhabited by Major, lately Captain, Mario Carità and his companions-in-crime.

The apartment house was hardly distinguishable from its respectable neighbours in this comfortable upper-middle class district, inhabited by prosperous business men, lawyers and other well-paid professionals. A tidy, concrete-paved court-yard led past a low line of narrow windows which let in a fitful light into the extensive sub-basement, lined with coal-bunkers, to an entrance hall with tall, square grey marble columns, built in the strict functional style of the 'Thirties. The close-carpeted corridors, and sumptuously large apartments, gave the house the impression of an ocean-going liner, which had docked unaccountably in the midst of a peaceful countryside.

From the upper stories of the apartment house one could see the Giardino di Orticultura, and the horizontal panorama of the city, broken by the rising cupolas of the Duomo, Giotto's belltower, and the crenellated outline of the Palazzo Vecchio. At the back of the house stretched the hills of Il Pellegrino, with the Convent of the Carmelites on their crest.

The house on the via Bolognese was a desirable property in every sense: so desirable that early in January 1944, the insignificant-looking pasty-faced S.S. Captain Alberti, took over the ground and second floor of the building for his Gestapo "post", leaving the first floor and sub-basement to Carita and his hundred-strong army of investigators, torturers, ex-variety artists, masseurs, bodyguards and cooks.

The stone of the apartment house was innocent, of course, like its present inhabitants. But in the summer of the same year when S.S. Colonel Eugen Dollmann was invited to inspect the sub-basement to see for himself how the S.D. and its minions dealt with the "brigands" who dared to challenge the vestigial authority of the Salò republic, and the greater power of the Reich, he stood like a frightened schoolboy before the doors of the inferno where Carita had established his torture chambers[1].

When Dollmann finally summoned enough courage to enter this hell-hole his nostrils were assailed by the acrid odour of sweat and blood. Squelching through the bloody grime of the coal-encrusted floors, he came across tables ladened with thick whips, rods of steel, pincers, manacles, the whole paraphernalia of mid-twentieth century persuasion, until he stumbled on a heavy wooden triangle on which a man had been recently splayed and beaten until his lacerated flesh hung in strips from his body. The S.S. colonel was decently appalled by all this. He was, after all, only a drawing-room S.S. officer, a political appointee, and a student of Italian art and language, and not a lowly S.S. thug who pulled gold teeth out of the mouths of corpses. On his own evidence he remonstrated with Carità on a number of occasions, but without much success. His relations with the Consul were friendly, although he had taken a great dislike to the Ambassador because of the influence Dollmann believed, Dr Rahn exercised over S.S. General Wolff, the all-powerful police chief of Italy, who was Dollmann's closest friend. In any case Eugen Dollmann helped the Consul in a number of "minor matters", and therefore has some place in this chronicle.

A less fortunate visitor to the Villa Triste on the via Bolognese, however, was the lawyer Roberto Papi, a devoted member of the Resistance, who was dragged by S.D. men past a sumptuous bedroom where Carità and his boon-companions were regaling themselves on delicacies, before resuming their ghoulish work in the sub-basement.

Papi was thrust into one of the coal-bunkers, a hole barely nine feet long and six feet wide, which served as his prison cell for forty long days and nights. During one of his interrogations, he met the gallant "Penna" Ferdinando Pretini who had been held in solitary confinement for almost seven months.

Papi reported the most dreadful scenes which he himself witnessed. Men and women were dragged down into the cellars and subjected to high-voltage electric shocks produced by medical equipment filched from the hospitals: Carità was not an electrician for nothing. Rough carpentry tools were used to extract teeth or to tear off earlobes of recalcitrant victims. But even these horrors had their "comic" side. When Carità threatened to break the teeth of a certain Signor Stucchi, that brave soul pulled out his set of artificial teeth from his mouth. Laying them boldly in front of Carità he invited him to break them! Even Carità could not forbear to smile (so the story goes), but this did not save Signor Stucchi from a severe beating.

It seemed a triumph for the Consul, when as a result of urgent pleas to Alberti, the latter agreed to release the five leading members of the Resistance's military committee, whom Carità had captured early in November. These men had been subjected to tortures "far in excess of the usual torments inflicted on his [Carità's] victims", the Consul complained in a later memorandum to the Ambassador[2]. The flimsiness of the charges against General Gritti, the colonels Mastropierro and Frassineti, the leading Christian Democrat Adone Zoli, and the magistrate Barile, was proved when the Gestapo took over the investigations, the Consul wrote. He had pitted the Gestapo against Carità, and the five men were released on January 31st 1944, despite the mounting tension in the city.

This surprising act of clemency on Alberti's part was an obvious appeal to the city not to judge the Gestapo too harshly. In a further burst of chivalrous behaviour, Alberti remitted the sentence passed on Francesco Vannucci Zauli, who had been arrested by the S.D. on January 26th on a charge of armed conspiracy, and on whose behalf the Consul had intervened[3]. Carlo Comberti, Signora Comberti's inquisitive son, was also released from the Villa Triste. But all these favours and mercies were part of Alberti's calculated plan. He not only wished to ingratiate himself with the Consul so as to destroy him, but by carefully balancing one favour against a refusal, he hoped to provoke a head-on clash between him and the higher S.S. and Gestapo authorities in Verona, who had become highly suspicious of the unorthodox consul of Florence. S.S. General Karl Wolff the head of the police and the "fighting" S.S. in Italy, who had once been Himmler's adjutant, was more than lukewarm in his appraisal of the Consul, who he said was "a most estimable man, much admired in army circles, but somewhat weak on military and police matters". The Consul's weakness stemmed from the fact that "he carried every complaint he received from the population to his friend and university colleague, Ambassador Rahn[4]".

On February 23rd, the Consul was again appealing for Dr Rahn's assistance. His two friends Hans Wildt and Erich Poppe had received their final call-up papers. The Consul had spoken to the disciplinarian General Unruh about them, pointing out that he had the smallest consular staff in the whole of Italy, but "the Thief of Heroes" (Unruh's job was to comb staff headquarters and civil agencies for manpower), was adamant. "Wildt has stomach trouble, and Poppe is so delicate and so short-sighted, that he can only be used in an office," the Consul wrote plaintively.

Two days later, he was badgering the Ambassador again. This time it was on behalf of Count Corrado Cini, the naval commander of the destroyer *Selle*—"which had been accidentally torpedoed by the Germans". The unfortunate commander of the *Selle* had been rescued, severely wounded. On his recovery he volunteered for service with the Republican Navy, but was unaccountably arrested in Venice and taken to Germany. The Consul now asked for his release, adding the obligatory formula—"unless there are reasons for his continued detention unknown to me". Whatever those reasons, Corrado Cini, a close relative of Count Vittorio Cini, Mussolini's former Minister of Communications whom the Duce had once accused of "defeatism", was released from Dachau some months later.

On February 26th, the Villa Triste erupted into furious activity. The exultant Carità had scored his most brilliant coup against the Resistance by swooping down on the Action Party's arsenal on the via Guiccardini, where he seized a large quantity of arms which had recently been parachuted onto Monte Giovi by special Allied agencies. The weapons had been brought with great daring into the heart of the city and deposited in two arsenals. Carità himself found a cache with an Allied parachute still attached in a stationary car outside one of these arsenals. A check on the registration number showed that the car had belonged to Luigi Boniforti, who was in Carita's hands!

Carità was beside himself with joy. He now had all the evidence he needed connecting Boniforti with the Armed Resistance, evidence which the Consul could not contradict. The brave, tense, good-looking young lawyer Boniforti, was dragged upstairs to the first floor of the Villa Triste and confronted with Max Boris, a leading Florentine business man who had used Boniforti's car to transport the arms to the Action Party's arsenal, but had been trapped together with five or six of his associates by one of Carita's spies.

Carita shook the tell-tale parachute in front of Boniforti's nose, telling him that it had been found in his car and that he would certainly be shot for this crime. "He was in a particularly ferocious mood," Boniforti recalled. "I saw scenes of the most appalling savagery that night. Carita put out his cigarette on the face of one bruised and bleeding prisoner. Then he drew on some boxing gloves and began to pummel Max Boris. He wounded at least five or six people who had already been "prepared" in the cellars of the Villa Triste. And then, at a certain moment, a German vice-consul, whose name I cannot remember, came to see what Carita was doing. I remember that Carita behaved extremely rudely, saying 'We are looking after Germany's interests, while you people at the Consulate are not!'[5]"

The vice-consul whose name Boniforti could not remember —he was hardly in any condition to remember anything— was none other than Erich Poppe, who was so short-sighted "that he could only be used in an office". But Poppe held his ground without flinching, trying to persuade Carita to abate his enthusiasm for "Germany's interests". When the Consul complained to Alberti about Carità's behaviour to his prisoners, the S.S. Captain explained that "he had nothing to do with the uncontrollable Carita", this, despite the fact that they shared the same premises together.

But on March 1st, Alberti's composure wilted when thirteen thousand Florentine workmen went on a general strike together with thousands of other workmen throughout Northern Italy. The Germans reacted by declaring a public holiday for a week, threatening everyone who did not turn up for work at the end of that period with deportation to Germany. The Consul was furious. He vented his pent-up bitterness against his own authorities and Alberti in particular, in a memorandum of March 27th 1944 which he headed: "Errors committed in the execution of the order to remove striking workers to Germany".

"As the Embassy must be aware," he began, "the local chief of security services [Alberti] was instructed to arrest twenty per cent of all striking workers during the recent strike outbreak in Tuscany, earlier this month and to send them to Germany. Since he had no adequate forces at his command, he handed the job over to the local Fascist militia, *expanding his directive by ordering all 'loafers' were to be rounded up as well.*"

Here the Consul took the opportunity of striking back at Alberti. "In Florence, where the strike was almost over, entire streets were cordoned off; pedestrians were arrested, and diners removed from restaurants, bundled into lorries driven off by German soldiers, and taken to the station where they were put into goods wagons. In the smaller provincial towns of Prato, Empoli, and Montelupo, the Militia carried off persons against whom it had a personal grudge. Altogether some 6,000 persons, including women, have been rounded up." Then with great delicacy he "absolved" S.S. Captain Alberti by despatching him with this rapier thrust: "Just how indiscriminately the militia acted is shown by the fact the Hauptsturmführer Alberti himself released two hundred persons after a cursory check". Despite Alberti's cursory check "a great number of totally unjustified arrests and deportations have taken place". The Consul added that he merely wished to indicate such errors as had come to his attention, since "the deportees included the deputy-director of an institution for the criminally insane at Montelupo: a factory owner, the owners of several important enterprises, a village doctor and his son, the former mayor, and the headmaster of a local school." If these were not enough, the Consul included a labourer with an artificial eye ("the other is being treated"), a student of architecture, and two employees of a "protected" enterprise working for the German Naval base at La Spezia. S.S. Captain Alberti had certainly expanded his directive by arresting persons engaged on vital war-work for the Germans.

"According to my information," the Consul continued, in a further indictment of Alberti, "there were wild outbursts of hatred against the militia and their German superiors throughout the entire Province of Florence during this clumsy and indiscriminate operation. The local Todt representative responsible for recruiting workers for Germany said that such actions complicated his difficult task even further. *He had not witnessed such incidents even in Russia.*"

Despite Alberti's check which may have reduced the figures a little, four hundred persons of both sexes were deported from Florence. "Relatives of these deportees come daily to the Consulate for news," the Consul wrote. He urgently asked to be informed of their fate, enclosing a long list of deportees sent to him by the Cardinal, requesting their immediate release.

He did omit to tell the Ambassador, however, about his own rescue operation, which he conducted with great aplomb when he pulled the young, English-looking Marchese Amerigo Antinori out of S.S. Captain Alberti's clutches.

Antinori, who belonged to an ancient Florentine family, whose vineyards were as famous as their Palazzo which had housed the British Institute and Consulate, had been caught with some twenty-one other persons in a round-up at Montelupo on March 8th. His wife telephoned the Consul, who rushed off to the detention centre on the via Palazzuolo near the Central Station where he managed to persuade one of the guards to bring Antinori to the Consulate. Here, he offered the guard a "receipt" for his prisoner, but the guard refused to surrender Antinori. The Consul then produced a fifty lire note, telling the man to go off and have a decent lunch. The militiaman, who was inexperienced in the ways of the world, scratched the back of his head, but accepted the bait. Once he was out of the way, the Consul bundled the young Marchese into his car and drove off with him to a secret destination.

On March 11th Allied air forces again raided Florence. Two days previously Berenson had noted in his diary: "There is sneering at Allied bombardments and how seldom they hit a bridge or any other aid to traffic, and how wicked it is to go on pelting at Prato and Ponte a Sieve[6]." The sneering disappeared as a squadron of American B-26 "Marauders" came out of a cloudless sky to bomb the Campo di Marte military marshalling yards. A young American bombardier who took part in this raid described it as "one of the greatest examples of precision bombing in the war[7]", but Berenson who was at the receiving end of this exercise, two or three miles away at Careggi, wrote: "The bursting of shells was deafening and made everything tremble. It sounded as if vertically overhead, and directed at one's person." The Americans were aiming at legitimate military targets, as the B.B.C. put out later, but the elderly art historian dreaded to think "what might have happened to Santa Maria Novella and other noble buildings in the vicinity of the railway station". He had obviously confused the Campo di Marte station with the Central station. However, no great edifices had been hit, "which does not mean that there were no human victims. Nor can I understand why, on leaving, they let fall bombs, as animals their droppings. Such bombs seem to have hit hospitals and houses at San Domenico, and done harm to life and limb.[8]"

The Consul, on the other hand used the air-raid as an excuse to prod the Ambassador into resuming the open city negotiations which had come to a dead end. The Consul cabled on March 16th: "Another air-raid on Florence on Saturday March 11th, in which a historic villa, now a children's hospital, was destroyed. I was visited in this connection by M. Comnene, the former Rumanian Foreign Minister, who had been asked to call on the Cardinal that same evening. The enemy has declared his readiness to spare Florence if all headquarters and forces are withdrawn from the city, as suggested by Herr von Weizsäcker. Repeated enemy broadcasts announce in Italian that the *suggested withdrawals have not taken place*, and that on the contrary, Florence has become a transport and supply centre for German forces. *Under these circumstances, there was no military reason why Florence should be spared.*" He went on: "Urgently request that the Commanding General should at last be given clear and firm directives that the Führer's personal order should be carried out." Everyone had forgotten about this "personal" order.

"Worse still," the Consul continued, "there are rumours circulating that churches and hospitals are being used as German depots for petrol and ammunition. To counter these rumours the Prefect, with the consent of the military commandant and myself, has set up a commission, consisting of the Cardinal, neutral consuls, and a representative of the Red Cross to evaluate the inaccuracy [sic] of these reports to pass on to the Vatican and the population. The Cardinal also asks for precise information regarding the evacuation orders to transmit to the Vatican and if possible, an official declaration of Florence's status as an open city, in order to present legal evidence to the enemy."

The onus was again placed on Hitler's shoulders where it rested for many weeks, while the Duce declared his open disinterest in the fate of the city of which he was the Honorary Freeman. "If Florence was to be declared an open city," he told the Ambassador, "then every Italian city would claim the same status!" he told Dr Rahn. And besides, the greater the destruction of Italian art treasures, the greater would be hatred against the Allied invaders.

The Resistance was also emphatic in its opinions. In thousands of leaflets scattered around the city, it repeated the rumours of German malpractice, adding for good measure, that the enemy had stored high explosives in the cellars under the Medici Chapel. What kind of "open city" was this where hundreds of Nazis could be seen wining and dining in the city's exclusive restaurants and hotels? "*...ecco i pericoli per la popolazione fiorentina!*" Out with the Germans who rob us of our bread and provoke Anglo-American bombardments[9]!

A few days later, the Consul was appealing to Rahn for some fifty-four Italian officers serving in the Military Geographical Institute who had been arrested the previous month for refusing to take a "voluntary" oath to the Salò Republic, and shortly afterwards he was reporting how on the morning of March 22nd, Carita and General Adami Rossi had dragged five young men who had refused to join the levy, to the Campo di Marte Stadium. "In vain General Adami Rossi, head of the regular army here, was entreated to commute the sentence," Berenson wrote in his diary on the next day. "He ordered recruits of the regiment to which these victims should have belonged to act as a firing-squad. Whether they did not want to aim or aimed badly, the poor victims were an hour being murdered[10]."

The Consul in his protest to the Ambassador at this slaughter confirmed the gruesome details. They had been shot "by shaking recruits who missed their aim several times," he stated. Carità himself stepped forward to give the *coup de grâce* into the heads of two of the mangled lads, who were piteously crying for their mothers. To add to this tragedy, both Alberti and the local commandant had told the Consul that "there was neither arms nor equipment" for the five executed youths, even if they had volunteered.

The forces of law and order were breaking down in the face of such brutalities. The forcible incorporation of the Carabinieri into Ricci's hateful Black Militia added to the general deterioration, the Consul reiterated in a stream of telegrams and letters. "I agree with Hauptsturmführer Alberti that this move will occasion the greatest surprise and alarm among the Carabinieri," the Consul cabled. He had sounded out opinion among the Carabinieri, both high and low, who assured him "independently of one another, that their oath of allegiance to the King did not prevent them from co-operating with the Occupation Forces or the Republicans, since the King apart from all his latest political actions, had done nothing for the Royal Guard of the Carabinieri." A local Carabinieri General had been so shocked by the incorporation of his men with Ricci's teenage gangsters that he told the Consul that "he did not believe that the order really originated with General Ricci, who issued it, but among certain political circles, so as to create unrest and prepare for new treasons".

The treatment meted out to some leading industrialists was no better. Franco Marinotti, the chairman of the powerful Snia-Viscosa rayon combine had been under arrest for some weeks, although he had the distinction of being "attacked over the London and Bari radios" and was "generally considered pro-German by his business associates". Marinotti had fallen out with the Duce over his "socialisation" plans, but "if such individuals were not safe from arrest," the Consul wrote to Dr Rahn on March 27th, "the inevitable result would be that other industrialists would withdraw or reduce their co-operation with Germany."

On March 21st, 28th and 31st, the Prefect's fact-finding Commission, consisting of nine prominent citizens, met under the chairmanship of Cardinal Dalla Costa to investigate rumours of German malfeasance. Among the commissioners was Marchese Serlupi in whose villa Berenson was hiding. Although the honorary Swedish Consul Mario Gobbo took part in the proceedings, the Swiss Consul Steinhäuslin had withdrawn on instructions from his Government. The German Consul, of course, took no part in the commission's proceedings. On March 23rd, he reported a further air-attack on the city to the Ambassador, adding that despite "the grateful recognition that Florence had been declared an open city by the Germans, the new air-raids are attributed to the overcrowding of the city with German troops and military vehicles". This expression of gratitude was accompanied by the hope that the "new resolute instructions which have recently been given by Kesselring to the military commandant, will be carried out". The Commandant had at least offered no resistance to the Prefect's fact-finding commission, which was hardly surprising, since its purpose was to appease the suspicious Florentines. But then suddenly a new and unexpected meteor streaked across the heavens, like a portent of salvation. The well-meaning, but impatient Rumanian ex-Foreign Minister, N. Petrescu Comnène, who had not been invited to sit on the "neutral" commission, took it into his head to write directly to the Führer. Comnène had known Hitler briefly during his hey-day as Foreign Minister, before being ousted from office by Marshal Antonescu and his Iron Guard revolution in 1940.

One can imagine with what overflowing generosity, and palpitating anxiety, Comnène approached this task of wringing the Führer's heart with sonorous alexandrines which he set down in impeccable French. Happily the setting for this exercise was as delightful as Comnène's prose.

The Villa Machiavelli which the former Rumanian Foreign

Minister inhabited, had, as its name signified, once belonged to the much maligned Niccolò Machiavelli, Florence's first civil servant and ambassador extraordinary, the author of a standard work on the behaviour of princes. A stone bust of "Old Nick" stood in a small inner-quadrangle which had weathered the passage of time and the contumely of enemies, retaining its air of long-suffering irony. In a nearby wall a plaque had been set, listing the names of famous authors and philosophers who had honoured "this modest little villa" with their presence during their great contemporary's lifetime.

This little haven built of "bel Maiano", as Comnene tells us, covered a good half acre, with its pretty garden, set amongst "immense pines, tall, cypresses, and odiferous magnolias". In such a setting Macchiavelli could be excused even the tortured Gothic style with which he addressed his "Exhortation to the Princes of Italy to deliver her from the Barbarians[11]". Only Comnene could have improved upon this rhetorical masterpiece. He did so with great splashes of Tyrian purple and Dacian indigo. He began his letter to Hitler by extolling the Führer's oft-expressed admiration for Florence, and then treated him to an extract from Baedeker!

"*Si Rome est la Ville de la Foi, Florence est incontestablement la Ville de la Beauté,*" he enthused. Florence not only belonged to Italy "but was part of the human patrimony of yesterday, today, and tomorrow". He was confident that Hitler shared all these sentiments. If this were so, all the Führer had to do was to instruct his Government or High Command to declare Florence an open city and to draw a line "in the air" of seven kilometres from the centre of Florence—the Piazzo del Duomo, would do—from which all military establishments and troops should be promptly excluded. To make his intentions quite clear, Comnene enclosed a map showing this circular demarcation line drawn "in the air" on which he ringed his own Villa Machiavelli in red.

"*En qualité de citoyen d'élection de cette ville—où je possède une modeste villa*", Comnène continued glowingly, he could not resist the appeal of friends and many high personages to give his plighted word "to millions [sic] of architects, sculptors, painters, poets, archæologists, and historians of all countries and epochs," to beg Hitler to give the necessary orders so that no one should ever accuse Germany of being "directly or indirectly responsible for the destruction of this inestimable jewel of the human spirit".

He then underlined the next astonishing sentence. "I know that it is a great sacrifice to ask numerous German military authorities and auxiliaries who have established themselves in Florence to leave the beautiful residences which they chose for themselves in the city and its environs (his underlining ends unaccountably at this point) but their merit will be all the greater, and the future generations will be all the more beholden to them.[12]"

Having drafted this letter, Comnene rushed round with it to the Archepiscopal Palace where he showed it to Dalla Costa. The Cardinal who was not a man to discourage good works, complimented the Rumanian on his noble initiative. Comnene then took the letter round to the Swiss Consul to ask how he could get it directly to Hitler, by-passing the usual channels, "*cosa tanto piu delicta*", because it was such a delicate matter.

Carlo Steinhäuslin advised him to confide the letter to the Consul "*persona, come e stato detto, amantissima di Firenze*" (a person, as previously mentioned, a passionate admirer of Florence). He arranged a meeting between the Consul and Comnene at the German Consulate, where the Consul greeted the ex-Foreign Minister "*con una squisita cortesia*". He was obviously impressed with the Rumanian's burning sincerity. ("After all, I would not have dared to send Hitler a letter like that!" he said.) He promised to have the letter translated into German, and have it delivered "*direttamente nelle mani del Führer*[13]".

The Rumanian diplomat thanked the Consul fulsomely (he really was a very polite and charming old gentleman) and then settled down to wait for a reply to his letter, which he dated March 25th, 1944. It took Hitler almost two and a half months to frame a suitable answer.

Meanwhile, on April 1st the Prefect's commission published its long-awaited findings. Despite all efforts, the commission could discover no trace of "war materials" beneath the Basilica of San Lorenzo, let alone in the cellars of the Medici Chapel, or under the great dome of the Duomo itself. A store of pharmaceutical and sanitary equipment had been found in the subterranean cellars of the Medici Chapel which had been rented by the Military Pharmaceutical Institute, but these inoffensive items had been removed at the insistence of the newly-formed "German Art Protection Commission", headed by Standartenführer Dr Langsdorf.

A small quantity of aviation spirit and petrol had been discovered in some hospitals, but these had served the exclusive requirements of hospital cars and ambulances. The mountain of rumour had travailed without producing even a mouse! The Prefect expressed his deep satisfaction with the findings, and invited Florentines either singly or in groups to visit their sacred edifices on feast days[14]. The Consul reported the Commission's findings in his April memorandum to the Ambassador in which he dealt with the state of the city's economy. Prices had risen beyond the reach of most persons, he complained: olive oil, a staple diet, had been reduced to a ration of one hundred grams per person a month. There had been no butter in the city since last December, and meat was unobtainable "even on the black market". The strikes which had occurred in March expressed economic grievances as much as political discontent. Slogans had begun to appear on the walls "showing only too plainly the unpopularity of the neo-Fascist government": the most favoured of these was "*Morte al Fascismo*" followed by "*Morte a Mussolini, Capo della Delinquenza Italiana*", to which the word "*Approvo*" had been added "many times".

If the Florentines were accused of being too harsh in their evaluation of members of the Duce's government, the Consul continued, it was because they were "particularly well-qualified to judge them" since most of them were Tuscans; Pavolini, the Party Secretary came from Florence; Buffarini, the Minister of the Interior originated from nearby Pisa;

Biggini, the Education Minister, also came from Pisa; Tamburini, the chief of police, a Florentine; Renato Ricci, the head of the Republican National Guard and the Black Brigades, hailed from Carrara; Mezzasoma, the young Umbrian from Perugia, was educated in Florence, he was Minister of Popular Culture. Little could be expected from Mussolini's "wild Tuscans" who were resisting every attempt to cleanse the neo-Fascist Party from undesirable elements. "When a distinguished member of the Fascist Party called for a thorough overhaul, Pavolini threatened to have him murdered![15]" the Consul wrote. What could be expected from Ministers whose government offices were scattered all over northern Italy and who themselves "lived mostly in luxury hotels, divorced from any links with the people, their sufferings and anxieties"?

German propaganda efforts also came under scrutiny, in the Consul's April report. It was no use pointing out "the short-comings in Allied occupied parts of Italy when similar things occur in areas under our control". Florentines could not be impressed by horrendous tales of over-crowded prisons in Sicily, filled with "the cries of unfortunate prisoners" when they had to endure Carità, Sauckel raids, forced military levies, and a black market where they had to pay for produce "at ten times its value". Crude attempts to stir up anti-British feeling by the publication of a forged letter which Winston Churchill was supposed to have sent Badoglio, made little impression on public opinion. "It was so long no Italian would bother to read it to the end." The whole thing was passed off as a joke in poor taste, as had been the issue of some excerpts from *Crux Ansata*[16] by H. G. Wells, "who although he is not unknown, in no way represents British public opinion", the Consul said. "The brochure lacks all value because of its total absence of historical insight and the recklessness of its attacks on the Catholic Church. The assertion, made in the introduction, that Britain's main war aim was the destruction of the Catholic Church and the downfall of the Papacy, as well as the elimination of Rome as the centre of Christian thought, is believed by no one, because people are accustomed to think soberly and objectively here. The Church refrains, on principle, from taking up a position for or against such diatribes, because it is convinced that neither of the belligerents is genuinely prepared to protect the interests of the Church."

The naïve fulminations against the Roman Catholic Church in *Crux Ansata*, whose opening chapter was provocatively titled "Why do we not bomb Rome?", was suitably answered by the son of a Protestant lawyer from Dresden. But the Consul's April report dealt with more pressing matters. The growth of the Partisan forces "had assumed alarming proportions[17]". This development could have been checked "if the measures discussed in my reports since September 21st 1943, had been avoided". Two German officers had been abducted near Arezzo, and shots had been fired at German passenger vehicles and lorries. A train had been held up some eight kilometres from Florence on the night of April 4th, and searched for Fascist militiamen. General Koestring, the former German Military Attache in Moscow who visited the Consul at this time had told him that if Soviet officers succeeded in giving these bands training in Soviet guerilla tactics then those "bands" would become "a serious menace to the country and to the security of German armed forces".

In Florence itself arrests by the militia continued. "Youngsters armed with machine-gun-pistols and hand-grenades, force their way nightly into peoples' homes, and threaten, manhandle and rob people," the Consul wrote. The hatred against Carita's and Ricci's adolescent gangsters had reached such a pitch that bomb attacks were now aimed at their masters. "Only recently a German soldier was shot at and severely wounded in broad daylight for the first time in Florence," he stated. "The reason for this is that the Gestapo and military authorities are using Fascist elements to do their work, and the latter after they have committed their excesses, say they are acting on German orders." The Consul had lumped the Gestapo and the military authorities together for the first time.

The repercussions which followed the wounding of the German soldier were immediate. The notorious "ten to one" ratio was applied in accordance with Hitler's instructions[18] and ten hostages were seized and condemned to be shot.

The Consul, although he makes no mention of it in his April report, had asked the city commandant to set aside the sentence against the ten hostages, but the latter refused. In a final gesture of despair, the Consul sent Hans Wildt and Erich Poppe to reiterate his plea, but the commandant did not bother to listen. The orders, he said, had come "from above" and there could be no argument. Wildt and Poppe were about to give up, when they noticed a young officer dressed in Field Security uniform, making frantic gestures behind the commandant's back. Stepping forward, he told his superior that the execution of the hostages had been fixed to take place on April 7th, a Good Friday. Such an act of deliberate blasphemy might be construed as a further example of *Deutsche Sturheit* —German bloody-mindedness, at its bloodiest. The commandant nodded his agreement and ordered that the executions should be delayed until after Easter.

When the two young vice-consuls left the office, the Field Security officer followed them, whispering that he belonged "to Admiral Canaris's circle[19]". The execution of the hostages in any case was postponed and finally abandoned on further pleas from the Consul.

On April 6th, the Consul and his two friends attended the opening of the Maggio Musicale, Florence's annual music festival, which began with typical Florentine perversity in April. The first item in the concert was Verdi's *Messa da Requiem*: it was Maundy Thursday. Sitting in front, a few seats away from the Consul and his aides, was the Prefect, Dr Manganiello, the Podesta (mayor) of Florence, the geographer, Professor Giotto Dainelli, and the Sicilian philosopher Professor Giovanni Gentile, who presided over the Accademia d'Italia, which had recently been transferred from Rome to Florence. Mirko Giobbi, the ebullient editor of *La Nazione* was also present among the glittering company of municipal and Party worthies, who listened with rapt attention as the *Dies Irae* soared to the roof of the Teatro Communale.

Nudging the Consul gently, Hans Wildt pointed at the

corpulent figure of Major Mario Carità, who sat sprawled in the front row in his resplendent uniform of the Black Brigades, with a gleaming machine-gun-pistol strapped to his back! Carità was yawning, showing his massive indifference to the *Dies Irae*, which would finally catch up with him, his pistol notwithstanding. But death first came to the plump, cherubic Professor Gentile. It came in the afternoon, a week later.

# 12

# The Gentle Professor

> A man can surely do what he wills to do, but he cannot determine what he wills.
>
> ARTHUR SCHOPENHAUER

Ante-dating Gentile's assassination by a few days was a political murder of a different order: Mirko Giobbi, the editor of *La Nazione*, Florence's influential daily, heard that he had been dismissed from his post on the instructions of the Minister for Popular Culture, Mezzasoma. The news had been relayed over the Fascist radio, but the prime mover behind the dismissal was none other than Pavolini, the Party Secretary, who had taken such an ardent dislike to Giobbi.

The connection between Gentile's murder and the dismissal of editor Giobbi may appear to be tenuous, yet these actions revealed a deep crisis in the political make-up of neo-Fascism, and, more surprisingly, a confusion of ends and means in the ranks of the Resistance which threatened to tarnish its image of self-sacrifice, patriotism, and heroism. The divisions which had rent the fabric of neo-Fascism, were paralleled in the ranks of its opponents, as the incoherent forces of fear and violence edged towards the nightmare which soon enveloped the city in the last months before its liberation.

The Consul, as has already been mentioned, had been greatly impressed by Giobbi's lively intelligence, his flair for popular journalism, and his covert criticism of the "new men" who surrounded the Duce. Giobbi, like Gentile, had preached some form of national reconciliation between those whom Giobbi called "idealistic rebels" inside the Fascist party and its ruling circles: like Gentile also, he had advocated a mild form of "loyal opposition" which could temper the excesses of neo-Fascism and give it some form of respectability in the eyes of the majority of non-aligned Italians. Yet Giobbi diverged profoundly from the Consul's own views in his support for the execution of Ciano, and even more when he defended "the bloodthirsty, sadic [*sic*] Captain Carita, because he was so 'sincere' ...[1]". Giobbi had also affected great admiration for Pierre Laval—"the only person left to collaborate with the Nazis". Laval's calculated ambiguity in his dealings with the Nazis, may provide some clue to Giobbi's own motives and character.

Giobbi's actual dismissal followed closely on an article which he had published during the Easter holidays in which he made his tortuous distinction between "idealistic rebels" such as himself, and others, whom he designated as Allied spies and hirelings, but the storm had been brewing over his head ever since the appearance of an even more provocative article which he called "Epurazione" (Purification), which appeared on February 23rd.

Pavolini summoned Giobbi to explain such unambiguous statements which included an attack on "the musty atmosphere in which treason survived" in the Duce's inner cabinet. It was necessary, Giobbi had written, to purge the ranks of the neo-Fascist Party from all time-servers and saboteurs and replace them "with those new men, who in the critical days after July 25th, 1943, were prepared to make vital decisions, without regard to personal advantage and without any support ...". When Giobbi attempted to explain his motives, Pavolini cut him short with a reminder that he was not prepared to tolerate any criticism of the new Republican Party, and such statements as Giobbi had allowed himself to make, were sufficient to have him shot.

The Consul who reported these somewhat undignified proceedings to the Ambassador, commented on this unorthodox method of dealing with recalcitrant chief editors: "I think that it is regrettable that the few honest and intelligent followers of Mussolini, who are also our friends, should be treated in this manner. In my opinion, the present situation in Italy makes it imperative to allow Italian journalists some measure of free discussion. Only then will it be possible to gain friends for our cause among those individuals who have an open mind, but who are still reluctant to come forward, but who read Giobbi's articles with considerable interest."

The Consul himself made a spirited attempt to re-open the issue of Giobbi's dismissal in a personal interview with Pavolini[2]. He admitted that Giobbi "had not always, perhaps, adhered closely to the line pursued by the government, but he had given life to what had been a very dull paper, and by doing this he had carried many of those who had still hesitated". Pavolini remained unconvinced by these arguments, and Giobbi's star set behind the cloud of "watchful waiting" of those who still refused to commit themselves fully either to the Germans or to the Allies. But even this became a diminishing pastime as Allied forces carried Cassino and began their advance on Rome.

Four days later, after the curtain of oblivion had fallen on Mirko Giobbi, came the murder of the gentle professor. Shortly after one-thirty on the afternoon of April 15th 1944, Professor Gentile left the Palazzo Serristori which temporarily housed the Accademia d'Italia over which he presided. He was returning home early in his small, chauffeur-driven car to the Villa Montalto, situated between Florence and Settignano, to visit his son Fortunato, who was seriously ill at this time.

On reaching the drive of the villa, the chauffeur left the car to open the gates. In those few seconds, a group of four or five youngsters—the evidence is hazy on this point—rode up on bicycles. Peering inside the car, they enquired for Giovanni Gentile. The old gentleman smiled benignly at his assailants: he himself was an ardent bicyclist, fond of taking long rides through the city without any thought for his safety. He nodded and identified himself, asking what he could do for them. The youths then drew their revolvers and poured three or four shots into the astonished professor at short range. The chauffeur ran back to the car, but by that time, the Professor's murderers had fled, as swiftly and mysteriously as they had arrived.

By the time the chauffeur had driven Gentile to the hospital at Careggi where one of the professor's sons worked as a doctor, Gentile's life had ebbed away: a look of astonishment never left his face.

The murder of Gentile caused a profound shock to the city's psyche, as well as some considerable heart-searching. Whatever Gentile's faults may have been as "the patriarch of the Fascist church" (the description is Berenson's), people remembered that he had once been Croce's disciple who had wandered into the foggy mists of Fascism, but "he had never been unjust, let alone cruel to individuals. On the contrary, he was helpful and good to everybody[3]".

The Consul who shared Berenson's opinion, heard of the wanton assassination while he was at Fasano where he had gone to consult with Dr Rahn and Professor Prinzing. Justice, he realised, was not a casualty of one side only: the slaying of Gentile would not only provide the Fascists with an aura of sanctity for their growing list of "martyrs", but might also provoke reprisals. On his return to Florence the Consul cabled Prinzing (whose association with the Gestapo was known to him), asking him to discount "the alarming reports" which had been spread by a German journalist, a certain Schmitz-Forst, about conditions prevailing in Florence[4].

Schmitz-Forst had visited Florence for only one day, and despite his outward calm "he had the reputation of dramatising events among his colleagues", the Consul informed Prinzing. The events in and around Florence were dramatic enough without this gentleman's embellishments. The main reason for the unrest in the city, the Consul pointed out, was the growing intensity of Allied air-raids on the city's outskirts and the shocking accounts brought in from the countryside of the Hermann Goering S.S. Division's punitive expedition against the Partisans over the Easter period.

Although the Consul did not connect Gentile's murder with the activities of this S.S. Division, there were others who did. Avv. Gaetano Casoni, a respected advocate and head of the Florentine Red Cross who was a close friend of Gentile's, traced his assassination to that fount of all evil, Major Mario

Carità himself[5]. It was a view which Berenson also supported.

"It seems that Göring's 'merry men', while sweeping the lower slopes of Monte Morello clean of 'communists', killed the favourite secretary of Gentile, who was spending the Easter days with his mother in a villa in Cercina," Berenson wrote. "When Gentile learnt this, he threatened to go to Mussolini and tell him what was going on here, that it was sheer anarchy and misrule. Thereupon, as is by no means unlikely, Major Carità, who under S.S. protection still runs the province, had him assassinated.[6]"

All these conjectures—and they were no more than this—were reinforced by the seizure by Carità and the compliant Prefect Manganiello of three leading University professors, Ranuccio Bianchi Bandinelli, Renato Biasutti and Francesco Calasso, two days after Gentile's murder, on April 17th. That the three men happened to be friends of Gentile's without being admirers of his political credo, confused the situation even further. Two other University men whom it was intended to arrest at the same time, managed to escape.

"Since the Gentile family has expressly requested that no hostages should be arrested, one of my representatives who is a close friend of one of Gentile's sons, made enquiries regarding the reason for these arrests," the Consul wrote to Prinzing on May 3rd, "the Prefect told him that he had issued the order against his own wishes on instructions he had received from the Ministry of the Interior. I spoke to you about this, and asked you to discuss the matter with Buffarini (the Minister of the Interior), but so far I have received no reply." The Consul himself knew that the order for the arrests had not emanated from Buffarini because he had been told "very confidentially" that the Prefect had been instructed "to take the strongest possible measures to find the criminals, but to desist from reprisals".

Armed with this information he went to confront the Prefect, but since he could not reveal the source of his confidential information, he told Dr Manganiello that he had learnt about the instructions while he was in Fasano. The

Prefect was now in some difficulties. "Put on the spot by me, he admitted that he alone was responsible for the arrests, but claimed that the three professors were merely in 'protective custody' for a few days, and that this had nothing to do with Gentile's murder." The Consul then expressed his astonishment at "this obvious lie, because all three men were asked during the first day of the investigation where they had been on the day of the assassination".

To make things quite plain the Consul then asked Prinzing to confirm his findings by telegram, absolving Buffarini and his Ministry from any complicity in the three professors' arrest which he proposed to show the Prefect. Meanwhile, both he and Dr Heydenreich went to the Murate prison to comfort the incarcerated men.

Their visit to this inhospitable mansion, made "a great impression" on Professor Calasso. Another prisoner, the eminent archæologist Professor Bandinelli, stated that while he had known the Consul for some time before the German occupation and at that time "was naturally on my guard and somewhat prejudiced against him", after the occupation, however, his opinion had changed since he "frequently applied for his help for persons threatened with danger[7]".

Now the life of Professor Bandinelli and his two colleagues hung in the balance (Carità was openly urging the Prefect to shoot them) as wave after wave of murder and reprisal struck the city without Carità discovering the real perpetrators of Gentile's murder.

The Tuscan Liberation Committee, with the exception of the Communists, in a dignified statement disclaimed any responsibility for Gentile's murder. One of its principal adherents, the Action Party, stressed that Gentile was "neither a spy nor a criminal", however reprehensible his cultural and political activities may have been. Later evidence showed that Gentile's assassination had been engineered by the terrorist bicycle squads of the G.A.P.[8] in revenge for the horrors which the S.D. and S.S. had exacted on their comrades in Rome and elsewhere. And there the whole tragic matter rested. The Cardinal-Archbishop of Florence, no friend of clandestine murder, attended a memorial meeting at the Lyceum where Gentile's name was solemnly added to the list of Fascism's "saints and martyrs". The Consul obtained the release of the three professors on May 6th, and Avv. Casoni opened a special fund in Gentile's memory to aid refugees and the homeless. But the death and obsequies of the fuddled old professor who preached his hopeless message of conciliation, and who spoke of Mussolini's return as a restoration to the Italy of Vittorio Veneto, brought no peace to the tormented city.

On April 22nd, the Consul sent another of his routine telegrams to the Ambassador. It went uncoded over the military teletype in flagrant disregard of Dr Rahn's advice and instructions. The cable read: "The Consulate is visited daily by relatives of Italians arrested during the round-up of striking workers on March 8th, who ask for information about them. Enquiries at the S.D. (Gestapo) office, the labour recruitment agency, concentration points and the militia are without results. Relatives in the greatest anxiety and distress. Request arrangement of immediate despatch of list of those who have been arrested and facilities for correspondence."

Five days later, on April 27th, the storm broke over his head. The Ambassador wrote telling him that he had just been handed his telegram, the text of which he quoted back to him in full. "This telegram was despatched over the military teletype," he fulminated, "and was therefore available to the German military authorities. May I remind you in this connection of our recent conversation. In principle, I should like to say this to you: the German authorities have done everything conceivable, under the most trying circumstances, to ensure supplies for the Italian civil population, and especially the workers. Yet strikes, assassinations, and acts of sabotage continue on an increasing scale. This has involved the shedding of innocent German and Italian blood. We must see that such tendencies to hostile behaviour on the part of the Italian population is brought to an end with the greatest severity and energy, until it is gradually eliminated. That is why I gave instructions during the recent political strike that the ringleaders of the strike movement should be taken to German labour camps, without their families being informed of their fate for the time being."

Dr Rahn admitted that this was "a severe measure, designed to create a certain mood of anxiety among their families, so as to make other workers less inclined to take part in such movements. This psychological shock had produced some good results in a number of cities, and would be only one way of ensuring that less innocent German and Italian blood will be shed in future." But the Ambassador, realising that the Consul would not be prepared to follow his argument to its logical conclusion, hastened to reassure him: "I am, of course, ready to examine every case where the innocence of an arrested person can be proved beyond doubt, and to arrange for his release. But it goes without saying that I have to apply the most stringent criteria, even at the risk that one or another person may have to remain in a labour camp, leaving an unhappy family behind him, anxious about his fate." This scarcely concealed rebuke stung the Consul, but there were more blows to come. Dr Rahn continued: "If I don't deal severely with these matters, we shall have to face unpleasant surprises in the coming weeks—probably during the first days of May—which will have to be paid for dearly with German blood and the blood of their Italian Allies, to the distress and tears of their families. I should be glad if I have been able to convince you of the correctness in my point of view, which you ought to take into account when compiling your reports."

TheAmbassador ended his letter "in sincere friendship and in the comradeship of battle".

The Consul began drafting his reply, regretting any misunderstanding which might have arisen between them, but insisting that he had not appealed for any "strike leaders". He could personally vouch for the innocence of the arrested men who had been torn from their families. He did not even object to the tone of elevated reprimand with which the Ambassador had reproved him. The letter might, after all, have been intended for other eyes besides his own. Surely Rahn realised that every repression merely deepened Italian resentment and that "innocent blood" could not be saved by such measures?

He then noticed the Ambassador's postscript. He screwed up the draft of his reply and threw it into the wastepaper basket. The postscript began: "You have placed me in a rather difficult position over the Coletti affair . . .".

For two days and nights the Consul had hammered at the doors of mercy, pleading for the lives of three young Italians accused of "desertion" and refusal to obey the military levy who had been sentenced to death by a military court. The Ambassador had made representations to Graziani to hold up the executions for two days because the Consul believed that there were "technical" reasons which had prevented the young men, or at least one of them, from answering the levy.

Now, as the Consul read the Ambassadorial postscript, all hope disappeared. "Damn them all," the Consul said quietly to himself. "Damn the just and the unjust, those who shed innocent blood, and those who seek to prevent it."

# 13

# Postscript

> . . . exorbitant mercy has an ill-effect on the universality, whereas particular executions extend only to particular persons.
>
> MACHIAVELLI

P.S.
You have placed me in rather a difficult position in the Coletti affair. Immediately after your telephone call I had Marshal Graziani wakened at 1 a.m. (he was already in bed) so as to prevent Coletti's execution. I did this in the certainty that the information which you provided was correct, namely that Coletti had arrived from Switzerland in order to report for military service, but had been prevented from doing so for technical reasons only.

Marshal Graziani came to discuss this matter with me personally today. He showed me a voluminous file of papers dealing with this case, which proved that Coletti had returned from Switzerland months ago, staying at first in the mountains, probably with the Partisans, and later hiding in his father's house. It is difficult to speak of "technical reasons" for this delay in reporting for military service. There is an added suspicion; I have been told confidentially that Coletti's father is in contact with anti-Fascist bands and that a brother has absconded. Coletti's parents moreover tried to "influence" the judge.

There is an Italian decree supported by us, according to which Italians who do not report for military service are subject to execution as is the case in Germany. It is absolutely impossible for us to intervene with the Italians in a case which has been prosecuted in a proper legal manner. Such intervention would be interpreted by the Italian population as an act of partiality by the German military authorities for persons with aristocratic connections even when they have clearly violated the law, a law which was introduced on German orders.

I wish to draw your attention to the fact that the introduction of the death penalty for failure to report for military service, as well as the arrest of the parents of young men who fail to do so, has resulted in the recruitment of 50,000[1] men, who would otherwise be in hiding or with the Partisans, or who would have become an easy prey for them. These have now reported for duty, and have been incorporated into the framework of the German army. Thus German blood has been spared, in both the active and passive sense of the phrase. There is, for example, a reference in Marshal Graziani's file to the effect that the German Military commandant intervened, reversing his earlier decision, at the request of the German consul. I consider your intervention in this case unjustified both from a human and political point of view. *It is liable to expose you to criticism which may undermine your authority in cases which are justified and which may be useful, and which have always had my support.* Please do not resent this admonition. Only those can qualify as defenders of justice who are also prepared to uphold the law in its inexorable severity.

R.

The Consul replied on May 3rd. Far from resenting the Ambassador's admonition, he showed a strenuous determination to argue the issue out with him step by step. This was no dry legalism on his part, although the "Coletti affair" had become largely academic since the three young men had already been shot. But the Consul was groping towards an expression of independence outside of the confines of his close friendship with Rudolf Rahn. He could no longer shelter behind the certainty that he and his friend would see eye to eye on every issue. The dichotomy which existed between Law and Mercy could not be resolved until Caesar wore the face of Christ, Nietzsche had once said, but neither Hitler nor

Mussolini had shown signs of such transformation. The Ambassador had tried to avert the fate of the three young men by appealing to Mussolini and Graziani to hold up the execution for two days, but had deliberately been misled by the Consul, who had allowed his heart to subdue his reason. The tragedy which had overwhelmed the executed men marked a new development in the Consul, who now understood that there was no escape from "tragic and evil circumstances". The Platonic ideal had crashed in the stark reality of that execution. The Consul had to accept defeat, to be powerless in the face of others' suffering and death, if he were to discover those resources of courage which the changing situation would demand of him. His letter of May 3rd to Dr Rahn showed the emergence of this side of personality.

Florence, May 3rd 1944.

Dear Rudolf,

Sincere thanks for your friendly letter of April 27th. I should like you to know the following so as to clear up the affair of the three Italians sentenced to death—Onorio Coletti Perucca, Alfredo Ballerini and Luigi Ferro, who have been executed in the meantime.

On the morning of April 26th, I received a visit from the local lawyer Bruno Puccioni. Puccioni is known to you: he is a friend of the Prefect's, a disabled veteran who had been awarded the Iron Cross. He asked me urgently to prevent the execution of the three twenty-year-old Italians, which was scheduled for that same afternoon, until pleas for clemency addressed to the Duce by their families could be considered. The aunt of one of the men, who is highly respected in Florence and whom I know to be a Fascist[2], also asked for my help in the matter. I was informed by an Italian officer whom I consulted that the case rested solely with General Adami Rossi. Lieutenant-Colonel Pischely, on instructions from the military commandant, tried to contact the General but was fobbed off. Pischely then contacted the General's chief of staff and conveyed the military commandant's request that the execution should be delayed until the Duce had made his decision. I then tried to reach the General myself to discuss the matter with him. Since he [the General] persisted in pretending that he was not available, I expressed my surprise to his adjutant that a General in such an important position could not be located. I repeated the request to delay the sentence until the clemency plea had been considered. When I returned home I was told by the military commandant that our joint request had been complied with. The 'phone call which I had put through to you earlier came through and I told you about the matter, although it had been settled in the meantime. It is untrue that the intervention of the German military commandant took place at my prompting, against his previous decision.

Had General Adami Rossi had a clear conscience, he would not have avoided a discussion with me on this matter. If three men are suddenly picked out of the many thousands who have not reported for duty and who are liable to the death penalty, one may assume that personal motives are involved. My suspicion was strengthened by a dramatic account which appeared in a newspaper of the circumstances surrounding Coletti's arrest by the National Republican Guard. This account was not in accordance with the facts.

If General Adami Rossi had been willing to discuss the matter either with me or the military commandant, I would not have even bothered you.

The Cardinal-Archbishop and Mussolini's niece had made a far stronger representation for mercy to General Adami Rossi. The General is understood to have told them that he had done his best, but that the Germans had demanded the execution of the death sentence. This is renewed proof that we are constantly charged with final responsibility.

In the meantime a heroic myth surrounding the death of the three young men spread among all sections of the population. It is said that on the morning of their execution they had celebrated Mass and had sung the *Te Deum* on their way to the place of execution. They died "like saints". As a result martyrs have been created who are held up as an example to young men here.

*

The Consul's letter may be interrupted at this point to establish a number of salient facts. Onorio Coletti Perruca, who had not turned twenty, had returned some months previously from Zurich, where he studied. He had served with the Partisans on Monte Giovi, an area where allied arms had been parachuted. When he returned to Florence on a mission he was arrested while hiding in his father's library. He had been betrayed by "an anglophobe and pro-fascist" woman who had ingratiated herself with his family[3].

The second victim, sub-lieutenant Luigi Ferro, had the distinction of having his photograph reproduced in *La Nazione* on March 2nd. His face showed signs of torture which he endured at the hands of Yugoslav partisans from whom he subsequently escaped. The third victim, Alfredo Ballerini, was a young peasant lad.

The "heroic myth" which surrounded the execution of the three young men was exploited fully by the Resistance and its clandestine press[4]. Having arrived at the place of execution Coletti turned to the prison chaplain, Father Naldi and said: "Father, it is not good to die at twenty: but I would not change places with those who ordered my death."

The three young men had been given extreme unction at five o'clock in the morning. Coletti appeared calm and serene. As they were driven to the Caserma di Rovezzano where they were to be shot, one of them turned to another: "What street are we on?" he asked. "What does it matter?" the other replied, "All roads lead to Paradise."

Despite all the efforts made by the young men's lawyer, Olga Monsani, the pleas directed to Mussolini by his niece, the Cardinal-Archbishop and the Consul's unremitting efforts to secure an audience with General Adami Rossi, the youngsters died on the morning of April 28th.

The Consul was not disposed to let the matter rest there. In his letter, written shortly after Whitsun on May 27th, he told the Ambassador: "Unfortunately, my apprehension that the execution on April 28th of the three young men who failed to report for military service on time was a serious psychological blunder has proved to be justified." He went on to argue that "people feel that this was not an act of justice, but was motivated by other reasons. It is thought that Coletti's execution was intended as a blow at the Florentine aristocracy, and that his two fellow-victims were sacrificed to class-hatred. One must take into account that the Florentine aristocracy has very close ties with the countryside and—with few exceptions—enjoys its warmest sympathy, as I pointed out in my report of October 8th, 1943.

"I am in complete agreement with your view that only those can qualify as defenders of justice who are prepared to uphold and enforce the law in all its inexorable severity. But it seems to me that this principle is not applicable in this case. The decree of April 18th announced an amnesty for all members of Partisan gangs and other persons who were in hiding but who reported voluntarily by May 25th. The somewhat ambiguously worded appeal made on May 20th by the chief of staff General Mischi, was taken as an offer of amnesty covering also all those who had so far failed to report for military duty. Public opinion in Florence maintains—and this is difficult to refute—that the May 25th deadline should have applied to the three men shot on April 28th."

Having disposed of the legal arguments beloved by all "defenders of justice", the Consul admitted that he had known all along that Coletti had not only "just" returned from Switzerland to report for military duty.

"It is true," he wrote, "that Coletti had returned from Switzerland some months earlier. He had every intention of reporting for duty, according to his aunt. But having learned the view of others of his age group about the general situation, he was assailed with new doubts and remained in the country beyond the date when he should have reported for duty. His aunt eventually persuaded him to report, and he was arrested on his return to Florence. I have already told you of the myth of hero worship which now surrounds the three men, a myth which extends to all sections of the population."

Although the Consul admitted that he had not provided the Ambassador with all the relevant facts of the "Coletti affair", he remained adamant in his belief that a blunder had been committed. "The impression that an act of injustice was committed is strengthened by the knowledge that Mussolini had exercised his right of pardon in other cases, and by the widely-held opinion that General Adami Rossi had accompanied the plea for mercy with a letter advising such clemency," the Consul wrote as a final amen to the affair.

Signora Comberti herself can testify to the fact that at least on one occasion such an appeal for clemency succeeded in moving the Duce. An entry in her diary reads: "Translated a petition for pardon for six Italian boys who had been sentenced to death. The father of one of them, who was quite wealthy, engaged a first-class lawyer. The sentences were not carried out."

Why then had an appeal for mercy succeeded in one case, and failed in another? The full answer cannot be given: the quirks and oddities of fate, as well as changing circumstances, all played their part in condemning Coletti and his two companions, although the elusive General Adami Rossi, the military commander of the Florence district, must take a large share of the blame. He already had the lives of some twenty-three young deserters on his conscience. But in ordering the execution of Coletti and his colleagues, Adami Rossi was interpreting the directives which he received from his superior, the chief of the Republican Army, Marshal Graziani himself.

Whatever one may think of him otherwise, Graziani had shown little of the bloodthirsty hysteria associated with Pavolini or Ricci: his sympathies towards Fascism had been "lukewarm", and he had little love for the Germans[5]. He had accepted the unenviable post of commander-in-chief only after considerable pressure and argument from Dr Rahn. The Ambassador had succeeded in persuading Graziani and the Duce that the more powerful the Republican Army became, the better their chances of reaching some kind of "productive compromise" with Hitler[6]. Here Dr Rahn's "Jesuitic tricks" had the fullest scope, although Hitler did his best to discourage such ambitions. He felt that Ambassador Rahn "should be told for God's sake not to be taken in by the Italian soul, and fall into the same mistakes as his predecessors". One of these mistakes was the belief that the Republican Italians could be forged into an effective fighting force. "A really reliable battleworthy formation could not be set up either by us or our allies. Ambassador Rahn, under the influence of his surroundings should not lose sight of this sober reality[7]."

The sober reality was daunting enough. The harsh measures which Dr Rahn had outlined to the Consul, which included executions and the seizure of reluctant recruits' parents, may have brought some 50,000 recruits to swell Graziani's "paper army" of 100,000 men, but these could barely face the scattered detachments of some 70,000 Partisan forces. Ricci's own black brigades, although they had priority in men and equipment, could field only 3,000 troops against the Partisans[8].

The unholy competition for man-power between Graziani, Ricci, Sauckel and other German recruiting agencies, reduced the numbers of Graziani's army still further. Coletti and his comrades was sacrificed to the myth of this paper army, for whom there was neither arms nor uniforms, as the Consul had repeatedly pointed out.

In Florence the slaying of the three youngsters was answered by instant reprisals on the day of their execution, the Consul told the Ambassador in his letter of May 3rd. One of Carita's commanders, a Colonel Ingaramo, who had arrested Coletti, had been seriously wounded and his driver killed. A bomb had been placed on the road leading to the offices of the military commandant, and another bomb had been hurled at a militia officer who was supervising the removal of a "Morte ai Repubblicani" inscription from a wall.

As for the "misunderstanding" which had arisen over his open cable of April 22nd, "there were hardly any strikers among the persons arrested in Florence and who were deported: they were mostly people who had nothing to do with the strike. I have therefore not intervened on behalf of any ring-leaders of the strike and their families"—the Consul shot back at the Ambassador—"but only for victims of the indiscriminate implementation of this order. I therefore repeat my request to allow communication between them and their families as soon as possible."

This tussle over the "strikers" went on for some time, until the Consul finally wrung a concession from the Ambassador to allow this communication between the unfortunate deportees and their families. The Consul himself knew the meaning of family separation, but his wife had returned for a brief visit to Florence. "I am glad to have Hilde with me," he told the Ambassador, "although she has not arrived at a very happy time."

He thanked the Ambassador for his continued help, but ended his letter "with sincere regards, and in old friendship. Heil Hitler!", an incongruous note which may have been intended to sting the Ambassador. But the Consul had sense enough to send his letter through their old Heidelberg friend, Dr Paul Lips, who was visiting Florence, on his way to Fasano.

Despite these protestations of friendship, a distinctly cold note had entered their correspondence. But there was little trace of the caution which Dr Rahn had so earnestly enjoined on the Consul. The breach which had grown between them would heal, when the war approached Rome and threatened Florence, but at the moment, the Consul had to rely far more on his own talent for manœuvre and pacification, without constant appeal to the Ambassador.

Such a situation arose almost immediately after the execution of Coletti and his comrades. Colonel Ingaramo had succumbed to his wounds, and Carità and the Prefect promptly ordered the arrest of between fifteen and twenty-five hostages whom they proposed to hand over to the execution squads.

The Consul sent no telegrams to the Ambassador on this occasion. The night before the executions had been ordered he telephoned the Prefect telling him "that the shooting of the hostages was not wanted by the Germans, and that he would get himself into great trouble if he carried out the executions the next morning without being able to prove that all the prisoners chosen for execution were equally deserving of death, under the existing laws".

The Prefect, Dr Manganiello, prevaricated, but finally

agreed to postpone the executions, pending a meeting with the German military commandant Colonel Maurer, at which the Consul asked that he should also be present.

"At that meeting the Prefect and S.D. leader (S.S. Captain Alberti) showed their annoyance at my intervention. Colonel Maurer, the military commandant, insisted on checking the lists, stating in accordance with the view which I had expressed to the Prefect, that only two or three of those listed had committed any crimes which could justify the death penalty. The discussion then moved on to various technical points, by the end of which the Prefect and the S.D. representative had given up all idea of shooting the hostages[9]."

Foiled in his attempt to execute these hostages, "under the existing laws", Carità resorted to indiscriminate "execution" by stealth, as the Consul himself indicated.

"I have repeatedly pointed out in my reports that total anarchy had prevailed in Florence for months over the methods employed in making political arrests," the Consul wrote in his memorandum headed "Senseless Mass Arrests: Amateurish and brutal methods of interrogation and the systematic use of violence[10]".

"In every instance I was told that the *Ufficio Investigativo Politica* of the GRN had refused to co-operate with the S.D. (Gestapo), the Questura and the Carabinieri (in other words, the qualified police forces), in order to undertake the investigations alone. So far they have never been successful." This lack of "success" on Carità's part encouraged him to take the law into his hands. He had rounded up a number of well-known anti-Fascists whom his men "killed in out of the way parts of the city".

Among those who were slain in this brutal vendetta were Bruno Cecci, a businessman, Lioniero Lemmi, a butcher, Gino Cenni and Fernando Traquandi, a businessman "who was never active politically, but who was killed in place of his brother, who happened to be absent from his home".

The Consul ended his report by stating: "According to information from a well-qualified source the disorganisation of the law enforcement agencies in Florence appears to be due to differences in top governmental circles. On one side there are Pavolini and Ricci, and on the other, Buffarini and Tamburini (the Chief of Police). The latter, whatever one may think of them otherwise, are certainly better qualified. They complain that lack of German support for their authority makes their position difficult."

While the Consul was busy drawing up this report, he was visited by the Marchesa Iris Origo who had been accused of a variety of misdeeds in a local Fascist newspaper. He asked both her and her husband to send him a full statement of their case, which he could show to the S.S. if they had the misfortune to be arrested. "Finally, the consul, with a certain humour, warmly implored us not to get arrested both together! He is spending his whole time, he said, in getting innocent Italian families out of prison—but it is so much more convenient when at least one member of the family is free to take some steps about it himself[11]."

On May 16th, the Consul sent a lengthy report on the atrocities committed by the Hermann Goering S.S. Division, which had raged through the Florentine provinces over Easter, and to which Berenson had alluded in his diary. It was the first mention the Consul had made of atrocities committed by German armed forces. The report itself was sent to S.S. General Karl Wolff, the head of all S.S. forces in Italy, although he later disclaimed all responsibility for the Division's actions, since that Division had been attached to the Luftwaffe. Wolff was anxious to secure the necessary evidence to present to Fieldmarshal Goering, he told the Consul.

The Consul began by apologising for the delay in sending the report, but he had had great difficulties "in securing reliable evidence." He had now spoken with the Cardinal-Archbishop, who had paid a pastoral visit to the affected provinces, as well as to humbler priests, policemen and farmers. The evidence they supplied about Goering's favourite division was incontrovertible and hardly made for good relations with the Italian population.

At Cercina, for example, all the male inhabitants had been pulled out of their beds at night, and many of them had been slaughtered. "The dead were discovered in a ditch, covered with rocks." The landowner, Leonarda Ginori Lisci "suffered losses amounting to 310,000 lire, due to theft and arson," the Consul told the S.S. General. "A young married woman was dragged out into a wood and raped by three soldiers. The men threatened to return and revenge themselves if she reported the matter to the police. The family was so frightened that they did not dare to make any charges. The woman's husband merely had his wife examined because of the risk of venereal disease. The unmarried sister of the woman, who made a confidential report to the Consulate, is afraid of returning to her own family for fear of reprisals. . . .

The villagers had all agreed that "the rebels had occasionally appeared and asked for food", but in contrast to the German soldiers, none of the rebels had harmed them.

In Sesto Fiorentino, a state-controlled powder magazine had been blown up: the damage amounted to 3,850,000 lire. In the Villa Tempesti at Vaglia, some fifty head of cattle were driven off—"some of the animals were slaughtered and the meat sold to the population". The gamekeeper, Gabriello Mannini, had been dragged from his bed and shot in the presence of his family, accused of possessing a pistol "which he had been authorised to carry for the performance of his duties . . .".

At Sitriano, a farmer was taken out of his homestead which the S.S. looted at their leisure. "They then took him into the yard and shot him in the presence of his mother, his brother and children." The house of the miller Faustino Bucchi was burned to the ground and two of his relatives were shot in front of his eyes. "The miller, and two of his grandchildren had to be admitted to the mental hospital at Bibbiena." At Vallucciole, the town was burnt down, and twenty-five persons slaughtered, among them two blind children. The daughter of the merchant Trento Santi was found hacked to pieces.

To cap this tale of horror, the Hermann Goering S.S. Division entered the small village of Fragheto after a skirmish with the Partisans on Good Friday. "The troops set fire to ten houses and murdered every inhabitant they could seize, without regard to sex or age. The parish priest, who was busy at a nearby village, had his soutane torn off on his return and was kicked and beaten and driven out of the village. His sister died in a burning house. Thirty-two persons in all, mainly old men and women and children, had been killed. A child held in his mother's arms was struck by several bullets: his mother was left lying on the roadside, severely wounded."

The Consul's report ends abruptly at this point, but shortly after he had completed this document, he turned to Dr Hanna Kiel, exclaiming: "My God, shall we always be looked upon as a nation of pillagers and murderers? We are decent people, after all, and we must behave as such. . . .[12]"

He himself had set up a reparations office, where he listed claims against the German Army, without having the necessary funds to settle them. "The reputation of the Wehrmacht demands that requisitioned goods should be paid for," he wrote in another memorandum, trying to cut through the mass of red tape which surrounded the regulations[13]. How could a man be expected to remember the registration number of a lorry which had been used to "requisition" his goods at pistol point, he asked? "If a cow has been stolen from the pastures, a farmer cannot be expected to produce witnesses and a certificate of requisition." He had a hundred such claims to deal with, he complained, and the only claim which had been satisfactorily settled to date was the payment of 500 lire "for a lost coat for which 1,000 lire had been claimed". The Questura should be given adequate funds to meet claims up to half a million lire, he stated.

The transportation of food supplies into the city were hampered by the wholesale requisitioning of lorries. Three hundred motor vehicles had been requisitioned in Florence alone. The few which remained had no tyres, which were in greatly reduced supply. The creeping paralysis of the city's transport system prevented workers from getting to their place of work. Promises had been made to remedy the situation, but they remained only on paper.

The Consul's communications with the Ambassador at

Fasano remained on this rather stiff official plane until the end of the month when he learnt that Dr Rahn had undergone an operation for appendicitis. "I would strongly advise you to take things easily for a while," he wrote on May 27th, "since recovery after this sort of thing usually takes more out of one than one suspects. If one disregards this, the consequences may be serious."

Having expressed his concern for his friend's health, the Consul thanked Dr Rahn for arranging a meeting with Alessandro Pavolini, the neo-Fascist Party's Secretary "with whom I have been able to discuss all important issues at leisure". Pavolini went out of his way to impress the Consul with his moderation and reasonableness. He said that the many difficulties facing the neo-Fascists arose "from the general situation and the lack of suitable leaders". A certain amount of consolidation had taken place recently, however. The Consul "was able to agree with him to the extent that satisfactory co-operation based on mutual confidence has developed between the Prefect, the Podesta, the newly-appointed Federale, the Quaestor and myself." He added, however, that he had to point out that because of the many blunders which had been committed, neo-Fascism had not yet been able to gain sympathy among the masses.

Pavolini readily admitted these blunders and "agreed with me that in the interests of the Party's reputation it was desirable that these should be remedied as soon as possible". This admission gave the Consul the opportunity of impressing on Pavolini that one of the greatest of these "blunders" was Major Mario Carità himself. "I gained the impression that he had already arranged with the Prefect for the transfer of Mario Carità, who is particularly hated by the population, and to see that his successor is more closely supervised. I should be grateful if you could give him your support in taking this step." The Consul obviously did not expect Pavolini to remove Carità without considerable prompting.

The Consul also drew Pavolini's attention to a recent order which obliged all former reserve officers, and more ludicrously all Red Cross nurses, to take an oath of allegiance to the

Duce's Republic. "This has created fresh disquiet and conflict of conscience," the Consul observed. "In my opinion such oaths sworn under duress are of little value. One should therefore put aside all political considerations and be content with the co-operation of those who are prepared to do their duty towards Italy."

Although Pavolini showed no enthusiasm for the Consul's suggestion to abandon "political considerations", their conversation "took place in the spirit of greatest cordiality, and may have some constructive effect on our relations with the neo-Fascist authorities," he added.

The Ambassador replied on June 3rd. His operation had been successful, but he was prepared to heed his friend's good advice and go away for a fortnight "probably to the mountains which are not far from here. My wife will meet me there with the children. I am looking forward to this meeting which is somewhat rare, and hope it will not be cut short by unpleasant developments."

"I'd rather not discuss the points raised in your letter today. I am looking into them and hope to be able to talk to you personally about them soon," Dr Rahn wrote, admitting a little tardily that the Consul's constant prodding on postal communications and money transfers between Italian voluntary labourers and detainees had had some effect.

"These questions," he wrote, "have already been settled with Berlin some time ago. The postal service has been speeded up, and money transfers will be handled in future by the Banca Nazionale del Lavoro which will make payments in all authorised cases." Unfortunately, however, only one third of all Italian workers in Germany had agreed to make such payments to their families. "Most of them seem to think that their families in Italy will somehow be able to get along without their assistance." The German authorities seemed reluctant to deduct such family allowances compulsorily.

This situation was far from satisfactory, the Ambassador admitted, and would affect the prospects of recruitment of voluntary Italian labour "but for the time being nothing can be done about it". But the Consul would now be in a position "to explain the circumstances to all Italians", and as a further consolation, the Ambassador himself would deal with any cases of specific hardship which were brought to his attention. "Our experience shows that there has been a great deal of loose talk about hardship which is spread by word of mouth, without any substance in hard facts," he added in passing.

The Ambassador ended his letter by thanking the Consul for buying a number of gifts and presents for him in Florence. These were small antiques which the Consul purchased on the Ambassador's behalf, so that he could distribute them on official occasions. "I hope you know my taste better than you did in Venice!" Dr Rahn joked, referring presumably to some purchases by the Consul in Venice which had not entirely met with Dr Rahn's exacting standards.

On this rather light-hearted, anti-climatic note their ten-month-long correspondence ended. From now on there would be no time for lengthy memoranda and personal letters with which to assail the Ambassador's sorely tried eyes and conscience. The two friends would rely increasingly on personal meetings, since the telephone and military teletype services were increasingly censored by the Gestapo. But on the same day that the Ambassador wrote his last letter to the Consul in this period in Florence, a special messenger arrived from Hitler's headquarters at M. Comnène's "modest little villa", named after Machiavelli, bearing the Führer's long-awaited answer to the Rumanian diplomat's missive of March 25th.

The letter was dated May 12th, but had reached Florence only on June 3rd, barely a day and a half before Rome fell to the advancing Allies. Jove had not sent his bolt from the blue himself, but left it to one of the lesser deities in the Nazi Pantheon, his chief of staff Alfred Jodl, to propel this damp squib into the sagging heart of the open city negotiations. The *gioello di Europa* (the phrase could only have been Hitler's!) as Jodl glowingly expatiated on Florence, would soon turn to paste in the heavy crown of the Führer's imperium. And Florence, that golden city, for all of Hitler's flattery, would prepare to face siege and destruction, with unnerving certainty.

# 14

# The Order of Humanity

> Who once has circled the flame
> Always follows the flame!
>
> STEFAN GEORGE

The letter which Comnène received on June 3rd, although it bore Colonel-General Alfred Jodl's nominal signature, had the unmistakable stamp of Hitler's personality. It was as subtle as the purr of a tiger which Jodl had to convert into his own elephantine phraseology, as he trumpeted his disapproval of the intensified Allied "terroristic" attacks on the cities of central and northern Italy. But he offered no explanation why a letter dated May 12th, had taken nearly three weeks to reach the anxious Rumanian diplomat.

Having castigated the Allies, Jodl began to extol all the measures which the Führer had taken or proposed to take to defend Florence whose preservation, he assured Comnène, "is considered by Germans as one of the highest duties incumbent on European civilisation". Hitler had ordered the evacuation "of all superfluous German military establishments" from the city. The few which remained were subjected to stringent controls. The Wehrmacht had even by-passed the city "although this presents many inconveniences".

Jodl was obviously either misinformed about the true situation which prevailed in the city, which the Consul had repeatedly outlined in his reports and telegrams, or he was deliberately justifying Hitler's untenable "unofficial" declaration which he had authorised Ambassador Rahn to make on November 12th, and which the local military command had occasionally ignored. Jodl himself was forced to concede that:

"After completing these measures, the number of German establishments remaining in Florence will be so low that the presence of German soldiers may be considered from now on as *practically* non-existent." The few units which remained "are *almost* exclusively sanitary formations". These formations would be billeted "far from the centre of the city, whose presence, assuming the enemy intends to honour the Geneva convention, should restrain, rather than attract, enemy offensives against the city".

Sweeping aside this lush foliage of Nazi propaganda one point may be pertinent to the situation which faced Florence. No amount of declarations, official or unofficial, proclaiming an "open city" ever saved such a city from attack unless all belligerents were prepared to honour such an undertaking. Belgrade, for example, was almost totally destroyed on Easter Day 1941 by the Luftwaffe, although it was proclaimed an open city by the Yugoslav government of the day.

Equally relevant to Florence's impending fate would be to enquire whether a city could be considered "undefended" merely because all enemy forces had been withdrawn from its centre. One authority has stated that "There is no virtue in mere lack of defence. Unless accompanied by its corollary of freedom of entry (by enemy forces) the exemption of the undefended town would lead to the absurd result that a belligerent would secure the immunity of his production centres and lines of communication from lawful bombardment simply by omitting to defend them, and thus concentrate all his arms for attack." Additionally, "it is ludicrous to suppose that a town shielded by an army holding a line in front of it, is undefended[1]".

It could not have escaped Jodl that Florence whether it was "open" or not was still part of the defensive "Arno Line" on which Kesselring hoped to hold the Allies if other lines were overrun. Yet Jodl had the effrontery to tell Comnène that "from the moment your letter was directed to the Führer, which occurred long before the reinforcement of the measures taken by the Wehrmacht to protect Florence, conditions in the city have changed a lot".

Jodl was not convinced, however, that all these self-denying ordinances would prevent enemy aviation from attacking Florence "even if there is no German soldier present in it. We have had too many examples of the brutal destruction of important cultural sites by the enemy's terroristic attacks, sites lacking in all military significances, and I am therefore obliged to tell you with deepest sorrow that *I have little hope that Florence will emerge intact from this war.*"

But despite this gloomy prediction, with its detectable Freudian undertones, Jodl assured Comnene that "the Wehrmacht would continue to make every effort and take every safety precaution not to give the enemy any military excuse to attack this jewel of Europe (*dieses Kleinod Europas*)". This last phrase which had undoubtedly been culled from Hitler's favourite thesaurus, struck a warm response in Comnène's generous heart.

The Führer himself had designated Florence the "gioiello di Europa" (the phrase translated into Italian easily enough). The jewel might quake a little in its ancient setting while the "terroristic" Allies waited for Hitler's promises to be turned into concrete action, but it would not go down in a cloud of debris with Coventry, Belgrade and Rotterdam which had fainted into dust before the onslaught of the Austrian corporal.

So with his usual infrangible optimism, the Rumanian diplomat rushed out copies of Jodl's letter to the Cardinal-Archbishop as "the spiritual head of this city", as well as to Dr Manganiello, the Prefect, its temporal head. A copy was also handed to Steinhäuslin, the Swiss Consul who represented Anglo-American interests in Florence, and to the Consul himself who was asked by Comnène to circulate it widely among the military, and if possible, get it into the hands of Kesselring himself. This the Consul promised to do, although he noted with heavy sarcasm that on the day following Jodl's letter, all pretensions of Florence as an open city had been hastily swept aside. The Allies had entered Rome on June 4th, and two days later, invaded Normandy. Tanks and reinforcements streamed through Florence to the assistance of

Kesselring's retreating armies, tramping recklessly through this jewel of Europe!

When the Consul arrived at Kesselring's headquarters at Monsummano, bringing a copy of Jodl's original letter in German, he found the commander-in-chief considerably put out. Kesselring complained bitterly that despite his "unilateral" acceptance of Rome as an open city, the American Fifth Army had streamed over the Tiber bridges which he had left intact, capturing some 10,000 of his men[2]. Never again would he allow such gentlemanly behaviour on his part to override tactical considerations. But he did tell the Consul that he had no intention of reducing Florence to a heap of rubble, although he would give no specific assurance that he intended to abandon the defence of the city. Despite repeated approaches, the Allied commander-in-chief, General Alexander, had refused to discuss the issue of making Florence an open city, showing the same refusal to commit himself as he had displayed in refusing to honour Kesselring's "unilateral" Rome declaration[3]. The Vatican would continue to make representations, but no one could be certain of the outcome. Kesselring did promise, however, to implement the assurances given by Jodl to Comnène that all troop concentrations and military offices would be removed from the city proper and that movement of personnel would be strictly controlled and supervised.

The Consul had no reason to doubt Kesselring's sincerity on these points. He returned considerably heartened to Florence, only to find that the city had been plunged into official gloom. The Duce had ordered three days mourning to mark his heartbreak at the fall of his capital city to the Allies,[4] following the precedent set by Hitler after the debacle at Stalingrad. Of more immediate concern to the Florentines was the cut in the cigarette and tobacco rations.

For the Resistance, the early part of June was marked by the tragic loss of some of its most intrepid and valued collaborators which took place with the seizure of the Action Party's "radio commission" (CoRa) by S.S. Captain Alberti and Carita. CoRa's exploits had long been legendary, a constant irritant to the Gestapo and military authorities who had made every effort to silence it. As early as September 1943, German radio-interceptors had picked up the weak signals emanating from a clandestine "radio-station", packed in a suitcase, which had been improvised by the inventive Carlo Ludovico Ragghianti. The members of CoRa had "grass-hopped" from one locality to another, broadcasting intermittently, a few minutes at a time, from offices and private apartments. An improved radio transmitter had been constructed by the air force captain Italo Piccagli. CoRa's code-signals "The Arno Flows Through Florence" and "The Monkey Laughs" had long made a mockery of all of S.S. Captain Alberti's efforts to trap their senders. The radio pirates fed a constant stream of vital war information to the Allies, giving particulars of gun emplacements, troop locations and other significant details of the "Gustav" and "Gothic" defence lines on which many of the Action Party's secret helpers were working. Equally important, CoRa directed the flow of parachute drops of arms and supplies which were reaching the Partisan forces on Monte Javello. The success of CoRa earned many commendations from Allied sources for its operators[5]. But the heightened optimism in the city, and hope of its early liberation, may have made them less than cautious.

On the night of June 7th, at around seven in the evening, a platoon of soldiers, supported by Italian militiamen, burst in on the transmission centre at Number 12, Piazza D'Azeglio, while Luigi Morandi, a young engineering student, was sending a message to the British Eighth Army. In an exchange of shots Morandi killed one attacker, wounding another, before he himself fell mortally wounded. Another five operators, including the gentle Enrico Bocci, a lawyer celebrated for the beauty of the roses he grew in the small garden of his house in an ancient part of the city, were also seized. Bocci's secretary Gilda Larocca, Carlo Campolmi, Franco Gilardini, Guido Focacci, were taken to the Villa Triste to face Carità's and Alberti's interrogation. Morandi, despite his grave condition, was also cruelly tormented, but expired with unyielding courage without saying anything. A more dreadful fate awaited the others. Enrico Bocci, despite a serious heart ailment, was mercilessly beaten, while his secretary Gilda Larocca made two unsuccessful attempts at suicide. When one of his victims asked one of the interrogators for a drink of water (they had been kept without water for some days), a receptacle filled with tepid urine was thrown into his face[6].

A few days later, Italo Piccagli, the technical brain behind CoRa, was captured together with three young parachutists. Both he and Bocci made unavailing attempts to take full responsibility for CoRa's activities in the hope of diverting their captors' attention from their comrades.

On June 12th, Piccagli, together with the parachutists and an unknown victim, were taken at dead of night to Cercina where they were mowed down by machine-gun fire. With them died another victim of Alberti's vengeance, the gentle, courageous, Anna Maria Enriques Agnoletti, the sister of Enzo Enriques Agnoletti, although she had no direct connection with CoRa. The tragic circumstances of her death and the lack of any decisive action on the Consul's part to prevent it cast a shadow over his record. It also destroyed the illusion that the Consul would always be able to rescue every victim from the extremes of Alberti's and Carità's savagery.

This beautiful and self-sacrificing young woman was a paleographer and archivist of some distinction, who had worked in the Vatican library. She had become a devoted Catholic (her father was Jewish), working with a Christian social movement where she drove herself unstintingly on behalf of prisoners of war (passing messages from British prisoners of war to their families), aiding Jewish refugees and others in need of help and protection. She also distributed clandestine Resistance literature in the writing of which her brother had taken such a notable part. Her activities in these manifold directions had long been known to the Gestapo, who finally managed to trap her through two agents provocateurs who had been sent from Rome for this purpose. On May 13th, Anna Maria and her mother were arrested and taken to the Villa Triste, and later to the Murate prison. Ration coupons, false identity cards and Resistance literature were discovered in her possession. Her situation was aggravated further by the fact that, as her brother himself stated: "The S.S. knew that she was my sister. They told Mme Wildt that they were looking for me everywhere and that, I think, aggravated her position.[7]"

Robbed of the brother. S.S. Captain Alberti exacted a sadistic vengeance on the sister. Anna Maria was made to stand without sleep for a week, in an effort to break her obstinate but dignified silence.

The Consul when he was informed of Anna Maria's plight made immediate representations to Alberti, but was fobbed off with the cynical assurance that the S.S. Captain thought that she had been sent somewhere northwards, although in fact, as the Consul said scornfully, "she had been taken a few steps to the north and shot down".

Not unnaturally Signor Agnoletti complained that although the Consul was able "to mitigate the rigours of imprisonment" of certain people "only if they were of a social standing", he showed "no interest in my sister, for example". Moreover, "Dr Wildt, who was a cousin of my sister's, tried to help my mother who was arrested with my sister, but thought it impossible to do anything for my sister."

The Consul had, in fact, asked S.S. Colonel Eugen Dollmann to take the matter up with Alberti "because he had a rank higher than Alberti's", but the S.S. Colonel told him that the Gestapo were not answerable to him— "a mere S.S. officer".

After all this hierarchical hand-washing there was little hope left of saving Anna Maria's life. But the accusation made against the Consul that he was interested in persons only "if they were of a certain social standing" is surely refuted by the evidence of the help which he was able to give persons of every kind and condition already given in these pages.

During the early months of the German Occupation, when both the military and the S.S. had gone out of their way to impress Florence with "gentlemanly behaviour", the Consul had been able to play on this sentiment: he had also the unfailing support of the Ambassador in "all justified cases". But with the approach of liberation the fanatical Alberti, acting under Harster's orders emanating from the Gestapo headquarters in Verona, was in no mood to listen to the representations made by one who was so notoriously "weak in military and police matters". The Ambassador had moreover been "misled" on more than one occasion: the Coletti case was one such example. The Consul could therefore no longer rely on the Ambassador's support in flagrant cases where the S.S. had ample documentary evidence of direct association with the Resistance, as in Anna Maria Agnoletti's case.

Moreover, the Consul had reached a pitch of moral and spiritual exhaustion which a constant attention to detail (never his strongest point) had induced in him. Apart from the open city negotiations in which he was involved, his attention was increasingly diverted to the problem of preventing the removal of Florence's art treasures from the city: he also had to pay close attention to the economic needs of the city, as his earlier reports showed. He could barely close his eyes for a moment, before a new crisis threatened to overwhelm him. The man who was so highly regarded in Florence could find such an attachment burdensome: more was expected of him than of other persons.

Yet none of these explanations in themselves could expunge the shadow of Anna Maria's death which fell upon him. There were no urgent telegrams to the Ambassador, no attempt to find the slenderest of mitigating circumstances, no midnight telephone calls. He had shut his eyes and surrendered to pitiless circumstances, and a young woman had died. But the Consul had not written the last of his biography in Florence: much of what he had done, much of what he still was to do, would of necessity remain hidden from his friends and critics alike. That is why Signor Agnoletti's estimate of his activities in Florence, influenced as it must be by his own personal tragedy, has its place in the tapestry of those June days.

"In other words, the Resistance movement considered Wolf a good person who tried to do something, but knew very well he would not jeopardise his position," Signor Agnoletti wrote. "He tried to stay in that position to which he had been appointed by the regime, even though he probably disagreed with it. This was already an exceptional thing, so it should be understood that what he did was already valuable, but it cannot be considered that Consul Wolf was part of the Italian or German Resistance.[8]"

The Consul was not inclined to argue the issue as to what Resistance, if any, he belonged. It was enough that they had begun to call him "the Consul of Florence". That road was lonely enough for a Platonist who had come to escape from "tragic and evil circumstances . . .". It would grow lonelier still.

The unflinching courage with which Anna Maria Enriques Agnoletti met her death at Cercina on June 12th, together with the members of the CoRa team of radio operators (others were executed later) threw into cruel relief the excruciating, slow and bloody liberation of the city which was now approaching.

Radio CoRa, despite Alberti's repressions, returned to the air on June 17th, and continued without interruption until the day of final liberation. The code signal "The Monkey Laughs" was repeated with mocking defiance.

A few days before the death of his sister Anna Maria and her companions, an appeal declaring a state of general mobilisation was issued by Enzo Enriques Agnoletti in the name of the Tuscan Liberation Committee, demanding the peaceful transfer of authority from the neo-Fascists. Negotiations were opened between the various party representatives of the C.T.L.N. and the Federal Party secretary Fortunato Polvani and his collaborator Uberto Puccioni. Among those taking part in these negotiations was the lawyer Mario Gobbo for the Liberal Party, whose arrest the Consul had forestalled earlier in the year. Another advocate, Gaetano Casoni, acted as an independent go-between. There had been considerable division in the councils of the Resistance whether to pursue such negotiations, but finally it had been agreed to "temporise" if it would save the lives of the numerous political hostages held by the Fascists. Among the conditions demanded by the Resistance was the release of these prisoners, the immediate removal of Carità, the disarming of Fascist forces whose arms were to be distributed to the Partisans, and the surrender intact of the city's stores of provisions when the Germans finally retired from the city. Polvani, who was also playing for time, agreed to most of these conditions if the Resistance itself discontinued its activities inside the city, and broke off its clandestine contact with the Allies. Neither side trusted the other, and the Germans who were the real masters of the situation, took no part in these early approaches. Although this horse-trading produced few concrete results, some 973 political prisoners were released out of a total of 1,083, but Carita still continued his regime of terror under S.D. protection[9].

He had now added a massive cupidity to his relish for torture. A senator whom Carità had arrested, together with his son, was asked to pay three million lire as ransom "at the present rate of exchange something like $25,000," Berenson remarked[10]. Jewish acquaintances of Berenson's had been called upon to find half a million lire immediately "and as much again next October". The S.D. was not interested in such deferred payments: Alberti's troopers broke into Florentine banks and confiscated all monies held by Jewish depositors. They also burnt down the city's synagogue for good measure. They now turned to less tangible, but equally valuable assets, the art treasures of the city itself.

The Consul who had managed to bemuse Alberti and the S.D. about Berenson's whereabouts, and had deflected their attention from the treasures at I Tatti, had found a staunch ally in the Director of the German Art Institute, Professor Heydenreich. It was Heydenreich, who some time in June, after he had received orders to remove all the remaining pictures and works of art at I Tatti which were to be sent northwards "managed to create so many difficulties by insisting on the agreement of the Italian sequestration office, that finally there was no time left to do anything about it[11]".

Both Heydenreich and the Consul were, in fact, doing all they could not only to prevent the seizure of Florentine works of art, which were to be sent to northern Italy and the Tyrol for "safe keeping", but also to arrange for the return of such art treasures as had already been removed from the city. First Lieutenant Frederick Hartt who was the Allied MFAA (Monuments, Fine Arts and Archives) regional officer for Tuscany wrote later: "While we were coming up from the south, working in the liberated areas of Tuscany, the devoted Professor Heydenreich, who under the *Kunstschutz* had charge of the protection of monuments and works of art in Tuscany and of whom we heard nothing but good, had intervened with the *Militärkommandantur* for military transport and fuel so that the contents of some of the deposits of the Mugello, at the foot of the Gothic Line, could be brought back to Florence.[12]"

Since Florence's "open city" status had been confirmed by Hitler in Jodl's letter to Comnene, there seemed to be no reason why the city should not again become the repository of its own art treasures. The German art protector in Tuscany, Dr Alexander Langsdorff, concurred with this point of view. He himself explained later that even if he had wished to remove more of Florence's art treasures for safe-keeping, he had neither the transport nor fuel available. He nevertheless assured the Consul and the Art Superintendent Poggi, with whom the Consul was in close contact, that he would return the 297 paintings taken from various Florentine art galleries to Montagnana back to Florence. There appeared to be no reason, at this stage, to doubt Langsdorff's word, although an order had arrived a few days earlier, on June 15th from the Fascist Ministry of Education demanding that all Florentine and Siennese works of art should be removed to northern Italy[13].

On June 18th, the Consul after a gruelling day with *Kunstschutz* officials, retired to bed early at Le Tre Pulzelle. He was woken by a messenger who had arrived from Careggi, bearing a letter from Bernard Berenson. The Consul opened the letter hastily, thinking that Berenson was in danger.

The letter which was unheaded, was dated June 18th 1944. It read:

"Dear Dr Wolf: When the war is over, if I had my way, I should institute a new Order—Pour l'Humanité. It would be given to those who had done their utmost—all that was compatible with their duty—to give a humane turn to enactments, and to alleviate the lot of sufferers. In such an order I would give you a high place. I cannot begin to tell you how much I appreciate all you have done here, and I can assure you that I have no friend or acquaintance who is not of the same mind with me. I hope to see you in my house some day soon. It would make me very happy. Meanwhile let me beg you to ask: should anything turn up that I could do for you. I should not fail to try my utmost. With all good wishes. Cordially yours, Bernard Berenson."

The purpose of this letter became clear to the Consul as he read it. It was not only a case of noblesse oblige. It was also a delicate reminder that he, Berenson would be ready to extend his mantle of protection over the enemy Consul in return for the Consul's efforts in keeping the S.S. away from the art treasures in I Tatti and his own person.

Although there is no mention in it of the letter which he sent the Consul on June 18th, two days later Berenson was wondering in his diary—"What will be the behaviour of Americans and British when they occupy Florence? Will they be pedantic or humane, gullible or sensible?" He himself deprecated the legend which had grown up in Florence: "Lord knows through no action or fault of mine, about my political importance as an American. They cannot believe that at home, to the extent that I am known at all, I count only as an art critic. As a citizen, alien-born, I should be of the second class, but living abroad and selling no American products, I rank best as of the third class. I have no political acquaintances whom I could influence, I have no authority. Catch Italians believing a word of that!" He goes on: "So I expect to be besieged by acquaintances and their relations, clients and dependants of acquaintances, expecting me to procure them exemptions, favours, privileges from the occupying Anglo-Saxons. As I shall rarely succeed, they will go away thinking that I, who could, would not help them.[14]"

The Consul had no such illusions. He folded Berenson's letter and stored it among his private papers. When the time came for the bestowal of honours, he would walk with S.S. desperadoes and cut-throats into the gehenna provided for defeated supporters of the Nazi regimé, without flaunting Berenson's letter in the face of his captors. The city of Florence, in her own time, would give him her own Order of Humanity. Yet the timing of Berenson's letter, coming as it did, barely six days after the death of Anna Maria Enriques Agnoletti, had its own irony. The Order of Humanity was elusive indeed.

On Thursday June 21st, the German commander-in-chief of Army Group "C" called a meeting at which the Consul, S.S. Colonel Dollmann and a military administrative officer Dr Seifarth were present. At this meeting, it was agreed to implement Kesselring's directive to clear the centre of Florence of all armed forces, and to take the severest measures to prevent undisciplined conduct such as were applied "after the September 1943 crisis in Rome and after the Nettuno landings in January 1944". The local commander expressed his disapproval of the labour-recruiting methods practised "up to June 19th in Florence". He ordered that forced recruitment of civilians should be discontinued forthwith, in line with the Consul's earlier recommendations. Such recruitment, however, would be continued in the fighting zone. In addition, the commander expressed a desire to stabilise the political situation, saying that "actions with wider political implications" should not be taken without prior consultation with the Consul and S.S. Colonel Dollmann[15].

From the Consul's point of view, this was a notable concession from the military authorities. On June 30th the first concrete steps to demilitarise Florence were taken. Notices appeared all over the city in German, informing the Wehrmacht that "Florence has been declared an open city by the Führer". No member of the Wehrmacht or the Waffen-S.S. would in future be allowed into the city without a special permit. Shopping and sight-seeing tours in the city were prohibited. The troops would find entertainment and relaxation outside the city limits which had been marked with signboards and ringed with barbed wire. All trespassing in the city would be severely punished.

In actual practice, Colonel Giessler of the Field Security Police and eighty military policemen managed to give effect to these measures in the remarkably short period of three days. The extent of these "off limits" included the so-called "English" cemetery where Elizabeth Barrett Browning was buried, a nice touch of "gentlemanly" behaviour. Berenson, less charitably, complained that these open city provisions applied only "to a tiny bit in the centre where they may not lodge but pass and repass, shop, stroll and loiter[16]".

On balance, however, *something* had been achieved to confirm the "official" nature of Hitler's declaration. Berenson had also heard that the Cardinal "has received assurances from the Pope himself that the Allies will do their utmost to spare Florence, and that only the most pressing military necessity will lead them to bombard it. It was gossiped that before they evacuated Florence, the Germans would blow up all the bridges. Then, however, that a commission went to Hitler imploring that they be spared. Now it seems that the Ponte Vecchio and the Ponte S. Trinita bridge will not be touched. The last is the most elegant and artistic thing of its kind in Europe, and its destruction would indeed be a loss, more than a dozen Monte Cassinos.[17]"

The Consul meanwhile had been fully informed of the negotiations which had been going on between the Federal Fascist Party Secretary Polvani and C.T.L.N. representatives for the release of political hostages. Signor Casoni who said that the Florentines always found in the Consul "a prompt and energetic defence of their legitimate interests against the demands of the German military authorities" reported that both he and Avv. Gobbo had seen the Prefect Manganiello and had pleaded with him to remove Carità and to release two prominent citizens—Eugenio Barsanti, a lawyer, and Professor Amaldi who had recently been arrested by the detested major of the Black Brigade[18]. The Prefect had hotly defended Carità, although he admitted that Carita had often resorted to brutal measures, but that "it should be remembered that distinguished Fascists such as Senator Gentile and others had also suffered at the hands of their adversaries". But he added that Carità, in any case, would be leaving "within a few days" and his victims would be released, among them Luigi Boniforti who enjoyed a certain relaxation from the rigours of imprisonment in the Villa Vittoria clinic, where he had been operated on for a stomach ulcer.

A few moments later, the son of Eugenio Barsanti burst in on this conversation, to inform the Prefect that he had tried to reach Carita on the Prefect's instructions, to urge the release of his father, but Carità could not be found. On the following day, Barsanti's son again visited the Villa Triste, but was given to understand that the Major Carità was at lunch and could not be disturbed.

When the younger Barsanti returned to the Palazzo Riccardi, he again told the Prefect that his authority was being flouted. The Prefect who was thoroughly irritated by now tried to reach Carita on the telephone, but without success. He then got into his car and drove to the Villa Triste where he released Avv. Barsanti and Professor Amaldi on his own authority.

Boniforti, however, did not wait for the Prefect's favour. On July 3rd, he was visited by an Italian S.S. lieutenant who enquired about the state of his health. Boniforti, who had every reason to be suspicious of such concern—his name was high on the list of hostages who were to be shot at the approach of the Allies—waved a certificate in the S.S. lieutenant's face showing that he was too sick to be moved from the clinic. On the following day, Boniforti managed to elude S.S. surveillance and rode off on the back of a bicycle propelled by one of his friends in the Resistance.

On the same day that Boniforti escaped, the Consul received an urgent summons from the Superintendent appealing for his help. A Counsellor Metzner had called from the *kommandantur* demanding a list of all the most important paintings at the villa in Montagnana since he proposed to transport these "for security reasons" beyond the Apennines —in flagrant disregard of the promises made by the "art protector" Langsdorff and the *Kunstschutz*. The Consul immediately asked Dr Langsdorff to come to Florence to settle the matter.

The elaborate game of "hide and seek" with Florence's art treasures had now reached preposterous proportions. The Germans, while promising to return these treasures to the "open city", were in fact heavily engaged in taking them further and further away. The paintings from Montagnana had already been taken to a village near Modena when Metzner came to ask for "a list of the most important paintings", a fact which the Consul himself reported to Signor Poggi some days later[19].

It may be interesting to note at this stage that Ambassador Rahn had personally intervened with Hitler to prevent the removal to Germany of art treasures stored in the outlying districts of Tuscany. He had no reason to doubt that the Führer would accede to his request as he had done previously in the case of the art works of Monte Cassino and the Naples National Museum[20]. Rahn with his usual circumlocution told Hitler that it would be rather "bad form" to deprive the Italians of their own art treasures, to which the Führer replied: "You may be right." He added, however, with a smile: "But I always thought that antiquities have been generally considered the victor's perquisites throughout all ages!"

In any case, he turned down the Ambassador's request that Tuscan art treasures should be placed under Vatican protection. Such a transfer was hardly feasible under the prevailing military conditions. The Ambassador who had no way of judging Hitler's true motives, then instructed the German Art protection service to draw up two copies of all Italian works of art which were to be taken to the Tyrol. This was done with the help of Italian art specialists. Dr Rahn then went with S.S. General Karl Wolff—"whose testimony seemed valuable to me" and gave one copy to Mussolini. "Thus I hoped that I had done my utmost to prevent looting," the Ambassador stated. The Consul, on the other hand, although he understood Dr Rahn's precautionary measures, went against these general instructions for the removal of Florentine art treasures "for safe keeping" to Germany, as his subsequent actions showed. He supported the Art Superintendent's efforts to have as many as possible of Florence's art treasures returned to the city. Dr Rahn, however, could not comply with these requests for "technical reasons".

But on July 6th the Consul's attention was diverted from Florence's art treasures back to the "open city" issue. Shortly before midnight two German officers arrived at the Archiepiscopal Palace opposite the Duomo, bringing an urgent letter from Kesselring. Despite the lateness of the hour, the Cardinal invited the Consul and S.S. Colonel Eugen Dollmann to be present at the meeting[21]. Dollmann takes up the narrative: "The subterranean hall into which I was ushered was lit by torches in sconces fixed on the marble walls. It was all very romantic, like a shot from a Rennaissance film, but it struck me as an incongruous background for the business which we had in hand . . . Dalla Costa stood opposite me: 'I have asked you to come here, Signor Dollmann, because I want to implore you to leave Florence without first laying the city in dust and ashes'." The S.S. Colonel could not resist elaborating on his scenario by describing the Cardinal's appearance. "He was dressed in a brown cloak with a hood which was over his head. In its shadow his dark brown eyes gleamed fiercely. It was not difficult to think of Savanarola. From Cardinal dalla Costa I went straight to Kesselring and told him what the Cardinal had said.[22]"

It may be more important at this stage to consider what precisely Kesselring had in mind when writing to the Cardinal. Omitting the long preamble in which he wrote that he had made every effort to protect "places of Western and Christian culture and civilisation", Kesselring now demanded a clear and unmistakable "open city" declaration from the Allies.

"I cannot tolerate, in any case, a repetition of what occurred in Rome, which was spared without any restrictions whatsoever by the Germans, while the enemy took advantage of these circumstances egotistically and recklessly," he wrote, repeating the arguments he had used on the Consul. Kesselring asked the Cardinal to obtain "a clear and valid undertaking from the Allies that they will recognise Florence as an 'open city', i.e., not to make any military use of the city area in any way, in which case I am ready to maintain the measures already taken". He added that he would give this undertaking "despite the senseless destruction of the cultural centres of my own country[23]".

With this ultimatum Kesselring skilfully placed the onus for the possible destruction of Florence on the Allies. The fate of the city was thus tossed like a shuttlecock between the belligerents, neither of whom believed in each other's protestations or disclaimers. Yet something more emphatic than a declaration from Hitler or Kesselring was required to impress on the Allies the real danger the city faced if they attempted a frontal attack. The Cardinal, together with the Consul, Steinhäuslin and Comnène, then hit on the bold plan of sending emissaries directly to General Alexander. But only Kesselring could give the required permission and a safe conduct to the Cardinal's delegates, and Kesselring himself was not easily accessible. Moreover, to add to this feeling of helplessness, all telephone communications between Florence and the Field Marshal's headquarters were abruptly cut off for thirty-six hours on July 7th.

At one o'clock that same afternoon a mighty explosion had rocked the city, as a group of youngsters belonging to the Action Party blew up the telephone exchange at the Porta Romana, severing German military connections with the city.

The S.S., who failed to catch the culprits, arrested four hostages, without consultation with the Consul. Among these was Giancarlo Zoli, who had been released earlier in January, a prominent industrialist Count Giuseppe de Micheli, and two other lawyers: a fifth hostage, Avv. Casoni, was shortly added to the list.

But another event overshadowed all these misfortunes. On the same day, Major Mario Carità, together with his mistress

Milly and huge Alsatian dog, left Florence for ever, in a stolen ambulance taken from the Misericordia[24]. But before leaving he stamped his hoofmark on the city he had desecrated for almost a year, by arresting the proprietor of the "Cloetta" bar, one Carlo Grifoni, an anti-fascist who had a great liking for the ladies.

While waiting for a girl friend on the Piazza Vittorio Emanuele, the evening before Carita's departure, Grifoni was arrested by his thugs who accused him of breaking the curfew and took him to the Hotel Savoia where Carita had an apartment.

On the morning of Carità's departure, the unfortunate Grifoni's body was found on the via Pergola. His wallet, diamond ring and gold watch were missing.

Old Berenson at Le Fontanelle had just celebrated his seventy-ninth birthday. "The house shook after midnight," he wrote in his diary, "as if the cannonading was overhead. Yet it could not have been nearer than sixty miles as the crow flies[25]." And now even the crows were leaving Florence.

# 15

# The Jewel of Europe

> Let us while waiting for new monuments, preserve the ancient monuments.
>
> VICTOR HUGO

Kesselring's unequivocal demand that the Cardinal-Archbishop should obtain a clear undertaking from General Alexander that he would regard Florence as an open city—on Kesselring's terms—provided a dramatic twist to the serpentine negotiations which had meandered backwards and forwards between Weizsäcker, the British Ambassador and the Vatican authorities.

No one seemed able to hit on a formula which would satisfy all sides. A victorious commander hot in pursuit of a retreating enemy such as General Alexander had a natural suspicion of "open cities" which were thrown up like so many sandcastles to block his advance. He may have concluded that Kesselring was using this open city offer as a protective barricade behind which he could rest and refurbish his battered troops so as to delay a final showdown on the Gothic Line.

All these fine declamations about "the jewel of Europe" and "a monument to Western and Christian culture" might have been little more than an elaborate piece of blackmail to hold over the heads of the advancing Allies, an implied threat that if they did not accept Kesselring's terms, he would "defend the town of Florence square by square, street by street, house to house" as Berenson believed[1].

The Consul knew that Kesselring would not lightly abandon the strategic advantage of holding onto Florence for as long as possible, but he might be induced to trade this advantage against another of equal or greater worth if the Allies themselves agreed not to occupy the city. This would call for discipline and self-sacrifice on the part of the Allies, but was Florence not worth such a price? Yet so far General Alexander had met all of Kesselring's overtures with silence. Only a direct appeal from the Cardinal might allay Allied suspicions of Nazi trickery which had bedevilled all these negotiations, since Elia Dalla Costa could not be accused of playing such a game.

Kesselring's emotional letter of July 6th had hinted at such a possibility without indicating how this could be affected. The Consul was not to know that when Kesselring went to Hitler's headquarters on July 3rd, the main purpose of his conversation with the Führer was to discuss forthcoming operations in, and forward of, the Gothic Line. Florence itself was not mentioned by name. Kesselring was ordered by Hitler to fight forward of the Gothic Line for as long as possible, to consolidate the latter and to deny Livorno and Ancona to the enemy[2].

Two precious weeks had now slipped by before Kesselring was due to return to Hitler's headquarters for fresh instructions, and with each passing day, the Allies drew nearer to Florence.

The city itself was caught in the fever of Liberation. A German woman, a British subject by marriage, who had renounced her British passport during the German occupation, now hastened to reclaim it. The Consul who had consigned it to his safe, handed it back to her without comment.

In the Tuscan hills and in Emilia, some seventeen thousand well-officered Partisans stood poised to harass the retreating Germans, cutting their lines of communication[3]. Kesselring himself had expended considerable manpower in fighting these "bandits". In Florence, the underground war against the Germans and the neo-Fascists continued with unabated violence.

In place of S.S. Captain Alberti who had left the city on June 18th, and Carità who left around July 7th-8th, there arrived the equally-ferocious Captain Giuseppe Bernasconi, a member of the Italian S.S. This Florentine-born ex-squadrista, who had fourteen different crimes marked on his penal certificate[4], had gained his apprenticeship as a torturer in Rome in the company of Pietro Koch, one of Carità's chief lieutenants. Bernasconi turned up in Florence with "un grosso cane bianco", a huge white mastiff, which some said he had filched from the Royal kennels! There was certainly little else to recommend this dog-lover, except a reputation for "fearlessness" which he quickly established in his brief three weeks sojourn in the city: the work in the Villa Triste on the via Bolognese continued uninterrupted, as Signor Casoni, who was a reluctant visitor to the House of Sorrow was able to testify[5].

On the morning of July 8th, three German S.S. men in khaki uniforms entered Casoni's office on the Via Conti, demanding that he should come with them for questioning. The astute lawyer, who had acted as an independent go-between in the negotiations between the Fascists and the Resistance, realised that something serious was afoot. Since it was a particularly sultry day, he excused himself to fetch his panama hat, managing to instruct his clerk Eugenio "to go immediately to Signor Kraft", and tell him what had happened. The Swiss hotelier, Gerardo Kraft, the owner of the luxury Hotel Excelsior, was a close friend of the Consul's to whom Casoni had sent his regards "only yesterday".

Just as Casoni was being led into the vestibule, he met his daughter Anna, who made no sign of recognition. The elderly lawyer was then bundled into a car and driven at great speed to the Via Bolognese. Fortunately for him, another acquaintance, Gerardo Kraft's daughter, Anna Fantoni, a Red Cross sister who had once ordered Carità out of an ambulance, and who happened to live on the Via Bolognese, saw the S.S. men taking Casoni into the "casa malfamata".

After a few preliminaries, Casoni was taken down to the sub-basement, where Carità had once held sway, where he met the four other hostages, who like himself were scheduled for execution on July 10th on the Piazza d'Armi. To divert their thoughts from this melancholy prospect Casoni and his friends busied themselves translating Horace's *Satires*, a copy of which had been left by a former prisoner. Casoni lamented bitterly that his Latin had grown somewhat rusty after the passage of fifty years.

While Casoni was struggling with Horace, his daughter Anna and Nora Fantoni were frantically trying to free the elderly lawyer. The Consul who had been apprised of Casoni's fate, immediately contacted S.S. Colonel Dollmann. The Cardinal and the Prefect were also involved, and a deputation waited on Puccioni to plead on Casoni's behalf, pointing out that he enjoyed a measure of "diplomatic immunity" as an official negotiator.

Thanks to all these efforts, Casoni was liberated from the Villa Triste after a residence of little more than twenty-four hours. He immediately went to thank the Cardinal, and sought out the Consul at the Excelsior to express his gratitude, appealing to him to save the other four hostages. The Consul, according to Signor Casoni, showed greater concern for three of the men, and was markedly lukewarm towards Giancarlo Zoli, whose anti-German and anti-Fascist record had been firmly established[6]. But this surface manifestation did not prevent the Consul from demanding that "the S.S. should not execute these hostages even if further acts of sabotage did occur". It also earned him a warm testimonial from the Zolis[7].

While the Consul was negotiating the release of the hostages, the young "gappisti" in the city took the law into their own hands by conducting a daring rescue operation. Ten young men disguised in Fascist militia, led by an S.S. "officer" appeared at the Santa Verdiana women's prison, demanding the custody of seventeen political prisoners. The alarmed superintendent of the prison, thinking that her charges would be shot like the unfortunate Anna Maria Agnoletti, cried out in despair: "Can't you leave these poor women in peace!" The "Fascists" brushed aside her protests, making off with seventeen women, among them three unnamed Englishwomen, and the wife of a prominent Communist, Tosca Bucarelli, who herself had been brutally tortured by Carità and the abominable Milly[8]. The Consul, less demonstratively, managed to obtain the release of one Hubert Kramer, a German refugee who had been imprisoned in Berlin and the south Tyrol before coming to Florence where he again landed in prison[9].

Some days later, the "gappisti" struck again, this time at Bernasconi himself as he emerged from a hotel on the Piazza Santa Maria Novella, but only succeeded in killing a police spy who was by his side. The vendetta between Bernasconi and G.A.P. was moving towards its own tragic climax, as Fascists bigwigs began leaving the city. The few city authorities who remained belonged to a less-compromised group of neo-Fascists among whom there was a genuine desire to save the city from destruction and the worst excesses of "the scum of the Fascist Party". But in the Excelsior where the Consul was staying to be closer to the centre of events, he could hear the nightly carousings of the band of Blackshirt snipers and saboteurs whom Pavolini had left in the charge of their "general", one Alberto Coppo di Cesare. The Consul's attention, however, was more closely devoted to the problem of safeguarding the city's artistic treasures, as well as reporting on the menacing concentration of armed forces, than in listening to these nightly revels.

On July 12th, he received assurances from the city commandant that the Villa Reale at Poggio a Caiano would be evacuated by the German military and placed off limits[10], but on the following day the sudden influx of a strong parachute detachment of tough, seasoned paratroopers, led by a Colonel Fuchs, sent the Consul hurrying to the military teletype.

"My impression that Florence is to be maintained as a strategic bastion is reinforced by statements and activities of the military authorities", he cabled the Ambassador. "If the Führer's personal order to protect Florence has any validity, urgent measures for its implementation are imperative. My situation vis-à-vis the military would be strengthened if Allied guarantees to respect Florence as an open city could still be obtained through Weizsäcker." On the same day, Signor Casoni noted gloomily in his diary: "We will now be entirely at the mercy of this man Fuchs now that they say that Consul Wolf is leaving. . . ."

The rumour of the Consul's imminent departure was premature, however, because on July 15th, both the Consul and S.S. Colonel Dollmann were invited to lunch at Le Fontanelle by the Serlupis. Berenson made some pertinent observations in his diary about this luncheon. "Friends of mine have seen the German who represents Himmler in the whole of Italy," Berenson wrote. "He is a certain Dollmann, good-looking, in the early forties, cultivated, affable, a man of the world, and claiming to have spent sixteen years in Rome. In just what capacity remains uncertain. . . .

"Although the Swiss consul considers the Fascist Prefect here an angel compared to those of Pistoia and Grosseto, Dollmann puts him down as a blackguard and holds him responsible for many of the brutalities and massacres committed by Major Carità and others," Berenson continued. The expansive Dollmann also confessed that he had "induced" Carità to leave Florence "not by ordering as he could have but by assuring him that he could not protect him against enemies who were hotfoot after him." How, asked Berenson, "can a civilian of such culture, sense, and judgment, be the lieutenant of Himmler[11]?"

Marchese Serlupi who must have reported these remarks of Dollmann's to Berenson, omitted to tell him that during the course of the lunch, the S.S. Colonel had suddenly looked up, saying, as an afterthought: "One thing we shall never know, and that is where Berenson is hiding!"

Dollmann was not aware that at that precise moment Bernard Berenson was lunching in an upstairs room, together with the Duchess of Ancona. Neither the Serlupis nor the Consul thought it necessary to tell Himmler's cultivated colonel where Berenson could be found. An aura of dread still clung to Dollmann's well-cut S.S. uniform[12].

By the time the luncheon party in Le Fontanelle was over, Bernasconi was able to announce to Dollmann that he had wiped out the entire command of the G.A.P. organisation in the city. He had not only captured their leader, Elio Chianese, a bicycle-mechanic, but had also seized the intrepid Bruno Fanciullacci, who had escaped from Carità's clutches. The story of their heroism and torment belongs to the record of the Florentine Resistance[13]. There was little the Consul could do for these "armed" rebels, but he had managed to hold up the execution order against the other four hostages, whose release was promised shortly.

On the evening of the 16th, while the Consul and Dr Poppe were dining with Hanna Kiel in her villa at San Domenico, their meal was interrupted by a telephone call from an agitated paratroop officer who asked to speak to the Consul. The Consul, who was available at any time of the day or night to the military authorities, listened to the garbled story which this officer poured over the telephone. He had stumbled, he said, on a fantastic treasure-trove of some of Florence's finest paintings which had been deposited at the Sitwells' villa at Montegufoni, some ten miles south-west of the city. This villa and the art treasures were now under direct fire from British artillery, this officer claimed. He therefore proposed returning as many of these paintings as possible to Florence, and a convoy of three trucks would arrive early next morning at the piazza San Marco with the paintings "but not wishing to be taken for a looter, he asked that the Consul and other officials should be present to receive them.[14]"

The Consul complimented the officer on his initiative, and the moment he put down the telephone he sent Dr Poppe hastening to the Art Superintendent to warn him about the arrival of the convoy. That much was confirmed by Signor Poggi's own report[15]. A convoy of three trucks did arrive at eight o'clock the next morning "from a non-specified place in the Valdelsa", at the *kommandantur* on the Piazza San Marco, accompanied by the paratroop Colonel von Hofmann, a Captain Tweer, and other officers and men. Among the works which were unloaded at the Museo San Marco were eighty-four paintings, twenty-three crates and five pieces of frames.

When Signor Poggi came forward to thank the paratrooper colonel, the latter saluted stiffly, turned on his heel and went off. This somewhat puzzling behaviour by Colonel von Hofmann, reported by Dr Kiel, was explained later when Signor Poggi came to check the inventory of the paintings which had been returned to Florence either from the Montegufoni deposit, or the deposit at Oliveto. The Art Superintendent discovered that two panels by Lucas Cranach, the *Adam* and the *Eve* from the Uffizi Gallery, were missing.

According to one witness, the Cranachs had been loaded on to an ambulance on the orders of Colonel von Hofmann "but had never arrived in Florence". The Art Superintendent, who was understandably alarmed at the "disappearance" of these two famous Cranachs, immediately contacted Dr Langsdorff the chief "art protector", who promised to investigate the matter and to hold himself responsible for the restitution of the two panel paintings. It also emerged that neither Montegufoni nor Oliveto were as yet menaced by British artillery fire. What then was the purpose of this generous "rescue" operation?

The rumours about the "missing Cranachs" multiplied in the city. According to Signor Casoni, Colonel von Hofmann himself "had spoken in a friend's house of the two pictures, and had given to understand that they had been taken at the wish of Field Marshal Goering . . .". This was on Sunday July 16th. But on the next day "when Langsdorff was protesting to Poggi that he knew nothing about them, the pictures were in the Hotel Excelsior in Florence—in Langsdorff's room![16]"

The "search" for the missing Cranachs continued over many months. Like other "German" works of art they were probably destined for the Führermuseum in Linz, a prize possession to set against the many hundred of worthless German nineteenth and twentieth century paintings. "Stealing pictures was very much in fashion in these days," the Consul observed. "So Dr Langsdorff should not be judged too harshly. He did a great deal to protect Florence's art treasures.[17]"

But Sunday July 16th not only witnessed the disappearance

of the two Cranachs. The four remaining hostages were released from the Villa Triste and a new phase in the open city negotiations began.

On the night of the 16th, at a meeting between the Cardinal, the Consul, Carlo Steinhäuslin and Comnene, a message was drafted to Kesselring asking permission for two chaplains to be sent to General Alexander across the German lines. The Consul and Steinhäuslin volunteered to accompany the two chaplains to substantiate the "official" nature of this delegation, and Comnène, not to be outdone, offered to translate the Cardinal's proposals "in francese ed in inglese", an exercise which General Alexander was mercifully spared. The Consul himself cabled to Kesselring's headquarters requesting "a clear definition of the desired guarantees".

Meanwhile the battles outside the city took a new turn as General Mark Clark's Fifth U.S. Army began its advance towards Pisa while units of the mixed British, Commonwealth and Free French forces under General Sir Oliver Leese, the commander of the Eighth Army, captured Arezzo. The Xth and XIIIth Army Corps divided in a sweeping out-flanking movement east and west of Florence, hoping to avoid the historic heart of the city itself. Stubborn battles were being fought on such well-devised defence lines as the "Paul", "Lyda", "Olga" and Mädchen lines, but General Eisenhower's decision to withdraw some seven divisions, largely French and American, for the projected invasion of the south of France, weakened the Allied thrust towards Florence. This withdrawal was "a great blow which must have been particularly bitter for General Alexander", Sir Oliver Leese said, since it not only cut short the hopes of an early breakthrough into the Venetian Plain that summer but also held up operations outside the city. Enemy resistance had also stiffened: "At times, the parachute and S.S. Divisions fought almost fanatically," Sir Oliver Leese observed, "and it looked as if they had been ordered to hold on south of Florence at all costs[18]."

But the lull before the final phase of the battle for Florence was short-lived. The unanswered question which was in everyone's minds was whether Kesselring intended to fight for the city, or whether the whole of his preparation for the city's defence was a gigantic bluff.

On July 19th, the Consul himself provided the answer to this question, when he cabled the Ambassador:

"The General commanding the Parachute Corps Schlemm, informs me in strictest confidence that according to present orders Florence and its environs are to be defended. As this is in open contradiction of the Führer's personal order which is known to me and the assurance given to the former Rumanian Foreign Minister Comnène, now living here, request earliest possible clarification and the issuance of new orders."

General Schlemm who was subject to the overall command of Artillery General Lemelsen, commander of the 14th Army, had obviously expressed his disapproval of these orders to the Consul, or at least, wished to warn him of their existence, although the precise definition of these orders had as yet not been established. They had, in fact, emanated from Kesselring who was at Hitler's headquarters on July 19th. According to the O.K.W. diarist Ernest Schramm[19], Hitler had told Kesselring that Florence was not to become a battlefield "despite the experience of Rome" (viz. the Allies' military utilisation of the Tiber bridges and railway network). Hitler moreover ordered that the bridges were not to be destroyed as their cultural and historic importance must be acknowledged; the military disadvantages of this course had to be accepted and "were not to be over-estimated". The decision to exclude Florence from military operations, which according to Schramm had been communicated to the Allies via the Vatican, a fact established by both Dr Rahn and the Consul, was further manifested in Hitler's order given on July 19th, that the 1st Para Corps was to offer defence from a line ten to twelve kilometres south of the city. It was the substance of this order which General Schlemm had communicated to the Consul on the same date, although the General apparently had no illusion as to what this order really meant. The only hopeful sign was Hitler's apparent determination not to destroy the Florentine bridges, of which the Consul learnt later. This may explain some of the optimistic remarks which the Consul was to make whenever this subject was broached.

But of more immediate consequence to the Consul was Kesselring's reaction to the Cardinal's proposal to send emissaries to General Alexander to plead for recognition of Florence's "open city" status. On the day following Kesselring's interview with Hitler, a bomb exploded in his headquarters. The unsuccessful plot of July 20th 1944, not only cost thousands of persons their lives, among them some of the Consul's closest friends, but also destroyed every hope that Kesselring would allow the Cardinal of Florence to make contact with the Allies. "It was quite impossible for any one to ask, let alone receive permission to make direct contact with the enemy at that moment," the Consul observed. "Hitler would have considered it as an act of treachery on Kesselring's or Rahn's part if such contacts were made." But Hitler himself confirmed to Mussolini who visited him some hours after the explosion that he had given Kesselring explicit orders "to pursue his retreat, fighting to hold south of Florence as long as possible and to stem the enemy advance to the best of his ability. Florence itself would not be defended, so as to spare its art treasures.[20]" The Duce, whose interest in Florentine art was minimal, did not even bother to reply.

The Allies were now some fifteen to twenty miles at the nearest point from Florence where the flashes of their artillery fire illuminated the night sky, but the Consul waited in vain for the clarification of the Führer's "personal order" whether the city would or would not be defended.

# 16

## *Statue de Saxe*

> But singly, there I stood, when, by consent
> Of all, Florence had to the ground been
> razed,
> The one who openly forbade the deed.
>
> DANTE, *Hell, Canto* X

The Battle of Florence has been fought over in other pages, in official reports, on maps spread out at headquarters, and in the minds of the contending generals. In the overall strategy of the war, the issue before Florence may have seemed only of local importance, a bastion to be overcome, overrun or outflanked as chance and fortune of war may dictate. General Alexander, a not insensitive commander, wrote in an official despatch:

"We wanted Florence as quickly as possible, not for the sake of the name but because it is a centre of communications and the best operational base for the attack on the "Gothic" line. We planned, if possible, to capture the city by an outflanking movement on both sides of it, with our main strength on the west. The Germans were making promises to treat it as an open city but by this they appeared to mean that, while using its communication facilities themselves, they expected us to refrain from doing so when we should capture it; at any rate they had concentrated large forces immediately south of the city[1]".

According to the Allied commander-in-chief some four and a half German divisions "strong in artillery and heavy tanks", numbering, it has been estimated some 75,000 men, faced the British XIIIth Corps, with three and a half forward divisions, on the front from Figline on the upper Arno to Montelupo west of the city.

But the fate of Florence troubled every conscience from His Holiness in the Vatican whose secretary of State Cardinal Maglione and Under-Secretary Monsignor Montini (the present Pope Paul VI) had made unavailing attempts to secure some common acceptance of Florence's open city status by Germans and Allies alike, to Weizsäcker, Rahn and a host of minor officials, including Florence's own Consul. And all had failed to move the Allies, and their Supreme Commander, General Eisenhower and the Allied commander-in-chief, Italy, General Alexander, from their firmly-held conviction that the Nazis were determined to extract every ounce of "propaganda" advantage by posing as Florence's well-wishers while using the city until the very last moment as a concentration centre from which they could deploy their defensive forces for the more important military task of defending the vital "Gothic Line". Nazi trickery and the age-old fear of the rampaging Hun did their deadly work. The Allies may have been victims of their own propaganda, but who could blame them after the vileness of Lidice and Oradour-sur-Glane? The very obduracy with which Kesselring's young soldiers fought and died, made it doubtful that they had any artistic feelings for Florence in their hearts.

Yet there were decent men on all sides, just as there were brutes, fools and muddlers whose "Intelligence" services went awry. Who, for example, gave the orders for two American air attacks on beautiful Impruneta "after the Germans had left"? Or why was the "blanket order" to blow up towers obeyed "without regard to military usefulness[2]"? It is small consolation that the Germans frequently used these ancient towers as artillery observation posts, and demolished many of them when they retired. Blanket orders cannot cover the ugly nakedness of vandalism, that step-mother of war, and Allied hob-nailed boots ground many an irreplaceable fresco into coloured dust. There were no spotless heroes, no irredeemable villains. In a just cause much injustice was done: in a bad cause, hell was paved with the best intentions.

An Allied general who shall be nameless was asked whether he would have "destroyed" Florence if it would have saved the lives of a hundred of his men. After a decent pause, he said simply, "No". It was a stupid question, a syllogism, which deserved a stupid answer. One might as well "die" for a cup of tea, or a plate of *kartoffelpuffer*. Who can "order" one's men to die for a Botticelli, or the Ponte Santa Trinita? A man may choose to die for posterity, and no doubt a hundred men could be found on either side who would have willingly given their lives to save the peerless bridge. Perhaps if it were a matter of personal choice, Kesselring himself might have immolated himself on the bridge, or even his dreaded Führer (a pleasing thought), holding it like some latter day Horatio against the approaching Anglo-Saxon tide. History was denied this edifying spectacle. Instead, Kesselring's explicit orders to his field commanders, were to hold up the twin thrusts from the American Fifth Army moving round from the west, and the British XIIth Corps, advancing from the south to envelop the eastern part of the city.

General Frido von Senger und Etterlin, the German defender of Cassino, commander of the XIV Panzer Corps, now covering west of the city to Pisa, wrote that "The nearer the XIV Panzer Corps came to the Arno, the fiercer was the fighting, for here the divisions would have to make their stand." He added that "It was entirely against the practice of the O.K.W. to give up a position that had not yet been broken through by the enemy. The Gothic Line was not ready; indeed, a new position never is." Yet at the same time "there were weighty reasons for giving up the Arno positions, the most important being Florence. The German High Command was unwilling to bear responsibility for the possible destruction of the city. Field Marshal Kesselring had always advocated sparing the Italian towns. Moreover it was barely possible to feed the population."

Although Florence was not in General von Etterlin's sector he thought, "It was ridiculous to think that the destruction, for instance, of the unique Pisa square with its Cathedral, Campanile and Baptistery could be justified merely because the German military commander wanted to hold a defensive line along the Arno rather than one running slightly farther back, through the woods and hills."

This art-loving general, who himself had done much to salvage works of art, felt that "It was a tragic thought that all such efforts came under suspicion because of the concurrent "salvage" activities of Göring's special commandos.[3]"

The Battle for Florence began with the breaching of the "Paula" line, the last major defence work outside of Florence. But another ten days were to pass before the Germans yielded even partial mastery over the city. For the Consul the issue had narrowed down to this simple premise: would Florence become another Cassino? And if so, could his beloved Ponte Santa Trinita survive in the ensuing holocaust?

There had been pitifully little he could do to help any of his friends caught up in the July Plot[4]: fourteen of them were destined to perish, among them the scholarly Dr Hans von Dohnanyi and his fellow-Dresdener General Hans Oster, both of whom had visited the Consul earlier, as well as the Socialist Reichstag deputy Theodore Haubach. He was, however, more successful in diverting the Gestapo's attention from the Crown Prince of Bavaria. He advised Rupprecht and his son Prince Heinrich to leave their Florence apartment the moment he heard that the Gestapo had been issued orders to arrest them. Moreover, he sent a telegram on his own responsibility to First Secretary Bock, stating that the former Crown Prince had left "for the north to join his wife". He knew very well that Rupprecht and his son had remained in hiding in Florence, thus escaping the tragic fate of Princess Antonia, Rupprecht's wife, who had been seized and taken to a concentration camp where she was found by some Luxembourg doctor in a starved condition after the end of the war[5].

On the nights of July 21st and 22nd evidence of German withdrawal from the city became apparent. Loud orders of command rent the air as trucks and horse-drawn carriages began their slow procession out of the city, whose roads began to be systematically mined. At night Berenson, that keen-sighted observer, witnessed "a Neronian spectacle" as railway sleepers were soaked in petrol before being set alight so as to disrupt the train service to Pisa, which would shortly fall to the U.S. Fifth Army.

On July 22nd, the delicate mechanism of the two main telephone exchanges were scientifically destroyed with corrosive acids before being smashed with crowbars: only a few telephone lines connecting German military establishments, the German and foreign Consulates and the Consul's private residence at Le Tre Pulzelle, as well as the Art Superintendency, were left intact.

Despite promises made by Kesselring to S.S. Colonel Dollmann, the city's piped water-mains were also destroyed, and electricity worked fitfully until it was completely cut off at the end of the month. In the altercation between Kesselring and Dollmann, which followed this destruction, Kesselring denied giving these orders, exclaiming that "Field Marshals don't lie!" Dollmann, according to his evidence, riposted: "Field Marshals also lie![6]"

Equally ruthlessly, seventeen of the city's flour-mills and pasta factories were blown up. Ambulances belonging to the famous Confraternity of the Misericordia were seized. The hooded brethren of the order which included many of the wealthiest families, together with shopkeepers and workmen, complained to the city commandant that their "last" ambulance had been stolen: this "last" ambulance had in fact been hidden away from German depredations. But the sick could no longer be transported to hospitals, where even the beds had been confiscated. Funeral hearses were also requisitioned, so that the dead had to be manhandled or taken in push-carts to the Giardino dei Semplici behind the San Marco, where they were covered with chalk to control the spread of infection. Garbage carts had also disappeared, so that refuse was left festering in the streets, covered with black flies. . . .

Such was Florence, the Open City, the Jewel of Europe, the citadel of Beauty, as she had been described by such different admirers as Hitler, Jodl and Comnène. Now the old, sedate buildings, some of which dated back to the internecine struggles of the Guelphs and the Ghibellines, watched with lofty disdain as the tough young parachutists under Colonel Fuchs' command, so much worse than the S.S. according to Signor Casoni, went around looting, seizing watches, clocks, binoculars, cameras, microscopes and even instruments from the medicine chests of private doctors. A fur shop belonging to Zanichelli on the Via della Vigna was cleaned out, but due to the intervention "of poor Consul Wolf" the major portion of the stolen goods both here and elsewhere were returned to their owners[7].

It is not surprising that Signora Comberti up at her villa Belvedere, noted down in shorthand in her private diary: "Have hidden my jewels under the third olive tree at the left corner of the terrace". She had lent a German major the sum of one thousand lire, of which he returned five hundred together "with a parcel of Perugino chocolates, after the Germans had sacked the chocolate factory at Perugia".

But one of the most poignant and terrifying moments of the Consul's last week in Florence came when he was invited to attend a ceremony handing over the defence of the city to Colonel Fuchs' parachutists. This took place on "the third Sunday" in July, according to Dr Hanna Kiel[8], which would make it the 23rd of the month. A sympathetic young staff officer who noted the Consul's reaction at the sight of the rough, seasoned young parachutists with their campaign flashes sewn on their jackets, showing that they had taken part in the invasion of Crete, murmured to Dr Wolf: "*Und nun Gnade euch Gott....*" ("And now God have mercy on you.")

Even more alarming were the maps which a General of the Engineering Corps showed the Consul. On these maps were demolition zones on which all of Florence's bridges had been included. The Consul "was speechless for a moment", but he soon recovered and begged the General and his staff to accompany him on a tour of the city, during which he tried to explain to them that all of Florence's bridges were works of art. In particular he gave a lengthy and detailed history of the Ponte Santa Trinita, telling the assembled officers that its conception belonged to Michelangelo, a fact which had been established by the German savant Dr Friedrich Kriegbaum, his good friend, who had been killed in a British air-raid on Florence.

The Consul had been speaking for almost an hour, but his voice was not only his. He was speaking for Florence, with the anger of a man whose cause was just and whose love was stronger than the shallow patriotism of "military necessity" which his listeners pleaded when they showed him the emergency plans which had been drawn up.

"But don't you understand what all this would mean?" the Consul demanded. "The destruction of the Ponte Santa Trinita, of all great works of art, will leave scars which are the hardest to heal and which will fill people's minds with hatred against the perpetrators."

Another staff officer then produced an alternative map showing the demolitions which would have to be undertaken if the Ponte Santa Trinita were to be spared. This would have included the entire heart of the city from the Palazzo Strozzi to the Piazza Santa Trinita, as well as part of the Via Tornabuoni, with the Lungarni on both sides, right up to the Via Maggio to where the Browning' "Casa Guidi" stood, oblique to the Pitti Palace.

Yet another officer, however, assured the Consul more gently that "at least, the Ponte Vecchio would be spared". The Ponte Vecchio was the Führer's *Lieblingsbrücke,* his favourite bridge. "For heaven's sake!" the Consul exploded, "I'd rather save the Ponte Santa Trinita!" Then he murmured: "God willing, the Ponte Santa Trinita will be his favourite bridge. . . ." But whether he meant the Führer's or the Almighty's favourite bridge, was far from clear.

On his return to Le Tre Pulzelle later that afternoon, the Consul immediately telephoned the Ambassador at Fasano, but he obviously had some difficulty in reaching him over the makeshift telephone line, because he sent a message to Hanna Kiel asking her to come to Le Tre Pulzelle straight away. Her private telephone, like other phones in Florence and the vicinity, had been cut off some days previously.

When Dr Kiel arrived, she found the Consul considerably

shaken. He told her that he would get in touch with the Ambassador immediately. He then described to her all the events of the morning.

At about three o'clock at night, twelve hours after he had put his call through to Fasano, Dr Rahn was on the line. The Consul told Rahn about "the emergency plans" which he had been shown. The Ambassador assured him that he would go personally to Kesselring to elucidate those plans and to make a special plea for the bridges[9]. But he advised the Consul to leave Florence and to come to Fasano so as to be reasonably close to Recoaro where the Field Marshal had established his staff headquarters. Moreover, General Harster, the chief of the S.D. (Gestapo) had expressed his solicitude about the Consul's well-being and had urged the Ambassador to persuade the Consul to leave Florence immediately. "It would make my position rather difficult if you do not comply," Dr Rahn told the Consul.

Shortly after this conversation with the Ambassador, the Consul telephoned Steinhauslin to tell him of his decision to leave the city, but Steinhäuslin argued with him, "as I am very apprehensive what will happen if he leaves Florence"—Steinhauslin wrote in his private diary[10]. The Consul, however, assured him that "*auch im schlimmsten Falle in Florenz nichts geschehen wird*". ("Even if the worse should arise, nothing would happen to Florence.") By this the Consul meant that even if the "open city" negotiations broke down, he was sure that neither of the adversaries would harm Florence. He did not mention the "emergency plans" which had been drawn up by Kesselring's staff, because he was firmly convinced that they would not be put into effect. But in order to quieten Steinhäuslin's fears, he agreed to postpone his departure from Florence for a few days. He did not envisage that Steinhäuslin would have any difficulties with the German military authorities since he (Steinhäuslin) had taken over the voluntary protection of German interests in the city, but in the event of any trouble, he was to telephone him immediately.

On July 24th, after Colonel Fuchs' appointment as the city commandant (his elevated title was the Commandant of the

Piazza), the Consul went to pay his respects to this individual who was now master of life and death in the city and who, as the Consul stated, "was unapproachable except on strictly military matters".

According to Comnène and Casoni, Colonel Fuchs was an "*uomo freddo e brutale*[11]", a cold and brutal man of around fifty, with a square jaw, whose "hard face gave little ground for hope". The Consul, on the other hand, described him as a rather simple and uneducated soldier. Fuchs certainly appeared to be untouched by the Consul's arguments to preserve the Ponte Santa Trinita. He had come to Florence on Hitler's expressed orders so as to fight and not to sentimentalise over bridges, he told him. "For me a bridge is just a bridge," he said.

It is small wonder therefore, that the Consul confided to his friends, and to Steinhäuslin among them, that "for Colonel Fuchs—Florence is only another Smolensk!" And that if Florence were destroyed like that famous Russian city, Fuchs's only remedy for the Italians was "to produce another Michelangelo or something of that sort to build up their town again[12]". This was either the grossest cynicism on Fuchs's part or a touching belief in the fecundity of the Italian genius.

While the Consul was recovering from his encounter with Fuchs he learned of the precipitate departure of the Prefect, Dr Raffaele Manganiello. There had been little love lost between him and the Consul since the day he had confronted Manganiello at the Palazzo Riccardi to demand the release of the elderly "ladies in waiting" and although he had tempered his scorn for him in his official reports, it was rekindled again when he heard that this physician turned Prefect had decamped with four million lire of the city's funds. But even this sizeable horde did not save Manganiello from death at the hands of Partisans some months later[13].

S.S. Captain Bernasconi who had crowned his brief reign as Carità's successor with a massacre on the Piazza Torquato Tasso where a number of working-class women, children and innocent bystanders were mown down by a blast of machine-gun fire from two armoured cars, also disappeared from the city with a caravanserai of fifteen *cartellini*. The sole city authority was now vested in the Vice-Prefect Dr Gigli and the deputy mayor De Francisci, both of whom maintained contact with the Resistance and did their best to continue the administrative life of the city. Of the more boisterous Fascists few remained outside of the franc-tireurs and sharpshooters who were preparing for their last "stand" in Florence. Other evidence of the Fascist presence had melted away in the noon-day sun. Almost all that remained was a plaque in the crypt of the Santa Croce church which listed the names of some twelve "martyrs" headed by the lamented Giovanni Gentile, with a forlorn inscription that not only extolled "the sublime sacrifice of these heroes", but promised the return of Fascism "in the light of Victory and Peace" when the spirits of their fallen brethren would be finally placated[14].

On July 25th, Nicholas Petrescu Comnene noted that he had passed "a restless night". Two German officers, the majors Bachmann and Michelsen, had called at the Villa Machiavelli, ostensibly to ask Comnene to make enquiries through the International Red Cross in Geneva about a brother and cousin who were prisoners in the hands of the Russians. In their turn they comforted Comnene by assuring him that the diplomatic immunity of the Villa Machiavelli would be respected, although German troops might be forced to bivouac in its grounds during the last phase of their withdrawal from the city.

But the two garrulous officers, either deliberately or out of sheer bonhomie, also confided that the Allies were expected "with the next four or five days", and that while the city itself would not be defended, the bridges and the zones around them "stretching from 100 to 200 metres" would be demolished. All main roads leading out of the city would be "covered with fire" ("*mit Feuer belegt*").

Comnène, on his own evidence, was profoundly shaken by this news. He had none of the inhibitions, which he imputed to the Consul, about making the information public, or at least, of bringing it to the Cardinal's immediate attention.

The Consul, Comnène affirmed, knew about this decision on July 23rd, but being aware of the revulsion which would spread through the civilised world at such a dastardly deed had "through an understandable sense of shining and true patriotism" decided not to give prior information to anyone[15]! The Rumanian diplomat had not been informed of the moves which the Consul was making to have these "emergency" orders rescinded. In any case, he dashed off to the Cardinal and gave him a full resumé of his talk with the two officers. The Cardinal, after a moment's reflection, decided to consult with his Vicar General Monsignor Mario Tirapani and to seek an early interview with the local German military authorities, among them Colonel Fuchs. This confrontation took some days to arrange.

Meanwhile the Consul was interpreting his "sense of shining and true patriotism" in his own way. On the morning of July 19th, a certain S.S. Colonel Baumann presented himself, together with another officer and interpreter, at the Superintendency with an order from Himmler, demanding the immediate removal of all works of art from Florence "in order to save them from the rapine of American troops". The British were, curiously, absolved from this intended rapine.

This was not the first that the Consul had heard of this project. On a previous visit Baumann had hinted at Himmler's plans. The Consul had had his fill of these madcap romantics who were playing ducks and drakes with Florence's art treasures, so immediately after Baumann's first visit he, together with Dr Poppe, went round to the Superintendency to warn Signor Poggi what was afoot. "I still remember how Poggi received us and organised people to carry all the works of art still remaining in the Uffizi through a secret passage, to a place of safety," Dr Poppe recalled[16].

A heated scene nevertheless occurred between the Art Superintendent and the two S.S. officers on the morning of July 26th. Poggi told Baumann in no uncertain terms that the art treasures of the Uffizi and in other public galleries were the property of the City of Florence, donated under the will of the last of the Medicis, the Grand Duchess Anna

Ludovica who, Poggi declared had bequeathed all the pictures in the Uffizi which were the private property of the Medicis together with the bronzes now in the Bargello, Etruscan antiquities now in the Archeological Museum, tapestries also there, and books in the Laurentian library, to Florence for ever, *on condition that they should never be removed from Florence and should exist for the benefit of the public*[17].

This solemn agreement had been confirmed by successive Italian governments, and had been countersigned by the Fascist Party Secretary Pavolini, and the works themselves placed under the trusteeship of the Cardinal-Archbishop who acted in the name of the Vatican.

To round things off, Signor Poggi also told the rapacious S.S. Colonel that "there were in Florence no movable and easily transportable works of art, these being all in distant deposits". Such as did remain were largely works of sculpture, "but too large to carry away".

Baumann insisted that he had all the necessary labour and transport available, and his instructions were to remove the works of art "at all cost". Signor Poggi, who had been thoroughly primed by the Consul, suggested that both Baumann and he should go round to the Consulate to talk with the Consul. "We went, and the Consul confirmed what had been said," Poggi's report stated. But in order to ally Baumann's suspicions, both the Consul and Poggi went to the courtyard of the Pitti, and the shelter under the Loggia dei Lanzi, and the armour hall of the Bargello, to show Baumann some of the heavier sculptures which had been deliberately left on view! Baumann appeared to be persuaded, but he nevertheless returned the next morning (July 27th), and repeated his "orders". Signor Poggi, not to be outdone, promptly went over all his arguments, and said that he would consign nothing without the authority of the Cardinal. Baumann then asked if there were any private collections on which to lay his hands (the S.S. man was prepared to scrape the bottom of this barrel), but Poggi told him that most of the private collections had been taken out of Florence earlier to save them from air-raids. Baumann then took his leave "telling me he would return at eleven and go with me to Consul Wolf and inform me of his decision. He returned instead at twelve to tell me that he had given up his conversation with Wolf, and to take leave."

In the face of Poggi's and the Consul's obstinate refusal to yield, S.S. Colonel Baumann retired empty-handed from Florence. What he did not know, and what the Consul and Dr Poppe knew only too well, was that while he was being shown the "enormous works of sculpture, such as the baptistery doors and Cellini's *Perseus*", some of the finest works from Arezzo and Empoli, as well as "the entire contents of the *Gabinetto dei Disegni* of the Uffizi" which had only recently been returned from "outlying deposits" were still lying unpacked in their boxes, hidden from the S.S. Colonel's inquisitive gaze[18]. But the Consul's prompt warning to Poggi played no small part in the elaborate game of deception practised on the S.S. It was a sizeable, if melancholy triumph, to set beside the disasters which were to follow.

On July 27th, a Thursday, the day before the Consul's departure, an official announcement from the military command published in *La Nazione*, reaffirmed that the Germans would continue to treat Florence as "an open city", but warned citizens that anyone found impeding the passage of their troops would be promptly shot, and severe reprisals would be taken against their families.

The Consul who had been forewarned of what might happen to the city, now began his round of farewells. In this climate of fading hopes, he came to Le Fontanelle to pay his respects to the Serlupis whose hospitality and friendship he had enjoyed over many months. He brought them a small "statue de Saxe", a Dresden figurine, as a parting present, but refused their offer to hide him from the Allies in their splendid mansion. He asked to be remembered to Berenson and Nicky Mariano who were to continue through the next month's vicissitudes as the Serlupis' guests, and after he had admired the elaborate "air raid" precautions which the Marchese had made for Berenson's safety and for the protection of his books and paintings, he bade his friends adieu. A brief visit to

Maestro Gui and a call on Monsignore Meneghello, the gentle secretary of the Vice-Cardinal Florit, followed. The Monsignore noticed that the Consul was in considerable distress at leaving Florence, and offered him, what he believed to be "a strong drink". It was actually a "thimblefull of sweet wine", the Consul recalled with affection, years later. Dr Achille Malavasi also came, with a message from his neighbour Donna Beatrice Viganó, offering the hospitality of her house, but the Consul told him "he would have to follow his Fate". Many other offers of hospitality reached the Consul: there were even rumours that "the Partisans were prepared to kidnap him in the event of danger and take him North with them[19]". The city was finding it difficult to part with her Consul, who himself felt the wrench excruciatingly as the hour of departure drew near.

To Steinhäuslin, whom he saw in the afternoon, shortly before leaving, he repeated that even if the worse should arise, nothing would happen to Florence, adding in answer to Steinhäuslin's query, "even when the English come to Florence". He confirmed that he had been unable to get a positive answer from Kesselring on the Cardinal's proposal to send special emissaries to the Allies, but said that he would continue to press both Kesselring and Rahn to establish some kind of contact, as well as to make other provisions for the safety of the city. He also gave Steinhäuslin the names of a number of German officers who might prove helpful.

Among these were Major von Rathenow and Captain Thomas of the Infantry, Major von Seubert of field gendarmerie, Colonel von Hoffmann on the staff of Parachute Corps, General Trettner, Major von Roon and Captain von Sastrow of the IVth Parachute Division. All these were personally known to the Consul, and were destined to play their part in the ensuing drama which unfolded after his departure from Florence. But it was an unrewarding legacy which the Consul left Steinhäuslin, with whom he had endured so many buffetings, alternating between hope and despair. Even in these last moments, he seemed anxious to fortify his friend's spirits which were as constant as his own.

There was the bleakest despair in the Consul's eyes as he looked for the last time on the Ponte Santa Trinita *come era*, as it was. He turned to Hanna Kiel, who was accompanying him, and told her with all the pent-up bitterness in his heart that he was ashamed of the plans and intentions of the German military, and that if they did not change their minds, there was nothing he could do except to stand in the middle of the Ponte Santa Trinita, and be blown up with it!

He had done all he could to save Florence "in extremis", and had a diary written in a simple code, which he asked her to keep for him, so that his daughter should one day learn what he had tried to do for the city he loved. This diary, however, was lost for ever, but the Consul's sudden burst of passion moved Hanna Kiel deeply. It would most certainly have delighted Kriegbaum.

With the sun riding high over the city, accompanied by the cannonade of Allied guns a few miles away, the Consul's motorcade moved off from his country residence at San Domenico di Fiesole. Le Tre Pulzelle with its twin stone maidens, and its Medici crest high above the portico, saw no more of the Consul. "I hope," he said, turning to Dr Wildt, who was to follow him in another car, "you will be clever enough to take a wrong turning!" The Consul was trying to be jocular, but he could hardly shake off the mood of depression which was weighing on him.

"We left Florence on the afternoon of July 28th, with its hills covered with smoke from Allied guns and German explosives," he remembered later. "The enemy was still some two and a half miles away from the centre and might enter the town by nightfall. No one could tell what would happen."

At nightfall on July 28th, a troop of armed men called at Le Tre Pulzelle to check for themselves whether the Consul had left. They found no one in Le Tre Pulzelle except for the servants, but a few days later, a young law student, Alessandro de Tabarelli, came knocking at the gates. He had managed to escape from Colonel Fuchs's paratroopers and had gone to find shelter at Le Tre Pulzelle "which had been placed at my disposal by the Consul[20]".

It was a small, but characteristic gesture, that in his last moments in Florence the Consul had arranged to open his house to a fleeing student. "Nothing I ever owned can be filched by Time," Stefan George wrote. Nothing could be taken away from the Consul: the city bred her own kind of humanity even in this "unwanted partner in an unwanted war" who had come four years earlier to the golden city to escape from tragic and evil circumstances, but who fell on the thorns of life, and found that he could bleed.

Of course, he took the lithograph of Goethe which had hung in his office in the Consulate on the via dei Bardi, with him.

# 17

# Operation *Feuerzauber*

> For whoever conquers a free town and does not demolish it commits a great error, and may expect to be ruined himself; because whenever the citizens are disposed to revolt, they betake themselves of course to the blessed name of liberty....
>
> MACHIAVELLI, *The Prince*

The Consul and his party, which included Hans Wildt and Erich Poppe, arrived early in the morning of Saturday, July 29th in Fasano. It had taken them almost fifteen hours to make a journey of some one hundred and fifty odd miles from Florence to Lake Garda. Their motorcade had been interrupted frequently by R.A.F. spotter and fighter-planes which swooped low to take shots at them. The crossing of the river Po had been particularly hazardous, as the Consul recalled, but by nightfall on the 28th, their progress had accelerated and they reached the Villa Bassetti, the German Ambassador's residence, just as the stars had begun to fade in the dawn-streaked sky over the sleepy watering-spa.

The Ambassador who had only recently returned from Hitler's headquarters in East Prussia, a pilgrimage he had undertaken with Mussolini to visit the Führer on the day of the abortive July 20th plot, had barely time to brush his formidable bushy eyebrows before the arrival of the Consul and his party was announced.

It was Dr Rahn's first meeting with the Consul over many weeks, and he was immediately struck by his friend's extremely strained and worn appearance. Indeed, the Consul seemed very close to a nervous breakdown.

"Is there any news from Kesselring?" the Consul asked abruptly, without accepting the Ambassador's invitation to be seated. "Will he give orders countermanding the destruction of the bridges?"

The Ambassador explained that Kesselring himself had only recently returned from Hitler's headquarters and was studying the defence plans prepared by his staff.

"Then we must get to Kesselring immediately," the Consul said, "before those plans are put into operation."

The Ambassador put his arm affectionately round the Consul's shoulders. Rilke's impatient young cornet was always ready to jump on the first available horse and gallop off in every direction. Dr Rahn told the Consul that as far as he knew Kesselring's directives were to spare the Florentine bridges, and that there was no immediate reason for alarm on that score. He himself had established cordial relations with Kesselring whom he knew to be amenable to reason and who had often accepted his suggestions to limit the area of destruction in Italy[1]. Should the necessity arise, he himself would be prepared to intervene personally with Kesselring to prevent the destruction of the bridges.

"But is there any hope you will succeed?" the Consul asked anxiously.

"There is always hope, Gerhard," the Ambassador replied affectionately. "Now you had better get some rest."

The Consul retired to an upstairs bedroom and lay down on his bed. The warm, morning sun broke through the wooden shutters, striping the walls in delicate shades of pink and ochre. The Consul who had begun to run a high fever, studied the bars of light in an effort to concentrate his thoughts. A jumbled photomontage of impressions overwhelmed him—the garden at Le Tre Pulzelle with its two stone maidens, overgrown with leander and rhododendron bushes, his office at the via dei Bardi with its patrician Goethe lithograph and the scowling photograph of Hitler, the reception hall with its chequered black-and-white marble floor, crowded with visitors and petitioners, the sedate Villa Triste on the via Bolognese, that house of torments where

Carita and his minions had supervised their daily round of tortures, Coletti Perucca and his young companions shot to death for refusing to obey the levy; the whole tragic procession of his four years in Florence now rose like a phantasmagoria before him, exploding into a thousand fragments in his mind. And over all, through the hazy outline of his young daughter's face, the glorious curved sweep of the Ponte Santa Trinita, Kriegbaum's bridge, the most beautiful bridge in the world. The bridge was trying to express something to the Consul ("What hand will grasp a wheel careering down into the void?") but the words belonged to Stefan George.

The Consul was heartsick and conscience-stricken. Had he merely escaped "from evil and tragic circumstances" for the second time because he could no longer face the sentence of doom which had been pronounced on the Ponte Santa Trinita?

The Consul had no answer to all this self-torment. He could take refuge in sickness, in death even: a man's death is more the survivors' affair than his own, Thomas Mann had written.

But grief, like a tide, carries a man's thoughts to the farthest shores of reckoning. It was to Steinhäuslin that the Consul now turned in his fevered mind, pronouncing his name like a benediction. On the Swiss consul's uncomplaining shoulders, his charity and love for his native city, the mantle of the city's last defender had descended on him, and on such as he, the last, fading hopes rested. . . .

Shortly after the Consul's departure on the 28th, Steinhäuslin went to the Villa dell' Ombrellino at Bellosguardo to contact General Trettner, the commander of the 4th Parachute Division, one of the more approachable officers whom the Consul had listed before his departure. As the general was absent from his headquarters, Steinhäuslin had to content himself with the chief of staff, Major von Roon and his aide, Captain von Sastrow.

The first meeting between the Swiss Consul and the two officers was brief but not altogether unhopeful. Von Roon assured the Swiss representative that the Wehrmacht would do everything possible "to avoid irreparable and useless damage to the city". Steinhäuslin seemed satisfied with this assurance: he merely asked Major von Roon and his men to take particular care of the villa's fine furnishings.

This air of gentle optimism which seemed to affect everyone was shared by the London *Daily Telegraph's* special correspondent, L. Marsland Gander, who wrote in his newspaper on July 28th:

"The Germans intend to evacuate Florence, which they have declared an open city. There is no effective black-out. So far none of the city's bridges across the Arno have been blown up. All the signs therefore, are that Florence, like Rome, will be completely spared from damage as the war bypasses it and the enemy falls back on the Gothic Line."

Even among Eighth Army men, who had done some of the hardest fighting outside the city, an almost festive air prevailed. Shilling sweepstake tickets were being sold, betting on the date of the entry of Allied troops into Florence. The most favoured "bet" was Sunday, July 30th, although General Sir Oliver Leese's VIIIth Army Corps was still eight miles away from the city centre—and not two and a half miles as the Consul had surmised at his departure—and there was still plenty of hard fighting ahead on the slopes of Monte Scalari, the heights outside Florence.

Young German paratroopers belonging to the "famous 1st Parachute Division" (as General Alexander[2] called them) were fighting with superlative courage, hurling themselves with reckless abandon, grenade in hand, at Allied armour, their bravery matched by the South Africans, New Zealanders, and other British and Commonwealth forces outside the city. The hastily-dug graves of friend and foe laid side by side in the rocky Tuscan countryside were testimony enough of the particular savagery with which the last defences of Florence were being contested. Kesselring's defensive strategy before Florence too, was masterly, its main objective being to gain time to organise his main defences on the Gothic Line. The young paratroopers bought that time with their blood and thus prolonged the needless agony of the war by almost a year. But however much one may deplore this senseless battle before the gates of Florence, military historians will admit that they could not have fought harder even in a better cause, and Kesselring's generalship won him unstinting praise from his fair-minded foes[3].

In Florence itself, July 28th passed uneventfully. In the morning before the Consul's departure S.S. Colonel Langsdorff, the "art protector", visited Superintendent Poggi to tell him that he had located the "missing Cranachs", but although they were "in a safe place, he was unable to give me any more details . . .[4]".

On the night of July 28th and 29th, an air-raid carried out by U.S. bombers almost obliterated L'Impruneta: the roof of the Basilica was demolished almost in its entirety, killing numerous refugees sheltering in the ancient church building. First Lieutenant Hartt who visited the scene of devastation a fortnight later, said it reminded him of "a log jam on an Alaskan river, the smashed beams were piled over the ruins of the *tempietti* of Michelozzo and Luca della Robbia. . . . To add to the gruesomeness, the Renaissance tomb of Bishop Antonia degli Agli, who died in 1477, which had stood in the right transept, had been ripped open and the bones and pathetic rags of brown and dried flesh spilled out upon the wreckage[5]".

There was grief and bewilderment at this destruction of Florence's delightful daughter-township, whose bombardment Lieutenant Hartt put down to "perhaps another case of frequent failure of Allied Intelligence". And Avv. Casoni complained bitterly at "this sad episode since there were barely a dozen Germans in L'Impruneta . . .[6]".

Waking early on the morning of the 29th, Steinhäuslin noticed that the Germans had marked enormous arrows of variegated colours on all the main roads leading north out of the city during the night: a pleasant rosy hue was reserved for the streets running from the Porta Romana over the Ponte Santa Trinita to the via Bolognese. He also heard rumours which were bruited around Florence that one of the city's largest typographical works was printing special "evacuation" orders on German instructions. This rumour was suddenly reinforced by a request from the German military command to the Municipal authorities of Florence to provide a "detailed map of the area of the city adjacent to the bridges"[7].

Steinhäuslin immediately sallied out with his safe-conduct countersigned by the Consul in his capacity of protector of the triple interests of Great Britain, the United States of America and Germany, to seek some explanation for the cabalistic signs on the city's streets from Colonel Fuchs. Although he did not see Fuchs on this occasion, Fuchs' adjutant Baron von Münchausen confirmed that the arrows marked the retreat route of the German forces from the southern perimeter of the city. Münchausen said that these arrangements should leave the Allies in no doubt as German intentions to treat Florence as an open city: German forces would only cross the "Sperrzone" for purposes of retreat, without attempting to fight in the heart of the city whose buildings would obviously (although Münchausen did not say this) serve as a protective shield for the withdrawal.

Some reassurance was also felt in the publication in the German-controlled *La Nazione* of the 29th, of an expression of "thanks" made on behalf of the population to their occupiers and to "those who have promised and obtained for Florence the treatment of an open city[8]". If the Germans were thanking themselves for their good intentions and the Allies accepted these at their face value, then there was still some chance that the city would be spared any destruction. But such gentle and generous illusions were soon to be shattered.

In the early afternoon of the 29th, Steinhäuslin and Avv. Casoni managed to obtain an advance copy of the German evacuation order printed by the Tipografia Vallecchi. In this extraordinary order Fuchs commanded the complete evacuation of a sizeable area of the city around the bridges: the depth of this evacuation zone varied from between 100 and 200 metres. Some 50,000 persons (the figure has been trebled by some observers[9]) were summoned to leave their living quarters with a handful of luggage, by noon on the following day.

Steinhäuslin immediately returned to Major von Roon at Bellosguardo to obtain some clarification of this vicious order which he was told had emanated from Colonel Fuchs, who was responsible for *the defence of the city*. The Swiss Consul was greatly taken aback at this admission that the Germans now contemplated a defence of the city, in an open contradiction to the assurance he had received from Münchausen earlier the same day. Had Münchausen, like his more famous namesake, exaggerated out of all proportion the Germans' desire to retreat unmolested from the city, or had some new circumstances arisen which had made the Germans harden their attitude?

Nicky Mariano, who together with Berenson, and their hosts, the Serlupis, was listening to the radio, noted down in her diary their stunned reactions to the B.B.C.'s announcement of General Alexander's "Special Message to the Citizens of Florence" urging them to defend their bridges and to prevent the destruction of all vitally important installations. To this, Miss Mariano commented somewhat acidly: "As the waterworks and almost all the steam mills have already been destroyed, these recommendations sound a little comical. With what should this poor, peaceful, unarmed population prevent such military measures? Our host assures us that the proclamation will have very evil consequences and furnish the Wehrmacht with a good excuse for declaring Florence no longer an 'open city'....[10]"

The most disturbing phrase in this "Special Message" from the Allied commander-in-chief was the simple reminder that it was vital for Allied troops to cross Florence without delay to complete the destruction of the German forces in their retreat northwards[11]". This was not the right moment to invite the Florentines to rise up in arms against a formidable array of "Tiger" tanks and heavy artillery batteries straddling the Viale Michelangelo and the Viale Torricelli, trained on the heart of the city! And it was hardly surprising that Avv. Casoni, a liberal-minded man and an anglophile like most Florentines, called this "Special Message" which would soon rain down on the city in a deluge of leaflets "*una vera disgrazia*[12]".

If Major von Roon knew anything about this radio broadcast or these leaflets, he said nothing to Steinhäuslin. But his manner, which had been fairly cordial up to now, became harsh and uncompromising. He did agree to make one concession, however: he would recommend extending the evacuation order from noon the next day until three in the afternoon, and possibly until a little later. The final decision would rest with the Commandant of the Piazza, Colonel Fuchs, and it was to Fuchs that the Swiss Consul repaired in considerable agitation.

The hard-faced Fuchs told Steinhäuslin in the presence of von Roon's subordinate Captain von Sastrow that he could neither withdraw nor modify his order. It was "a purely precautionary measure", the decision to defend Florence would depend on the behaviour of the Allies. The Germans could not go on making military sacrifices merely to protect the beauties of Florence!

"I was then put in mind of the remark made by Consul Wolf," Steinhäuslin noted down in his diary, "that for Colonel Fuchs—Florence was only another Smolensk!"

They then launched into a complicated argument about the significance of open cities under International Law. Steinhäuslin asserted that according to his interpretation an open city was one which was open to the entry of enemy troops. If the Germans evacuated the city without fighting, the Allies would give immediate *de facto* recognition to its open city status. They had no reason, therefore, to give a declaration analagous to the Germans. Fuchs said that although he would have agreed with this interpretation "if Florence were a German city", the question of Florence's status was subject to tripartite agreement between the Germans, the Allies, and the city authorities. The Allies, therefore, had to make clear their intentions before such a declaration could become valid[13].

According to Comnène's version of Steinhäuslin's conversation with Fuchs, the Swiss Consul asked *ex abrupto*, whether the Germans would agree to revoke their evacuation order if some agreement could be reached with General Alexander not to occupy the city[14]. Fuchs was somewhat taken aback by this novel proposition. But he parried it easily enough by saying, "that if the Allies do not attack Florence, the Germans will naturally not defend it".

He did, however, agree to extend the time limit for the evacuation, a concession wrung from him with passionate insistence by Steinhäuslin. The population, Fuchs said disarmingly, need have no fear for their personal possessions nor furniture which they would be advised to leave behind, since German troops would be under severe discipline to prevent any looting. Then in a final burst of confidence, he added that the Führer's open city declaration was holy writ, his "norm" as he put it. But he, too, did not say anything about General Alexander's "Special Message", which he reserved for a more opportune moment. By four o'clock that same afternoon of the 29th, the city's walls were festooned with his evacuation order.

At seven in the evening Steinhäuslin, together with others, met at the Cardinal's palace to draw up the text of a final communication to Colonel Fuchs, asking him to allow the Cardinal to make contact with the Allies, and reminding him of all Hitler's generous promises to the city. Steinhäuslin offered to have the text translated into German.

By eleven o'clock on the evening of July 29th, the black-out in the city was complete. The Germans had destroyed the main electricity station and all supplies were cut off. Evacuation Sunday (the 30th of July) loomed gloomily. There was no sign of the Allies in the city and numerous Eighth Army men must have lost their bets. Nicky Mariano received "sad accounts from town, of the procession of wretched evacuees, pushing their few belongings and their old and sick people in little handcarts, of the endless queues of people carrying *fiaschi* and bottles wherever the water fountains are still running". At Le Fontanelle everyone was busy preparing candlesticks and small oil lamps for the evening. "Our hostess (Marchesa Gilberta Serlupi) who is an expert electrician and does all her repairs herself thinks it may take at least six months to repair such a radical destruction (of the central electricity station) as this one is likely to be," Nicky Mariano wrote in her diary.

At eleven o'clock in the morning, as Steinhäuslin passed by car through the Borgo Ognissanti, he saw the "gente piccolo", the poor people of the city, heaping their few precious belongings on to handcarts hired at the inflated price of 4,000 lire for the day before tramping off to the reception centres hastily improvised for them in the Pitti Palace and on the Campo di Marte. Chaos and confusion reigned at the orthopædic hospital of San Giovanni di Dio, where Steinhäuslin himself helped armless and legless patients into his car which was used to transport them to other hospitals outside the evacuation zone. Frantic efforts had been made by the hospital's director to clear the hospital by noon, since no one had told him of the extended time limit.

Steinhäuslin, true to the Red Cross traditions of his country, left his car at the disposal of the hospital authorities and went on foot to the Archiepiscopal palace. A few minutes before twelve, a seven-man procession, headed by the tall, venerable Cardinal Elia Dalla Costa made its way slowly on foot to the *kommandantur* on the Piazza San Marco for their confrontation with the dour regimental commander who had been suddenly thrust on the city's stage at the most tragic moment of its wartime history.

Fuchs received the Cardinal and his delegation with his usual show of cold politeness. It was not difficult to perceive that the Florentines were poor petitioners, whose civic pride and *gravitas* made it difficult for them to stoop before the occupiers' footstool. The atmosphere was electric, although the Cardinal maintained his usual serenity.

Avv. Casoni, who was also present on this occasion, took what comfort he could from the rumour that Fuchs' handsome young adjutant Baron von Münchausen, who acted as interpreter of these proceedings, had been born in Florence, where he occupied a villa[15].

Fuchs invited the Cardinal too explain the purpose of his mission, which he did very briefly. The memorandum which had been drawn up by Professor Poggi and translated into German by Steinhäuslin's son-in-law M. Zogg, the counsellor at the Swiss consulate, was then read aloud to Fuchs, who listened without making any comments "although the movements of his face betrayed an inner irritation at the last part of this memorandum[16]". In this part, the Cardinal insisted once more that a safe-conduct should be given to his emissaries to enable them to contact the Allied high command "to inform them of the situation in order that the responsibility for acts which could bring grave harm to a city of such importance, not only for the Florentines but for the Italians and for the whole civilised world, should remain clearly determined before the judgment of history".

Fuchs who obviously realised that the memorandum was directed as much against the evacuation order and demolition preparations as against any possible Allied "reprisals", replied tersely that since General Alexander had refused to treat Florence as an open city, Kesselring no longer had any obligation to exercise any restraint on his actions. The evacuation orders which had been given were solely in the interests of the population, designed to protect the city from unnecessary damage when the Germans withdrew.

He did promise, however, to get into immediate telephone communication with Kesselring about the request for a safe conduct to Allied lines, "but as the latter does not speak Italian, and the Cardinal, it appears, does not speak German, I shall take it upon myself to convey the substance of your communication to the Field Marshal personally and give you the answer I receive from my chief".

But he left little doubt as to what Kesselring's reaction would be as he dived into his pocket and produced one of General Alexander's "little proclamations" dropped by the Allies the day before over Florence. This was proof, Fuchs said, that the Allies did not consider Florence an open city!

With this calculated douche flung in his petitioner's face, the meeting dissolved. The Cardinal and his friends returned to the archiepiscopal palace, knowing that the salvation of the city "*e veramente attaccato ad un filo*", truly hung on a thread[17].

While this unedifying scene was being played out in the *kommandantur* on the Piazza San Marco, another drama was enacted at Kesselring's staff headquarters at Recoaro, which the Ambassador had reached after a night's journey by car, at about the same time.

When the Ambassador was shown into the German commander-in-chief's office, he found him seated behind "a huge Renaissance table". Dr Rahn gave this impression of his first words to Kesselring. "I can still see myself standing in front of Kesselring, telling him, 'Well, Field Marshal, I don't think you'd like to go down in history like that young Bavarian lieutenant who gave orders to fire on the Acropolis!' I think he was somewhat stung by this remark—comparing a Marshal to a mere lieutenant!" the Ambassador remembered.

The devil's advocate had produced his favourite anecdote with which he had previously regaled the Führer[18], waiting patiently for the explosion he was certain would follow. Kesselring reddened, but without uttering a single word, slammed down one of General Alexander's little proclamations on the table in front of the Ambassador. The impact which this leaflet made on the Ambassador took the wind right out of his argument about the Parthenon. "I felt that the leaflets were a violation of the open city principle, and I could understand Marshal Kesselring's very violent reaction and his refusal to treat Florence as an open city under these circumstances. The only concession which Dr Rahn was able to obtain from Kesselring was that the Ponte Vecchio would remain untouched under all circumstances and that he would limit all other destruction strictly to military necessities: his field commanders would judge how and when these circumstances arose.

The Ambassador was not to know that Kesselring the moment he received news of General Alexander's "Special Message" contacted Hitler's headquarters to ask for fresh instructions regarding the "open city" issue. He was told that his conduct of operations must be geared to ensuring that "it was only the enemy who disregarded the inestimable cultural treasures of this city" and that the Arno bridges were *only to be destroyed on the Führer's orders*[19].

On July 31st the 1st Para Corps received written orders

from the 14th Army command to prepare *Operation Feuerzauber* (Firecharm), which was only to be put into effect on superior orders (i.e., General Lemelsen, acting on Kesselring's instructions.) The AOK 14th's Army war diary[20] from which this information is taken explained that the code-name *Feuerzauber* covered preparations for the destruction of all the bridges "in and near Florence", with the exception of the Ponte Vecchio. In view of its historic and cultural importance, this bridge was not to be blown up but the houses on either side of it ("*vor under hinter der Brücke*") were to be demolished to an extent which would make access to the bridge impossible for some considerable time. In the relevant signal received by 1 Para Corps, the corps commander, General Schlemm, was reminded that by order of the OB Südwest (viz. Kesselring) no "military measures" were to be taken in respect of the Ponte Vecchio, and if any such measures had already been prepared, they were to be broken off forthwith.

Apart from Kesselring's theatrical use of General Alexander's "Special Message" which had impressed the Ambassador so much, there may have been other considerations in Kesselring's mind which deserve passing attention. The B.B.C.'s psychological war experts had undoubtedly galled Kesselring by their reiterated allegations impugning his loyalty to the Führer. They were quick to point out that unlike other German generals who hastened to send Hitler telegrams of condolence after the abortive attempt on his life on July 20th, Kesselring, for some unaccountable reason, had remained silent[21].

The suggestion therefore that he was in some way involved in the Plot—like Rommel, for example—might have irritated Kesselring. In any event, he refuted any such accusation in his "Memoirs". Goering had rung him up at his headquarters on the night of July 20th, but up to that moment he knew nothing about the conspiracy. Goerdeler, one of the chief conspirators, had tried to reach him in 1942, but had failed. Apart from a few officers who were involved in some measure in the Plot to whom he later gave his "protection", the reaction among the Armed Forces to the news of the attempt on

Hitler's life was a complete surprise. "Of this I was heartily glad," Kesselring wrote[22]. As a professional soldier he was not interested in politics, and as a professional he went out of his way to stress to Dr Rahn that he would not allow "any repetition of the events in Rome".

The Ambassador returned to his ailing friend in Fasano with the news that Kesselring would not destroy the Ponte Vecchio under any circumstances and that he would limit other areas of destruction to strict military necessity. It was comfort—of a sort.

# 18

# The Last Defender

I can endure my own despair,
But not another's hope.

WILLIAM WALSH, *Song*

The plight of Florence was worsening every hour. In the Consul's city the reek of dead bodies, fires and road demolitions, mixed with the stench of cordite which was wafted from the battlefields outside its boundaries, filled to suffocation the hot summer air. The price of a litre of water had risen to six lire—"*microbi di tifo compresi!*[1]" ("with typhoid microbes included in the price!")

The last issue of the subservient *La Nazione* to appear in Florence under German occupation repeated the accusation that since the Allies had failed to clarify their intentions towards the city, "it is not surprising if the German headquarters suspect a possible enemy action against the six Florentine bridges . . .". This, the newspaper said, "is purely a suspicion, and thus a form of precaution which does not in the least change the determination of the German headquarters to abide by the standards of international conventions up to now scrupulously respected. . . . Evacuation of the strip of habitations bordering on the Arno means only the prevention of possible injury to the population in case the enemy attempts to damage the bridges across the river.[2]"

More ominously, in the early afternoon of July 30th a person from an unidentified German unit telephoned Superintendent Poggi to ask if it would be possible to remove during the day the four statues of the Seasons from the Ponte Santa Trinita. Poggi told the unknown caller that this was out of the question, since the statues were so large that a scaffolding would be required, and also because it was impossible to find workmen at the moment, given the circumstances as well as the fact that it was a Sunday. No matter how quickly one tried to work, at least *several days* would be necessary: but the German replied that was not possible.

It would be pleasing to record the name of this would-be Samaritan from an unidentified German unit who made this call to the Superintendent, but alas, he must go nameless. It would be even more pleasant if the call emanated from Colonel Fuchs, but equally, there is no evidence of this.

Dr Ugo Procacci, the director of the Pitti, from whom this report is taken wrote: "When on Sunday I crossed Ponte Santa Trinita for the last time and in dark sadness climbed Piazza Pitti to enter the great portal, an atrocious spectacle roused me from that nightmarish sense of being lost that had seized us all, a feeling that we were tiny and impotent against the adverse development of events." The saddest spectacle of all, according to Dr Procacci, was "the most humble populace of the Oltrarno section who sought refuge in the great palace, finding that its massive walls gave a slight sense of protection and security[3]".

Miss M. Gladys Elliot, who lived next to the Ponte alla Carraia with her three sisters "found sacks in which we put all our furs, warm winter clothing, and went to live at the Villa Cardia, in an old *Torre*, with an English lady of about ninety, a Miss Eleanor Burnett, a Northumbrian. We placed four mattresses on the floor of her living room, and lived there. . . ."

The Tuscan Committee of National Liberation issued a protest against Fuchs' order and advised resistance to German demands, and the Communists warned Kesselring that if he valued his skin he would not attempt to destroy the city whose ruins "would become a tomb for the Germans[4]."

By nightfall, the city was plunged into total darkness. Nicky Mariano at Le Fontanelle noted down in her diary: "In the evening the spectacle is magnificent. The profile of the whole range of hills to the south of the town is lit up by dazzling flashes of lights." The Allied artillery was blasting the Germans out of their last defence positions in front of the city. But on the next day, Monday July 31st, she wrote: "A strangely quiet day. Nothing but the shrill voice of the cicadas to be heard and all around us the peaceful activities of the *contadini* among the ripening figs and tomatoes and grapes."

That morning, while First Lieutenant Hartt was eating breakfast in the Eighth Army officers' mess, he was "electrified by an astonishing announcement by the British Broadcasting Corporation". A B.B.C. correspondent, Wynford Vaughan Thomas, and Major Linklater (the famous British author) had "stumbled unawares on a group of the greatest masterpieces from the Uffizi and Pitti galleries" in the Sitwell's villa at Montegufoni. This is what Wynford Vaughan Thomas reported[5]:

"This war springs some strange and dramatic surprises. I got my strangest surprise this afternoon in an old Italian house within 2,000 yards of the German line. I was with Major Eric Linklater and we went into the house for a better view of the battle. We stepped into the quiet hall—there were bits of waste paper and broken glass about—and then both of us gave a gasp of surprise as we saw on the wall ahead of us a magnificently painted crucifix. I went on hurriedly into the main room and the mystery deepened. That room was stacked with canvases, most of them covered. There was one of the world's most famous paintings, the "Primavera" by Botticelli. Around us were the chief masterpieces from the Uffizi Gallery, the Pitti, the Accademia, and the San Marco Gallery. They'd been taken out of Florence to guard them from the dangers of bombing. Besides the "Primavera", I saw "The Coronation of the Virgin" by Botticelli, "The Battle of San Romano" by Uccello, "The Uffizi Madonna" by Cimabue and paintings by Andrea del Sarto, Giotto and Pontormo, all the great masters. It was the strangest Art Gallery tour I'm ever likely to make."

On the same morning of July 31st, the Swiss consul was told by a Municipal guard that all the bridges had been mined during the previous night. What lingering hopes Steinhäuslin may have had about Fuchs' precautionary measures in ordering the evacuation from the banks of the Arno, were now swept away. On the same afternoon, while arguing with a German sentry who could not allow him to cross the Ponte alla Carraia—the sentry insisted that he should cross by the Ponte Santa Trinita—a German staff car approached. Major von Seubert emerged from the car and introduced himself to the Swiss consul. The German consul had frequently mentioned Steinhäuslin's name, von Seubert told the Swiss consul.

In the conversation which followed, Carlo Steinhäuslin took the opportunity of making a special plea for the Ponte Santa Trinita. The Major listened attentively and then remarked sadly that "the military had a greater sentimental regard for the Ponte Vecchio than for the incomparable beauty of the Ponte Santa Trinita", and after deploring the measures which had been taken, added: "*Es ist schade, aber es ist nichts mehr zu machen!*" ("It's a pity, but nothing can be done about it!")

This expression of regret was all Carlo Steinhäuslin could obtain from the major. On his return journey, when the Swiss consul presented himself at the Ponte Santa Trinita, the sentry ordered him to cross the river by the Ponte alla Carraia! Steinhäuslin, however, insisted that both he and his counsellor should be allowed to cross the bridge named after the Holy Trinity. And this they were allowed to do at their own risk and peril.

Steinhäuslin's observant eyes soon noticed that five separate rows of boxes, measuring between 70 by 50 by 30 centimetres, had been placed under the great arches of the bridge, joined together with electrical fuses.

Steinhäuslin again went to see Major von Roon, urging him to convey a verbal message requesting the competent German military commander to spare the Ponte Santa Trinita. All possible security measures should be taken to avoid the useless destruction of the bridges—"at least the three central ones" through the thoughtless action of some subordinate, he said. Major von Roon, in his reply, insisted that no subordinate could give an order for the destruction of the bridges without a categoric order from "a superior officer who alone can judge whether the bridges are still useful to German troops".

The Ponte Santa Trinita was thus reduced to a mere utilitarian object. Not content with this, Major von Roon then produced another of General Alexander's leaflets in which he had underlined in red ink the phrase: "It is vital for Allied troops to cross Florence without delay to complete the destruction of the German forces on their retreat northwards?" "Have you seen this?" he demanded. "This will cost Florence dear!"

From this conversation with the tough, uncompromising chief of staff of the 4th Parachute Division, who had had earlier encounters with the Swiss consul, Steinhäuslin deduced the following:

1. If the Germans were not pursued by the Allies on their retreat from Florence, they would blow up non-artistic bridges (della Vittoria, alla Carraia, alle Grazie, San Niccolò).

2. That the Ponte Vecchio would certainly be reprieved, but that the streets leading into it would be inevitably demolished.

3. That these inevitable demolitions might occur before the destruction of the bridges, depending on the obstructions caused by the demolitions themselves.

4. That the Ponte Santa Trinita would be destroyed if the Germans were pursued by the Allies, or if they decided to defend the north bank of the Arno.

5. In any event, if the Allies attempted to cross to the right bank of the river, one or all of the bridges would be destroyed between Florence and the river-mouth[6].

Berenson made much the same deductions, but with this difference, when he wrote in his diary on July 31st: "I cannot believe that the Germans mean to defend Florence house by house. It does look, however, as if their plan is to blow up the bridges, including the Ponte Vecchio and the Ponte Santa Trinita. For my part, as I already have written, I could more easily forgive the destruction of any other building."

The Tuscan Committee of National Liberation also had few doubts about German intentions, although there had been considerable argument both inside and outside the controlling junta how best to cope with the situation. Broadly speaking, the political parties of the Right and Centre such as the Christian Democrats and the Liberals, together with the majority of the Action Party, had been inclined to support the Cardinal's efforts to reach some diplomatic agreement with the Germans regarding the open city status of Florence. Every effort which would mitigate the severity of German defensive preparations such as the destruction of the bridges had seemed worth making. There was also another more complicated and complicating factor: although the number of hostages held in German and neo-Fascist hands had been considerably reduced through earlier negotiations, or through skilfully organised escapes such as Avv. Boniforti's, enough of these hostages remained in enemy hands whose fate would have been instantly sealed in the event of a wholesale insurrection in the city.

On the Left and extreme Left, the Socialists and Communists shared none of these inhibitions. Communist prisoners and hostages had received short shrift from the Nazis and neo-Fascists, and expected none. For them it was war *a l'outrance*, even if the whole of Florence was to go up in conflagration. The example of embattled Stalingrad was in their hearts and some braver spirits were no doubt prepared to fight it out with German Tiger tanks and flame-throwers in the ruins of Florence.

Accusations of "intransigence" had evidently been hurled across the Tuscan Liberation Committee's council table. The Communists, in particular, noted this intransigence on the part of the Action Party "which had grown more rigid after the liberation of Avv. Boniforti[7]". Their clandestine propaganda never ceased calling for immediate armed insurrection, regardless of the consequences.

But more temperate counsels prevailed. In a report sent to Allied headquarters, the Liberation Committee pointed out that a frontal assault on the city might provoke the Germans to fight over every foot, bringing death and destruction to a population already swollen to nearly half a million persons, most of whom suffered from lack of food, water and the most elementary hospital and barest sanitary arrangements[8].

While the Partisan forces, deployed north and south of the city were prepared to advance on Florence, in order to harass German rearguards on their retreat from the city, a full-scale battle in the centre of the city was ruled out.

On the night of Monday July 31st, huge artillery salvoes rent the air. "The shells now fell close to the city," Dr Procacci recalled, "one could even hear the whistle. The terrified people were crowded into the lower parts of the palace (the Pitti) and into the air-raid shelters. To me, however the bombardment gave a sense of joy: if the Allies arrived in Florence now the bridges and the city would perhaps be saved, for the Germans would not have been able to place all their mines. But at dawn the bombardment ceased and by light of day I could see on the Piazza the motionless Germans guarding the entrance to Via Guiccardini.[9]" At the bottom of this famous street stood the Führer's favourite bridge, the Ponte Vecchio. The Cardinal and his associates waited in vain to hear whether Fuchs had contacted Kesselring to allow a mission to be sent to General Alexander.

By the morning of Tuesday, August 1st optimistic rumours of Allied strategy reached Le Fontanelle. These rumours suggested that the Allies "would cross to the north of Florence", Nicky Mariano noted down in her diary. She hoped that this was not "wishful thinking". In the evening Miss Mariano noticed that "large fires have broken out in the plain to our right and the discussions about which buildings are burning are very heated. In any case, it is a fascinating spectacle and the tall columns of smoke lit up from below remind B.B. (Berenson) of certain late very dramatic Altdorfers, particularly in the Sankt Florian series. In the night we hear for the first time sharp detonations which must come from a new German defence line somewhere behind us."

That same afternoon while Steinhäuslin and a Swiss newspaper correspondent were trying to console a woman who was complaining bitterly that her wristwatch had been stolen by a German soldier, the Swiss consul happened to remark that he had not abandoned all hope that the bridges would not be destroyed. A German soldier (to whom the woman had evidently also complained) interrupted Steinhäuslin's remark. The bridges, he said, would certainly all be blown up. This somewhat gratuitous piece of information was sufficiently important for Steinhäuslin to note in his diary[10].

The rest of the day passed uneventfully in the city, which was waiting impatiently for its liberators. On the next day the *Manchester Guardian* reported that "The battle of Florence is becoming one of the hardest of the Italian campaign. Basing their defence line in the city itself, the Germans are making a fantastic stand immediately to the south."

On August 2nd Steinhäuslin again repeated his request to move the four statues on the Ponte Santa Trinita to Baron Münchausen, and the Florentine-born captain undertook to draw Colonel Fuchs's attention to this problem yet again. The world of the possible had narrowed down to four statues on the bridge of the Holy Trinity.... No answer had arrived from Kesselring to the Cardinal's last request made on July 30th to contact the Allies, and all hope had faded from that brave churchman's heart[11].

Meanwhile, the savage artillery battle continued on the outskirts of the city. The O.K.W. diary recorded that the Allies had now begun shelling the city, taking the bridges under fire: the AOK 14th's Army war diary mentioned only the Ponte della Vittoria in this connection, but this was sufficient for the O.K.W. diarist to claim that it had now become apparent that the bridges were a military objective for the enemy, who had thus "defeated" the German intention to preserve them[12].

The official German News Agency announced that "the Allied Command, as was the case in Rome, must assume the responsibility if Florence and its cultural monuments are exposed to destruction by bombardment and street fighting". Nothing was said of the tragedy which would overwhelm the city in the next thirty-six hours.

The next morning, Thursday, August 3rd, while Miss Mariano and her hosts were busy "assembling all the art treasures in the house, among them B.B.'s finest pictures and placing them, protected by pillows and blankets in the safest corner of the library", Baron von Münchausen called promptly at eight o'clock, to inform Steinhäuslin that the statues on the Ponte Santa Trinita were too heavy and could not be moved without the help of a removal specialist and haulage equipment. Thirty men and a lorry were needed to remove these works of art. Steinhäuslin immediately contacted the Superintendent who told him that arrangements were being made with the *kommandantur* to remove the statues[13].

At two o'clock that same afternoon, an official German announcement ordered everyone off the streets, under penalty of death. The citizens of Florence were told to keep their doors and windows shut and to seek shelter in cellars and church edifices. The open city of Florence had, indeed, become open to war, as the *Osservatore Romano* remarked some days later. But the C.T.L.N. still hesitated to give the order for an armed insurrection within the city.

At Villa Belvedere, Signora Comberti had risen early at 5.15 a.m. and made *twenty-five* litres of "so-called coffee". She then peeled potatoes until eight, and had a long talk with a friendly German soldier, who quoted the motto of the House of Savoy, "Sempre Avanti" (Always Forward), adding mischievously, "on our retreat". He told Signora Comberti that he had been a farmer's boy from Silesia, but that he would never take up farming again because he suffered from heart-attacks.

At 9.30 in the evening, the soldiers began to leave the Belvedere, going downhill because the main road was mined. "We are alone!" Signora Comberti wrote in her diary: "I hug my daughter and say that for us the war is over! Then I notice one of the soldiers rushing back up the hill. My heart stops beating. But he says, 'Frau Comberti, I have forgotten to wipe the table we have used. Please give me a rag.' When he says goodbye, he is really almost in tears. . . ."

The departing soldiery had, however, left some of their dark bread, as a parting present for their hostess. "It is the only thing they get regularly," she observed in her diary, "for the rest, they have to manage somehow. I am delighted with the bread, but it is not edible. Their retreat is too quick, and the *Kommissbrod* was not properly baked and is green with mould inside. . . ."

Shortly before ten in the evening, the first explosion rocked the heart of the city. For Carlo Steinhäuslin, who still hoped for a last-minute miracle and who wrote that "not a single Allied shell fell on the city", this was a moment of supreme agony, whose bitterness he would drink to the full.

According to Dr Ugo Procacci, who was standing with his wife in the courtyard of the Pitti with a crowd of refugees, "It seemed that the earth was trembling and that the great palace would be conquered from one moment to the next; at the same time from every side glass and pieces of window rained on the crowd, and the air became unbreathable. Terror seized the crowd; a few began to cry 'The bridges, the bridges!' . . ," But Dr Procacci's thoughts rested only on one thing: "Ponte Santa Trinita—if at least that were saved! This idea became almost a nightmare; it did not leave me, and often, shaking myself as from a state of unconsciousness, I found myself repeating, 'Ponte Santa Trinita, Ponte Santa Trinita, Ponte Santa Trinita.' . . .[14]"

In distant Fasano, on the shores of salubrious Lake Garda, the Consul, too, turned in his nightmare. The bridge named after the Holy Trinity was running with blood. *Hellas ewig unsere liebe*. . . . Hellas, eternally our love, but Hellas had been truncated and all that remained was darkest hell where someone's brute hand had struck down the most beautiful bridge in the world.

# 19

# Requiem for a Bridge

Who would destroy such beauty? Surely neither their side nor ours....

FRIEDRICH KRIEGBAUM

"Time passed, then I heard a clock strike ten from a church tower close to us. Suddenly, in a flash, the silence was broken by a terrific, crashing explosion. The sky towards the Palazzo Pitti was magnificently turned to crimson. This was the first destruction: Via Guiccardini, on this side of the Ponte Vecchio, had been blown up and the street beyond also...." With these words, Miss Gladys Hutton, whose continued residence in Florence had been made possible through the intervention of the "kind, human, angelic German Consul", began her narrative on the destruction of the Florentine bridges[1].

She was sitting on some cushions on a stone terrace overlooking the Pitti, with an eighteen-year-old Italian, whose mother was German, and a vivacious Australian woman called Myra. As the explosion rent the air, the three friends looked in horror at each other, murmuring, "The bridges!" Myra bowed her head, exclaiming: "May God forgive them! How can they?"

Kriegbaum's words, "Who would destroy such beauty? Surely, neither their side, nor ours?" returned in the mouth of the Australian woman, to be shattered into a thousand fragments together with the ash, brick and the plate windows of shops and houses which rained down on the stricken city.

Avv. Gaetano Casoni who stood on the terrace on the

corner of the via Cerretani and the via dei Conti, felt the ground heave in a gigantic earthquake as great plumes of smoke preceded the two explosions which followed in quick succession, destroying, so he thought, the Ponte alle Grazie and San Niccolò.

Then a few hours of eerie silence followed.

Gladys Hutton threw herself down on a bed in her pension, hoping to get a few moments of rest: the other Gladys, Miss Elliot, "saw a small R.A.F. reconnaissance plane hovering over the bridges . . .[2]".

The hot air of the city gradually became choked with dust. Then at midnight the explosions returned, "loud, but not terrifying like the first two", said Ugo Procacci. Carlo Steinhäuslin in his office in the via Sassetti counted "about thirty explosions" which went on to dawn.

Between three and four in the morning two enormous explosions heralded the final destruction of the bridges. Huge lumps of debris struck the windows of the Swiss Consulate, which had been thoughtfully protected by mattresses, but part of this flaming shower fell through into the reception hall. The windows and roof of the German Consulate at 20, via dei Bardi were also shattered. A large sector of this ancient street from number 44 to 40 was destroyed up to the Palazzo Ambron. The Palazzo Bardi which gave this street its name, with two palazzos on each side, was also destroyed to block the entrance to the Ponte Vecchio. It was not sentiment which spared the Consul's own offices in the Evangelical Mission, but the fact that they lay at a reasonable distance from the doomed area which included the Lungarni on both sides of the Ponte Vecchio, part of Borgo S. Jacopo and the ancient via Por S. Maria—the "heart of Dante's Florence".

Hanna Kiel some six miles away at San Domenico di Fiesole was arguing with a paratroop officer who insisted on evacuating her together with a group of wounded. "I was trying to be as kind as possible, smiling all the time, when the bridges of Florence were blown up," she recalled. "The smile froze on my lips, but I could not show any emotion. I couldn't see anything of Florence for almost an hour or more. One couldn't even be sure whether anything was still left. The detonation was such that it might have destroyed the whole city. . . ."

Berenson, too, at Le Fontanelle, heard the great explosion which "seemed to burst from the heart of Florence", while Miss Mariano went to argue with a German officer who had insisted on placing heavy machine-gun emplacements on their terrace. She appealed to this officer to respect the extra-territoriality of the villa which was protected by the flags of the Republic of San Marino and the Vatican, but her plea met with "a very curt and sneering reception".

"We are not lawyers and know nothing of such diplomatic rights," the Captain "with a nasty, wolfish expression", told her.

She continued to argue with him, saying that the German consul himself had told Marchese Serlupi "how correct the *Wehrmacht* invariably was about all diplomatic privileges . . .".

The polite *Wehrmacht* had meanwhile blown up all of Florence's bridges, excepting the Ponte Vecchio which alone had achieved this extraordinary diplomatic immunity!

After some lengthy negotiations with a "superior" officer over the field-telephone, the captain with the wolfish expression agreed to remove his machine-guns from Le Fontanelle's terrace.

A beautiful, rosy dawn rose over the golden city. By five thirty in the morning, the last explosion had rumbled over the ruins which Hitler's demolition experts had caused. Dr Procacci who looked out of a window at the back of the Pitti towards the Piazza San Felice, saw two Partisans approaching.

"Where are the Germans?" he cried out.

"There are none here any more, but they are still across the Arno!" came the answer.

"And the bridges?"

"All blown up, except Ponte Vecchio!"

"Viva l'Italia!" cried one of the Partisans.

"Viva l'Italia!" Dr Procacci answered. But Italy no longer had the Ponte Santa Trinita!

When he went down into the courtyard he was weeping.

"What's the matter?" he was asked. "The Ponte Santa Trinita is gone," he answered.

One thread of hope, however, remained: had the Partisans been mistaken?

Disregarding the snipers who were firing from the ruins, he climbed up the stairs to the *Kaffeehaus* "and in the still feeble light of the early morning I saw the massacre of my Florence".

And this is what Dr Ugo Procacci saw: "That marvellous panorama which for generations had been admired by the whole world showed a tremendous gash in a tragic foreground along the Arno around Ponte Vecchio, and the dust and smoke were still rising from the rubble.

"I could not keep my mind long on these ruins. Already my thoughts had become accustomed to this destruction, but Ponte Santa Trinita could not be seen from here. I came down from the *Kaffeehaus* and went with the others towards the 'Cavaliere'. Suddenly shots passed close by. A sniper hidden in the Fortezza del Belvedere had aimed at us. For some time we had to hide and could not move. Not even from the 'Cavaliere' could we see Ponte Santa Trinita.

"I returned to the palace; now exact news had come from the outside. No illusion was possible any longer. Ponte Santa Trinita, they told me, collapsed only at dawn, after the third attempt by the Germans to mine it. In the immense sorrow, this gave me a little comfort: the giant had resisted to the very last the destructive rage of the bestial enemy.[3]"

The first explosion under the enormous piers of the Ponte Santa Trinita which had occurred at around two o'clock in the morning, had merely made the bridge heave its shoulders: it remained obstinately on its feet. Ammannati's masterpiece, the creation of Michelangelo's greater mind, had shaken off the first puny attempts to destroy it. So the lovely bridge was condemned to a slow lingering death by its tormentors, infuriated by its pride and endurance in the face of their mining skill and experience[4]. But by dawn, the holy bridge, like the bravest of Resisters, succumbed to the third explosion which burst out its heart, leaving two triangular piers and abutments still intact, despite the hideous pockmarks left by the explosives in their honey-coloured stone. The bridge's highly-ornamental, graceful statues of the Seasons, despite Fuchs' "arrangements" to have them removed, had been shattered into many pieces, flung like dross along the Lungarni, or into the deeper reaches of the Arno.

The maimed stone of the Ponte Santa Trinita cried out that night of August 3rd and 4th, but no one answered its summons. Florence's Consul who had struggled so long to move the conscience of his countrymen, lay on his bed of sickness in Fasano, withdrawn into himself. No one had as yet dared to tell him of the orders for the destruction of the Ponte Santa Trinita. And Friedrich Kriegbaum, that good and learned scholar who had divined the mystery of the bridge, was mercifully in his grave. But if death could come a second time to any man, Kriegbaum died again on that dreadful night when his countrymen, the darkest and most reckless, destroyed the bridge.

Rumour, legend and fact, mingled with recriminations, just and unjust, soon accumulated round the ghost of the bridge. One pleasing story was recounted by a young American pilot-bombardier who claimed that four young Italians died trying to remove the mines on the Ponte Santa Trinita, their venture cut short like their lives by the heavily-armed sentries who guarded the bridge. Their bodies, it was said, were blown up together with the bridge.[5] Dr Ugo Procacci, now the Superintendent of all Florentine art galleries, however stated: "It is not known to me that partisans tried to prevent the destruction of the Santa Trinita bridge. As it was absolutely forbidden for anyone to approach the bridge, it would have been quite impossible to carry out such an attempt[6].

One thing appeared certain, however; the order for the destruction of the bridges emanated directly from Kesselring. It was "entirely Marshal Kesselring's idea", Ambassador Rahn asserted, "who reacted violently to General Alexander's attitude with regard to our offer to declare Florence an open city". Yet, at the same time, when the Ambassador discussed the question of the bridges at Recoaro with him, Kesselring made the rather inert promise that if it came to the worst "he would only blow up a small part of the Ponte Santa Trinita to make it inaccessible to the enemy". It is possible that at some stage of the grisly business Kesselring may have contemplated demolishing the via Tornabuoni and via Maggio, the two streets at either end of the Ponte Santa Trinita. The prospect of destroying these two fine streets had filled the Consul with much alarm during his "tour" of the city together with local commanders on July 23rd. But if such an idea crossed Kesselring's mind, he sensibly made no mention of it in his "Memoirs", where he stated quite openly:

"I could not accede to the Cardinal-Archbishop's request to renounce the defence of the city as I could not obtain a similar concession from the enemy, so the road through it (Florence) was blocked by various demolitions, which unfortunately involved the destruction of the wonderful bridges across the Arno.[7]"

Yet a Lieutenant-Colonel Zolling (who was interrogated by Allied officers in the summer of 1945), who claimed to have been present at a meeting between Kesselring, Hitler and Goering, stated categorically that it was Hitler "who gave orders to blow up the bridges of Florence, saving only the 'most artistic one'[8]".

The Consul himself concurred sardonically when he observed that "the Ponte Vecchio was spared on account of its romantic character which the responsible generals thought were of more obvious artistic value than the other bridges".

S.S. General Karl Wolff, although he has described his own efforts to preserve the beauties of Florence, confirmed Zolling's view. "Hitler was very angry with Kesselring over his failure to blow up the Tiber bridges . . ." he stated[9]. The Marshal was therefore under "great psychological pressure" not to repeat his mistake by sparing the Florentine bridges. Yet when Dr Rahn had occasion to remonstrate with Hitler about their destruction, the Führer said: "But I told Kesselring on the telephone that the destruction of the bridges would be senseless." Hitler was also "very angry with Kesselring[10]".

General Sir Terence Airey who was Field Marshal Alexander's Chief of Intelligence, gave perhaps the most succinct explanation for the various dilemmas facing Kesselring. Hitler, as Sir Terence pointed out, had ordered Kesselring to pursue his retreat, fighting to hold on to his defensive positions as long as possible, but Florence itself was not to be defended (this policy was confirmed on July 19th to Kesselring and repeated to the Duce when Hitler met the latter at Rastenburg on the day of the July Plot). Since the Germans planned to make the "Gothic Line" their main defensive position and since this line was in fair proximity to the Arno, the orders given to Kesselring appeared to be conflicting. He was told, on one hand, to resist as strongly as possible but without making any serious defence of Florence, while on the other hand to gain the maximum time to consolidate his Gothic Line positions.

"This sort of order was typical of Hitler and the O.K.W.," Sir Terence affirmed. "They were trying to avoid responsibility for what might happen in Florence and at the same time impose on the fighting troops the task of fighting a delaying action over a short distance. In consequence Kesselring exceeded his instructions by blowing up the bridges, excepting the Ponte Vecchio, and even with that he took unjustifiable risks by blowing up the old houses at its approaches. This could well have undermined the structure of the bridge and produced some prodigious cracks in the fabric of the adjoining buildings, notably the Pitti. In view of the irreplaceable and priceless nature of the bridges, this operation seemed to have been stupid because it could only produce a short delay. For the rest, apart from the bridges, Florence was in effect, treated as an open city by both sides, and the Allies were able to occupy it intact."

As for the suggestion that Kesselring had been "provoked" into this action because of Field Marshal Alexander's "Special Message", Sir Terence did not believe that this tallied with Kesselring's character, experience and sophistication. "Commanders of Kesselring's calibre blow up bridges for solid military reasons," Sir Terence stated. "He did so simply because he hoped to gain time. Because of the priceless nature of the bridges, it was too high a price to pay for so little delay, especially in the light of O.K.W.'s policy, specifically laid down that no damage was to be done to Florence. The 'provocation' excuse, therefore, is something that could only belong to the insane Nazi twilight world[11]."

Opinion therefore appears to be fairly divided between those who found Kesselring's action militarily justifiable and those who did not, but it still remained far from clear who gave the final order for the destruction of the bridges. Was it Kesselring or Hitler? A brief chronology of events might help to clarify some of the obscurities. We know from the official diarist of the O.K.W. that, as previously mentioned, Hitler had instructed Kesselring on July 19th that Florence was not to become a battleground and that the bridges were not to be destroyed despite the military disadvantages of such a course, but on July 31st the O.K.W. (High Command of the Armed Forces) must have authorised Kesselring to order *Operation Feuerzauber*. This order was conveyed to the 1st Para Corps through the 14th Army staff headquarters when the necessary preparations for the destruction of the bridges (the Ponte Vecchio always excepted) started. The purpose of this order, as the O.K.W. diarist stated, was to ensure that the Allies did not cross as swiftly to the north bank of the Arno as they had done over the Tiber. This measure was taken "after the original order had been rescinded", which would certainly seem to imply Hitler's connivance, although there is careful absence of any reference to him at this point. It should, however, be borne in mind that the Führer was adept in ensuring that controversial orders or decisions were always outwardly taken by his field commanders, rather than by himself; a case in point being the evacuation of Sicily which was never the subject of a "Führer directive" but only of his commendation after it had been successfully concluded.

The order for the destruction of the bridges, however, is pinpointed in the AOK 14th's diary[12]. According to this source, at 1100 hours on the morning of August 3rd the 14th Army's Chief of Staff Major-General Wolfgang Hauser informed General Westphal, Kesselring's Chief of Staff (Army

Group C) on the telephone that 1st Para Corps was retreating to the north bank of the Arno according to plan, and asked if the destruction of the bridges could be carried out "as envisaged". Westphal (who must have consulted Kesselring) telephoned sanction for this measure at 1815 hours, with the proviso that there were to be no "unnecessary" demolitions. At 1930 hours, a signal was despatched from 14th Army headquarters to 1st Para Corps commander General Schlemm, ordering that the bridges should be blown up. The actual demolitions did not begin until some hours later: most witnesses place the first explosion at shortly before ten o'clock that same evening. The AOK 14th's diary gives no explanation for this brief reprieve, nor does it state which of the divisions under 1st Para Corps command, namely the 4th Para Division, 29th Panzer Grenadier Division, and the 362nd Infantry Division, were involved in the actual destruction of the bridges. The 29th Panzer Grenadier Division was operating south-west of Florence, with the 4th Para Division, in which Colonel Fuchs was a regimental commander, to the south. It is probable, but by no means certain, that a Corps Engineer Battalion, operating under the appropriate Corps Engineer Commander. carried out the physical destruction of the bridges.

According to Comnène, some Partisans told him that "the sappers under General Fehndrich" blew up the bridges[13], but no such general's name could be found in the military records consulted. They may have garbled the name, confusing "Fehndrich" with Lieutenant-General Richard Heidrich, the portly commander of the 1st Para Division who had a striking resemblance to Winston Churchill, but Heidrich's division had been moved to the Adriatic front on July 20th.

The identity of the actual destroyers of the bridges, and in particular the glorious bridge of the Trinity, hardly matter. In a sense, we all destroyed the Ponte Santa Trinita, the liberators as much as the fanatics who carried out "superior" orders with cold indifference and colder hearts. It would be too simple to place the entire blame on Kesselring for this collective crime which was one of the darkest fruits of the blood-soaked Nazi regimé.

Yet many taunting ironies remain: to save the Ponte Vecchio "a score of palaces, fifty mediaeval houses, a dozen towers" had to be rased; the ineptness of this massive demolition operation was such that the Germans did not even succeed in blocking the bridge. A few hours after the Allies entered Florence, sufficient loopholes were found in the rubble to make the bridge passable to light traffic. And the Arno itself was almost dry ...[14]. Within a few days an ugly Bailey bridge, looking like a giant Meccano set, swung slowly in the breeze over the sad ruins of the fair Ponte Santa Trinita.

The venerable London *Times* which has ached for many a good cause in its day, reported two days after the destruction of the bridges: "It remains to be seen whether the Germans will carry their vandalism to the extent of destroying the Ponte Vecchio, a famous example of bridge architecture.[15]" The Ponte Santa Trinita was perhaps not "priceless" enough to deserve even a passing mention. But it was left to the official statement issued by Allied headquarters to excel itself in an outpouring of cant and corn-syrup. This communiqué stated: "The enemy has taken advantage of the situation, knowing full well that our undisputed air power could not be used to destroy the bridges in Florence behind him (while the Germans were still on the south bank of the Arno) without damage to architectural buildings in the city." It then went on: "He has thus enjoyed uninterrupted use of the bridges over the Arno and has seen fit, when outfought south of the city, to destroy bridges of *military value* to deny us the use of the bridges which up to now he has enjoyed.[16]"

Thus in one unabashed statement the official communiqué and its framers fell into Kesselring's trap. What else did they expect the enemy to do except to deny them the use of bridges of military value?

It took six full years after these events for some corrective to emerge when Field-Marshal Lord Alexander of Tunis (as he then became) wrote in his official report:

"The local German commander had apparently been allowed discretion about demolishing the Arno bridges and exercised it by blowing up all except the Ponte Vecchio. The

Ponte della Trinita (*sic*), by many considered the most beautiful in the world, was a particularly severe loss; the Ponte Vecchio, though it had a certain charm of antiquity, is not so fine a work of art and in any case is too weak for all but the lightest traffic. It has been suggested that it was spared because it reminded the nostalgic parachutists of Nuremberg; but to ensure that military requirements were not unduly sacrificed to sentiment the ancient buildings at both ends were blown up in order to block the approaches. We were not, in fact, hampered militarily by all this destruction for *we never intended to fight* in Florence and, once the city was cleared, could build as many bridges as we wanted without loss of time or efficiency.[17]"

And if it *was* his intention not to fight in Florence, and quite obviously it was, why was it not made plain beyond shadow of doubt to the Vatican, who would have communicated this information to Weizsäcker and through him to the German Ambassador and Kesselring?

Both the Consul and the Cardinal-Archbishop and their associates had correctly surmised this intention, hence their despairing efforts to make contact with General Alexander to get some kind of "official" declaration from him, which he unaccountably refused to issue. Despite all the savage fighting, all the *ruse de guerre*, Allied intentions to by-pass the city were not only widely rumoured, but were also the subject of numerous press reports. A declaration to this effect that the Allies would be prepared to regard Florence as an "open city" under certain guarantees, involving the retirement of the German garrison without fighting inside the city, might have saved not only the bridges, but the brutal demolitions which accompanied their destruction.

General Sir Oliver Leese, not surprisingly, threw some light on the whole vexed question when he stated:

"At this moment the Germans declared Florence an open city. It was a typical German trick to do this sort of thing at the last moment, to cover themselves morally with the inhabitants and with world opinion: and also, I suspect, to protect their harassed rearguards. General Alexander refused to take any official action in this respect and quite rightly so. We were however most anxious not to do any unnecessary damage to Florence, and luckily it suited our books not to attempt, at this moment, to advance any further in this sector; but it was vital not to do anything which might let the Germans imagine that this was the case. It was just—'A little bit of luck'—as Stanley Holloway would tell us, that both sides were able to stay their hand, so that Florence could be spared.[18]"

One would hardly grudge this doughty commander or the tired men of his XIIIth Army Corps their well-earned rest, but the price paid for all this elaborate dissimulation, to prevent every possibility of "German trickery", was a formidable one. Neither side destroyed the entire city, and for this, the Muses will have danced their grateful roundelay, but the Ponte Santa Trinita nevertheless died, while generals remained to relive their memories, which any chronicler with a bias towards *his* generals, must quote, if only to preserve some semblance of impartiality.

The victorious General Alexander, like his Macedonian namesake, paid tribute to yesterday's foes when he wrote: "One must credit the Germans with a certain desire to safeguard a monument of historical interest, but it is sad, that of the many beautiful bridges over the Arno, the one they chose to preserve should have the least aesthetic value.[19]"

There remained one curious unlaid ghost of the bridge which also deserves its well earned rest. The great and generous-hearted Professor Piero Calamandrei, the "cantor" and inspirer of the Florentine Resistance, filled with all-too justifiable anger at the destroyers of the Ponte Santa Trinita, accused a "studious German, in the services of the S.S." of making a photographic record house by house of the streets and bridges which were to be blown up. This, he said, was proved by documents left by the Germans after their retreat, which showed the premeditated nature of their crime.[20]

The only "studious" German whom Dr Gizdulich (one of the leading architects responsible for the restoration of the Ponte Santa Trinita) could recollect as having any professional interest in Florence's architecture was Professor Ludwig Heydenreich, Kriegbaum's successor as director of the German Art Institute. According to Gizdulich, Heydenreich "knowing that some areas would not be spared, decided with a sensitivity to which we must pay tribute, to take protographs, with the help of Signor Barsotti, of both sides of the Arno." But neither Heydenreich nor Barsotti, who between them took more than three hundred photographs of historical Florence, photographed the Ponte Santa Trinita! Like Kriegbaum before them, they were certain that the Ponte Santa Trinita would be spared[21].

But if memories falter, a page from Signora Comberti's diary, returns us abruptly to that dreadful night when the Ponte Santa Trinita died. . . .

"At two a.m. on the night of August 4th, two S.S. men ring the bell and ask for water," she wrote. "I ask them to be quiet, someone in the house is ill. They are heavily-armed and not at all obliging. I bring them water (and a bottle of wine. which they do not touch). The gate must be kept open since our garden is a meeting-place for late-comers. The front door of our house is heavily barred, but we do not dare go to bed. Until four o'clock, more soldiers arrive and lie down on the grass. One of them tries to open the door, we can see him through the venetian blinds and are terribly frightened. But the first man, who seems to be the leader, drags him from the door. At four o'clock they leave. *We learned afterwards that we had sheltered the destroyers who blew up the bridges.*

At 5.30 a.m. the bridges were finally blown up. First, we felt a kind of earthquake, then we saw flames and then we heard the detonation.

At 7 a.m. I looked at the Piazzale Michelangelo with my field-glasses. I saw a big Negro walking up and down as a sentry. This sight was overwhelming because—after all these years of racialism—it was a "dark" liberator. . . ."

Between the time that Signora Comberti gave the glass of water to the destroyers of the Ponte Santa Trinita and the arrival of the "dark" liberator in Florence, the Consul was wakened in Fasano.

He rose from his sick bed like a man who was already doomed. Then they told him that the Ponte Santa Trinita had been destroyed. He received the news in stunned silence. What comment could he have made? The promise which he had made to Friedrich Kriegbaum, the oath he had uttered in his own soul when he first arrived in Florence, had not been kept: but he had made his compact with living men, not with dead stone. The law of decency, of simple courage, of care and protection of the weak, that law had not been broken. The German consul was dead, but the Consul of Florence was alive. He had become part of the city which he loved, a city where "the houses of men had become the House of God", as Professor La Pira was to say.

# 20

## *Alba e Serena*

> Anything more? The prayer, I think, is enough for me.
>
> PLATO, *Phaedrus*

The Consul's story in Florence had come full circle with the destruction of the Ponte Santa Trinita. Some part of him had died or had been irreparably damaged: the dissecting knife which time, the fury of the war and the sheer necessity of continued feeling had dug into his soul, produced no sensation. The knife itself had become blunted on the stone that had entered his soul; the man and the dead bridge had become one. "He seemed *absent,*" someone said of him, at this period. For long stretches of time, as he recovered from his illness, surrounded by the care which the Ambassador and his family lavished upon him, he remained silent. "I had the impression that all my efforts in Florence had been in vain," he recalled.

But sleep and the summer weather brought back some of his strength. He began turning over the newspapers, whose soggy diatribes and lavish self-praise, brought an occasional smile to his lips. Kesselring's masterly withdrawal from Florence, he read, had been designed to save "the jewel of Europe" from wanton destruction, but the Anglo-Saxon vandals had unscrupulously destroyed the Arno bridges, and were now deliberately firing at the Cathedral, Campanile and Baptistery—"a fine transmutation of fact to fiction", as Berenson called these extraordinary accusations which poured from Goebbels's propaganda mills and over the Fascist radio[1].

What had happened was actually this: General Sir Oliver Leese who until August 18th, was in command of the Florence sector, was as good as his word. No Allied shells fell on the northern part of the city, while German shells intermittently struck the Santo Spirito, Santa Croce, one side of the Duomo, the centre of the Uffizi and the Loggia del Bigallo, removing the head of a Madonna by Arnoldi. "Every morning the personnel of the Superintendency patrolled the streets of Florence to pick up the fragments of what German shells had knocked down during the night.[2]" The Madonna's head was discovered, miraculously intact but there still was no sign of "Primavera's" head, whose headless statue was being painstakingly restored.

The Ambassador occasionally brought the Consul reports from the city. From these he learned that when the first Allied patrols entered Florence, two hours after the destruction of the bridges, they found the Partisans already busy mopping up nests of snipers. By August 5th and 6th, the 6th South African Armoured Division had established themselves along most of the southern bank of the Arno. No effort was made by the Allies to "rush" the northern sector into which the Partisans themselves gradually infiltrated. For some two weeks this zone remained an undeclared no-man's land where Fuchs exercised control over half of Florence's population.

The *Manchester Guardian*'s special correspondent reported on the conditions prevailing in the southern half of the city. "The community of 5,000 homeless refugees who inhabit the Pitti Palace in the Boboli Gardens make an interesting study. It is as if a cross-section of London's population were camping out in Kensington Palace, sleeping on the floors of the royal apartments, among the old masters and bits of period furniture, cooking picnic meals while the Germans snipe intermittently from the roofs of Barkers and Derry and Toms' and lob shells on the Bayswater Road. Only this morning two civilians were hit by snipers[3]."

Three snipers, including a woman, were pulled out of the ruins, placed against a wall on the Piazza Santa Maria Novella and summarily executed. Two Englishwomen, employed by Prince Borghese's family, told the prince's children that the noise made by the fusillade occurred because "they were shooting pigeons[4]." Summary justice was also done on members of Carità's gang; among these was Pietro Chesi, a famous racing-bicyclist. The boxer Alfredo Magnolfi was shot, accused of being one of Pavolini's and Coppo di Cesare's sharpshooters[5].

The Consul also learnt that relations between the Allied Military Government and the C.T.L.N. junta which proclaimed itself the sole political authority in the city, had become strained. Despite the rapturous welcome which Allied forces received on their entry into Florence and the flurries of salutes which were exchanged in the first ecstatic moments of liberation between General Oliver Leese's battle-hardened soldiers and the Partisans, the sweets of liberation were soon soured by disagreements. "Florence gave AMG more headaches than any other liberated city in Italy[6]." This was hardly surprising in a city which during the siege of 1529 had the audacity to proclaim "*Jesus Christus, Rex Florentini Popoli S.P.Decreto electus*" (Jesus Christ, King of the Florentine People, elected by Popular Decree[7].)

After a few ham-fisted attempts to dole out "certificates of merit" and sums of money to the most worthy Resisters, which many of them, not unnaturally spurned, attempts were made to foist a "career" Prefect, the worthy Dr Paterno, on the civil administration, headed by the elderly eighty-three-year-old socialist Professor Gaetano Pieraccini. Flattering references were made to the Resistance not only by General Alexander but also by the news-sheet *Corriere Alleato* in which the Resisters were told that AMG preferred to treat with them because of the fine work they had done "rather than with the local aristocracy which had done nothing during the present crisis in the city[8]". Orders came from Rome to treat the C.T.L.N. "courteously", and permission given, to seek their advice[9].

But at 6.45 in the morning of August 11th, without waiting for anyone's permission, the great bell of the Palazzo Vecchio sounded the alarm of general insurrection: Partisan forces began infiltrating the northern sector of the city, where large pockets of them put up a stiff fight against the Germans. Two hundred and five laid down their lives for their audacity[10].

The Consul received these reports with a mixture of admiration for "his Tuscans" and bitter reflection on the failure to establish an open city in Florence. But even Fuchs, that dour man, who showed such little concern for the "beauties" of Florence, praised the discipline and endurance which the Florentines had shown in the long months of occupation from September 1943, as he confessed to Carlo Steinhäuslin, the Swiss Consul.

Steinhäuslin had come to ask him to improve the near-starvation rations in the northern sector of the city and to bring in supplies of milk for the younger population. "Think if your sons were dying of hunger," he told Fuchs, "if it was your wife who saw her child dying in her arms...." Fuchs promised to deliver fresh milk for 5,000 children by the evening of August 10th, but by the 11th, his paratroopers had begun to make their retreat to the hilly outskirts of the city. All that was left of the occupiers and their Fascist adherents was a shower of leaflets written in pathetic bombast that "We shall return ... God will punish the traitors and reward the faithful and constant[11]".

By the 13th, no trace of Fuchs and his paratroopers remained in the city proper. In the last week in August German shells no longer fell in the centre of the city, and a week later the rearguards had abandoned the city's environs. All threat to Florence had passed, although First Lieutenant Hartt was told that "the Germans had a V-weapon site in northern Italy, pointing in the vicinity of Florence[12]". On September 2nd, First Lieutenant Hartt arrived at Le Fontanelle to find Bernard Berenson "resting on a chaise lounge in an upper room, terribly pale and suffering somewhat from shock, but otherwise perfectly safe".

The old gentleman had good reason to be shaken. Despite the confidence which Berenson had often expressed to his hosts, the Serlupis, that the Allies would not shell Le Fontanelle because American Intelligence knew where he was, some thirty small-calibre shells from Allied guns had been fired at the villa. These had probably been aimed at German gun-emplacements in and around the lovely grounds of Quarto and Le Fontanelle, and miraculously, neither Berenson nor his paintings, received so much as a scratch. Providence had been clearly working to assist military intelligence.

Projects for reconstructing the Ponte Santa Trinita began almost immediately under a commission of experts appointed by the C.T.L.N. In the debris, carefully sorted out and buttressed by the architect Dr Riccardo Gizdulich ("Captain Bianco" in the Resistance) and his co-workers, the remains of all four of the Ponte Santa Trinita's statues were found, all excepting the head of Francavilla's gentle "Spring", as previously mentioned. Some said a New Zealander or a Canadian, had found her head and taken it as a "souvenir" in his knapsack. Professor Calamandrei was certain, however, that "some rosy and blonde" German soldier had absconded with it![18]

Darkness and light divide the course of time. "To be ignorant of evils to come," Sir Thomas Browne said, "and forgetful of evils past, is a merciful provision in nature, whereby we digest the mixture of our few and evil days, and our delivered senses not relapsing into cutting remembrances, our sorrows are not kept raw by the edge of repetitions."

The Consul, gradually recovering from his illness in Fasano. not only found it difficult to be forgetful of evils past, but he also discovered that his sorrows were kept raw by the edge of repetitions. Indeed, it was precisely the *repetitious* nature of those cutting remembrances which acted as a spur to his recovery. Removed from Florence, there was pathetically little he could do, lying on his sick bed in Fasano. He who had shown remarkable examples of civic courage when it came to protecting Berenson and many other helpless persons, hostages, deportees, and those whose bodies had been broken in the cellars of the House of Sorrow, turned once more to the intangible gifts of the spirit—the rich treasure house of Italian and Florentine art on which the S.S., acting under Himmler's instructions, had stretched their hands.

The Consul, who had repeatedly urged his authorities that the best way to "save" all these works—since this was their proclaimed intention—was to leave them under the care of their own highly-capable guardians such as the Superintendent Poggi, Dr Ugo Procacci, Professor Anti, and numerous other devoted antiquarians, had grasped only too clearly what the S.S. and Himmler's "salvage" operations really amounted to. The trickery and double-dealing which the chief art protector Dr Alexander Langsdorff had so ably demonstrated over the "missing" Cranachs, was now reproduced on a vaster scale.

On August 31st 1944, when the Consul had begun to take his first exercise in the gardens of the Villa Bassetti, a telegram was received from Berne by the Allied Control Commission (ACC) informing the Allies that "valuable artistic collections and archives concerning Tuscan Renaissance works" had been stored in the Villa Reale at Poggio a Caiano. The German Government, this message stated, were anxious to inform the Allies that no German troops were stationed in the Villa so as to spare the Villa and its contents from bombardment. Kesselring himself had expressly excluded the Villa from the German defence zone at his own direct order, following the complaints which the Consul had made on July 12th.

But despite all these precautions and "similar announcements" with which AMG was bombarded over the German radio, when First Lieutenant Hartt arrived at the Villa Reale on September 5th, after the German withdrawal from the area, he discovered that "the Germans had made off with fifty-eight cases of sculpture, including the *Saint George* of Donatello, *during the days when they were broadcasting appeals to the Allies not to bombard the Villa!*[14]"

The Consul and Heydenreich, whom he consulted, could do little about this *fait accompli*, but as Lt. Hartt stated, in his generous tribute to their efforts, "in October, Langsdorff received from those staunch friends of international culture and decency, Heydenreich and Consul Wolf, an astonishing proposal in view of the circumstances. They requested a special order from the Führer declaring that the works of art were held in trust for the Italian nation, a complete inventory to be delivered to the Italians, and a visit of inspection by an Italo-German team . . ." should be arranged. Langsdorff, as could be expected, made no reply. Indeed, he asked Heydenreich why he was "so interested in the Italians![15]" But under pressure from the Ambassador, some weeks later, on November 28th, Professor Anti was allowed to make his tour of inspection, and according to Dr Rahn two inventories were made out, one of which he gave to Mussolini.

At the end of November 1944, the Consul arrived in Milan where the last stage of his drama was played out, with the nominal rank of Consul-General, a promotion which the Ambassador made on his own initiative but which did not receive confirmation in Berlin. According to the Consul's personal file in the Foreign Ministry, Dr Rahn asked repeatedly for the Consul's promotion to Consul-General, "but the RAM (Ribbentrop) refused several times on the grounds that only officials actually in charge of a Consulate General could be so promoted[16]". This excuse did not deceive either the Ambassador or the Consul, since they both knew that all hope of promotion had been effectively blocked by high Party officials inside the Ministry, acting no doubt on advice they received from the Gestapo[17].

Milan however was sufficiently far from Berlin for anyone to quarrel with the Ambassador's administrative arrangements and the Consul was given both the rank and function of a Consul-General. The new Consul-General was not entirely happy in his post since he did not get on with his junior colleague Dr Hans Otto Meissner who was described as "very adroit and effective" on his personal file at the Foreign Ministry. The Consul-General also looked askance at the formidable arsenal of assorted weapons which his predecessor Consul-General von Halem had established in his quarters in the Principe di Savoia Hotel which Dr Wolf had now taken over. Gregarious by nature, he missed in particular the wide social and political contacts which he had established in Florence. Milan, he found, despite its antiquity, was a large sprawling industrial city, which lacked the compact beauty and graciousness of the Tuscan capital.

Although his official duties had been deliberately lightened by the Ambassador who sent him primarily to act as his eyes and ears in this important garrison town, he also attended conferences and meetings dealing with the provisioning of Italian cities under German control and similar routine matters. Great care, however, was taken by the Gestapo to keep him from meddling in "police" matters so that he knew nothing of the vicious interrogations which were again taking place under the auspices of his old enemy in Florence the scoundrelly Major Mario Carita.

Soon after his inglorious departure from Florence, Carità disgraced himself in a round of tortures which he had conducted in the ancient University of Padua where he tormented groups of professors and students belonging to the various medical schools attached to the University[18], before turning up with his henchman Koch in Milan. Here one of his victims, Augusto Chesne Dauphiné, a prominent Resister who had been accused of an attack on the life of one of Carità's notorious spies, Nello Nocentini, described Carità's "medical" approach to the art of torture. A man in a white hospital coat came up to Dauphiné, placing a wad of cottonwool impregnated with chloroform over his face—"just like in an Edgar Wallace story[19]".

Despite all the torments Carità could devise, Dauphine made his escape, a fate which a retributory Providence withheld from Mario Carità and his mistress Milly, who received their not-undeserved deserts shortly after the end of the war. Carità shot his mistress in an obscure hotel in north Italy where they were surprised by an American military patrol. Carità himself was killed in an exchange of shots[20].

At the beginning of 1945, Ambassador Rahn initiated the first approach to the Allies. He had already discussed the possibility of a "political solution" with Mussolini, without giving him any pertinent details. The need for secrecy was paramount if these negotiations with the Allies were to be kept hidden from the various Gestapo and intelligence agencies operating on behalf of Himmler. It was therefore left to S.S. General Karl Wolff and S.S. Colonel Dollmann who had been convinced of the uselessness of further struggle to make the first preliminary contacts with the Allies. At the same time, Dr Rahn instructed his Consul-General to open conversations with Cardinal Schuster of Milan and with Don Corbella, the Cardinal's representative, both of whom were in touch with leading members of the Liberation Committee.

On April 18th, Dr Rahn invited Marshal Graziani, the head of the Italian Republican Army to dinner in his villa at Fasano. After dinner, Rahn gave Graziani a brand-new revolver, making what appeared to a later observer "the irrelevant remark" that the port of Genoa would not be blown up by the Germans. He also invited Graziani to stay a few days with him[21].

Since the present of an inlaid-container with a chromium-plated Beretta pistol led to some misapprehension, the Ambassador's disclaimer that he intended nothing sinister in making this presentation to Graziani, may have some relevance. "It happened to be Graziani's birthday," he stated. "As an incurable civilian I never suspected that such a gift would be interpreted as an invitation to suicide![22]"

As to the remark that the port of Genoa would not be blown up, this was of considerable concern to the Genoese who depended on their livelihood on this port, which not only served as a maritime outlet for northern Italy, but for Switzerland and central European countries as well.

What actually happened was this: in mid-February Baron Hasso von Etzdorf (German Ambassador in London, 1961–1965), arrived in Genoa to take over the Consulate General. His arrival had been precipitated by his involvement in the abortive July plot on Hitler's life and he had gratefully accepted the Genoa post which his friend von Steengracht, the Secretary of State for Foreign Affairs, had offered him as an escape from the Gestapo's increasing attention. Ribbentrop was not informed of this arrangement "as he was busy with other things at the time".

Etzdorf's arrival in Italy was warmly welcomed by Rahn and Dr Wolf, who were both close friends of his. When orders were sent by Hitler, and later by Admiral Doenitz, that the port of Genoa and the huge Ansoldo shipyards were to be mined and destroyed before the entry of Allied troops into the city, Etzdorf, with Dr Rahn's concurrence, refused to sanction this order. Etzdorf then contacted the Genoese Resistance and the German military commander General Meinhold who came to an understanding about the preservation of the port. Etzdorf's part in these negotiations lie outside the scope of this chronicle, but they have been fully confirmed by Archbishop Siri of Genoa who himself played a leading rôle in these discussions, which lifted the menace of destruction from the port and city of Genoa[23]. Both the Consul-General in Genoa and the former Consul in Florence, in different ways and at different times, reconciled their conscience with their duties and served the wider interests of the community rather than those of their nominal masters in Berlin. The Gestapo, it should be recalled, was still breathing down their necks.

Meanwhile, in the middle of April 1945, Don Corbella, Cardinal Schuster's representative brought Consul-General Wolf a list of conditions for the immediate surrender of German forces in Italy, prepared with the concurrence of the Allied command. Since the Consul-General had no military status, he promised to transmit these conditions without delay to the Ambassador who, of course, was in contact with high German military authorities, not all of whom knew of the extent of the secret negotiations which Dollmann and Wolff were conducting with Allen Dulles, the head of the American Strategic Services in Zurich[24]. The Committee of Liberation was beginning to grow impatient "at the lack of any concrete move from the German authorities". On April 15th, the Ambassador "instructed his private secretary and also the German Consul in Milan to keep these contacts open[25]". Don Corbella was told that "Today the German Ambassador is not in a position to negotiate directly with the Committee of National Liberation as the Nazi regime still exists in Germany." S.S. General Wolff himself was absent from Milan and the final stage of his "secret negotiations" with the Allies was not fully known to the Consul-General.

On April 24th, the Consul-General and the Commercial Attaché of the Consulate, Tomicic, went to pay a courtesy visit to Mussolini at the Prefecture (the Duce had arrived in Milan on April 18th, disregarding Dr Rahn's pleas to remain in the "safety" of Lake Garda). Since this meeting with the Duce which took place "in the early afternoon" has nowhere been reported, it merits a full description: it provides a curious glimpse of the faded Caesar in his last days of life and authority[28]

The Consul-General noted that Mussolini looked like "a broken and tired man", as he sat behind a large table in Prefect Bassi's office, to receive his guests. Both the Prefecture and the office were guarded by numerous heavily armed S.S. guards. The Duce himself was in uniform.

The preliminaries of this courtesy call were conducted with great civility. The Duce made some passing enquiry about Kriegbaum whose death had been reported to him earlier and mentioned that he had read an excellent book on Rome, *Roms Ewiges Antlitz*, written by Dr Rahn's friend, Fritz Alexander Kauffmann. He also expressed his delight at reports of the "cool reception given by the Italian population to the Allies", which he now recounted to the Consul.

Once these nostalgic reminiscences were out of the way, they got down to business. The Consul-General tactfully reminded him that the "fixed payments" which the Italian Government had undertaken to pay for the upkeep of German Armed Forces had not been settled "in the current month". Mussolini promised to have the matter expedited. But neither the Consul-General nor Mussolini broached the subject of any secret negotiations with the Allies. On the following day, April 28th, Mussolini himself met General Cadorna and other members of the Liberation Committee in Cardinal Schuster's presence.

To the heated scene which followed, the Consul can add but a postscript, but it appears from Cardinal Schuster's own account that at the very moment when the Duce appeared ready to accept the Liberation Committee's terms of surrender, someone blurted out that the Germans had already begun their secret negotiations with the Allies. In a sudden burst of indignation, he declared that the Germans "had always treated us as their servants". He therefore demanded complete freedom of action for himself.

"To prevent a diplomatic incident," the Cardinal recounted, "which would have led the Germans to repudiate the negotiations now nearing completion, and which might also have driven them to a desperate defence of their position in Lombardy, I reminded the Duce that we had not yet reached any final conclusion. 'That does not matter,' Mussolini replied, 'simply to have begun negotiating without letting me know is a betrayal. I shall ring up the German Consul and tell him that I resume complete freedom of action[27].'"

General Cadorna, who was present at this meeting, picks up the account: "We begged Mussolini once more to make a decision. He finally said he would talk to Wolff (*sic*), and that he would give us an answer by 8 p.m."

The Cardinal and the Liberation Committee waited in vain for the Duce to return at 8 p.m. with his reply. Instead, the Consul-General and his assistant turned up in the Cardinal's study at that hour. The Consul-General denied having received any communication from Mussolini. But—according to Cadrona—the Consul-General was "aware of the urgency of a surrender if further damage was to be avoided". He described the Consul-General as "a typical diplomat, smiling and correct who showed "the best will in the world", but for all that he had not succeeded in communicating with S.S. General Karl Wolff "on whom the decision depended[28]".

After waiting for a further hour and a half, the Cardinal and the Liberation Committee representatives, tried to reach Mussolini on the telephone, only to be told that he had left Milan, having left instructions that a negative reply should be given to the demand for surrender.

In the account which Cardinal Schuster wrote, he correctly surmised that S.S. General Karl Wolff had been held up in Switzerland and had been prevented from coming to Milan. And Mussolini who had yielded to panic, "hoped to find refuge in Switzerland, himself". The Cardinal continued: "Had he accepted my humble advice, indeed my urgent prayer, he would have saved Milan—for capitulation would have spared it the guerilla warfare of those last days—and he would have also saved himself, protected, as he would have been, by the terms of The Hague Convention.[29]"

All these niceties of timing had considerable bearing on the fate of the Duce himself, even if they no longer influenced the course of the war which was rapidly coming to its end. At about the same time as the Consul-General had gone to visit the Cardinal at 8 p.m., the Duce left with a column of ten cars for Como. On April 28th, four days after his meeting with the Consul-General, both he and his mistress, Clara Petacci, were shot on the outskirts of the small village of Mezzagra near Dongo. His execution was followed two days later by the suicide of his friend and admirer Adolf Hitler. On May 2nd, the Germans laid down their arms in Italy.

The war for the Consul of Florence, now the Consul-General in Milan, was over.

A week before the final surrender of German Armies in Italy, the Cardinal-Archbishop of Florence, Elia Dalla Costa, in a letter to the people of Florence, dated April 25th 1945, wrote of the "valued collaborators" who had shared in his efforts to have Florence declared "an open city".

With fearless charity, he singled out the Consul of Florence, the consular representative of defeated Germany, as such a collaborator:

"In the first place we have in mind the German Consul, Gerhard Wolf, a true lover of his country, who would have wished that the glory of our city's salvation should enhance the fame of his country. He did much that Florence should be declared an 'open city , but found no response among his compatriots . . .[30]".

To Carlo Steinhäuslin, too, the "last defender", the Cardinal paid a justified tribute as the true representative of "his noble country". He went on: "Intelligent and active, he was unsparing in giving us wise and judicious advice, especially after the departure of the German consul." Comnène, too, received his portion of thanks, as did many others who played an active and not inglorious part in these sadly abortive "open city" negotiations.

The Consul in far away Milan, however, found that the local Partisans had received "three separate orders to shoot me". The "Matteotti" brigade was determined to make an example by executing the five principal officers in the German consulate as hostages: among these the Consul was included. The Consul communicated this unwelcome news to the local Questura, the Swiss Consul, the Red Cross and Cardinal Schuster, who managed to avert this last calamity through the intervention of the newly-appointed police chief in Milan.

But the Consul was less concerned for his safety than for the possible reprisals which might fall on the heads of his defeated countrymen. In a letter to Cardinal Schuster, dated May 10th 1945, he reminded him of his own efforts in Florence to aid the weak and helpless. He ventured to appeal to Schuster "as a Consul of the prostrate and outlawed German Reich, in my Fatherland's tragic hour, to ask your Eminence in the name of Christian charity, to extend the Church's protection to my countrymen, now without any kind of protection, abandoned in disgrace and exposed to every degree of violence". The guilty, he affirmed, should be punished "by the due processes of law", but in the hour of Germany's defeat the Church's influence on the hearts of the young, could return them to the eternal verities of hope, faith and charity and teach all belligerents the Commandment "to love our neighbour as ourselves".

The son of a Protestant lawyer in Dresden was crying out of the wilderness of despair at the gates of mercy in the hour of his country's defeat, a defeat which his own humanity and decency had done something to hasten. Yet he, too, had to taste the sting of defeat, the humiliation of cross-examination, imprisonment, and final release.

"I simply seemed to slip into internment," he explained. "One day I was 'free' and the next—I found myself in the company of S.S. thugs and cut-throats. It was a period of confusion. . . ."

His first internment in his hotel passed without any noticeable tribulations. Then an equally unrigorous month was spent at Montecatini, followed by some ten months at Salsomaggiore, in the company of his friend, the German Ambassador, who had also been interned with him.

But news of the Consul's internment created an immediate furore in Florence. The Cardinal Archbishop, Avv. Boniforti, the President of the Tuscan Liberation Committee, old Berenson, Marchese Serlupi, the Mayor and Prefect of Florence, together with Steinhäuslin and the honorary Swedish Consul, sent off a letter to the Allied Provost Marshal in Caserta appealing for the Consul's immediate release. Steinhäuslin, that good and generous man, amassed twenty-nine separate affidavits listing the Consul's services to the city and its citizens, of which one should perhaps be quoted: Maestro Gui wrote, "if during the German occupation every Italian city had such a 'German' as Consul Wolf, how many torments and griefs would have been spared us . . . [31]".

But Caserta replied with a stunning silence, as Steinhäuslin who came to visit him at Salsomaggiore, reported. Gladys Hutton, who wrote personally on his behalf, was told that Allied officials "knew all about his actions, but could not make a precedent" by releasing him[32].

A sympathetic U.S. sergeant who interrogated him, told the Consul that "we know all about your record in Florence—but who were the chief Nazis in Milan?"

"I was only four months in Milan," the Consul replied. "By the end of the war, very few showed much enthusiasm for Nazism."

In March 1946, the Consul was transferred to the security camp at Hohenasperg, near Stuttgart, a former woman's prison. Protests continued to echo from all corners of Europe: the Oecumenical Council in Geneva took up his cause, so did Bishop Wurm of Stuttgart. A professor wrote in the *Winterpark Herald* in the U.S.A. that "the sins of bureaucracy are many and are often more insidious than the overt acts of a dictator".

But tragedies, like comedies, must have their end. In July 1946, the Consul's wife who was in Switzerland with their daughter, learned that he had been released and "completely exonerated" from crimes which had not even been specified.

The Consul of Florence was given a free railway ticket to Stuttgart, where he turned up, without a penny in his pocket, in the same clothes which he had worn thirteen months earlier when he was arrested.

On May 14th 1945 Carlo Steinhäuslin, the Swiss Consul, when he was given the Freedom of the city of Florence, together with Cardinal Dalla Costa and Comnène, said with unaffected simplicity that "there is one more deserving than I who should receive this honour[33]."

Ten years later, on November 19th 1954, the Commune di Firenze voted unanimously, Communists included, to pay their tribute to the Consul of Florence. On March 20th 1955, in the Sala Clemente VII of the Palazzo Vecchio, with all the pomp and pageantry beloved by all Florentines in all times and ages, the Consul received the Freedom of the City he had served so well.

The spontaneous and warm-hearted address which the Mayor of Florence, Professor Giorgio La Pira delivered on that occasion will be found in the Prologue of this chronicle. But there are other remarks which La Pira also made, which deserve to be recorded.

He said: "I have the good fortune and happiness to know Consul Wolf, because he was to us in Florence, a living testimony of human fraternity and courage. In the most dramatic moments of the life of the city, he performed acts of true heroism: and it is for that reason that every party was in agreement in conferring on Consul Wolf the Freedom of the City of Florence; not as an act of courtesy or a piece of diplomatic tact, but as an expression of profound respect for a man who did so many heroic things. Rarely in the history of mankind does one come across people who are prepared to give everything they possess to the point of self-sacrifice.

In doing what he did, Consul Wolf rendered a great service to his own country, that is to say, to the real Germany, and not Nazi Germany. For that reason, the German people should be grateful to him, as the people of Florence are grateful[34]."

A few days after the city honoured her Consul, the physical work of reconstructing the Ponte Santa Trinita began. Sixty thousand working days later, at a cost of £176,000 generously subscribed by Florentines, other Italians, known and unknown donors from all over the world, the new bridge, a beautiful and faithful reconstruction of the old, was opened on March 16th 1958[35]. On October 6th 1961, the head of "Primavera" was found in the Arno.

# NOTES

1 NEITHER THEIR SIDE, NOR OURS

1 Information supplied by Dr Riccardo Gizdulich, one of the leading architects responsible for the reconstruction of the Ponte Santa Trinita. *See also* "La ricostruzione del ponte a S. Trinita" by Riccardo Gizdulich, *Comunita*, No. 51, July 1957, pp. 74–81.

2 *Ibid.* p. 74. Vasari's letter to Cosimo I reads: ". . . sono stato fino ad ora ogni dì seco (con Michelangelo), et aviamo atteso ai disegni del ponte S. ta Trinita, che ci ha rasgionato su assai, che ne porterò memoria di scritti et disegni secondo l'animo suo, con le misure ch'gl'ò portato secondo il sito. . . ." *See also* Carlo L. Ragghianti; *Ponte a Santo Trinita*, Vallecchi, 1948, p. 30, *et seq.*

3 Mary McCarthy, *The Stones of Florence*, Heinemann, 1959, p. 28.

4 Laura Fermi, *Mussolini*, University of Chicago Press, 1961, pp. 360–361.

5 G. Ciano, *Diary 1937–1938*, p. 114, English translation by Andreas Mayor, Methuen, 1952.

6 Max Krell, *Das alles gab es einmal*, Scheffler, Frankfurt-am-Main, 1961, p. 278, *seq.*

7 Bernard Berenson, *Rumour and Reflection*, Constable, London, 1952, p. 214. Arnold Böcklin, 1827–1901, a Swiss-German painter, and Anselm Feuerbach, 1829–80, both lived and painted in Florence.

8 Filippo Bojano, *In the Wake of the Goose-Step*, Cassell, 1944, p. 82. This refers to Hitler's second visit to Florence in October 1940. *See also* Rachel Mussolini, in collaboration with Michael Chinigo, *My Life with Mussolini*, Robert Hale, 1959, pp. 94–95. *See also* Eugen Dollmann, *La Vie Secrete de l'Axe*, Presses de la Cité, Paris, 1957, p. 91 *seq.*, for a general description of Hitler's visit to Florence, and Elizabeth Wiskemann, *The Rome-Berlin Axis*, Oxford University Press, 1949, p. 1100.

9 William Shirer, *The Rise and Fall of the Third Reich*, Secker & Warburg, 1960, p. 248.

Regarding Bernard Rust's visit to Florence, information supplied by Dr Gerhard Wolf. Also Krell, *op. cit.*, pp. 277–8.

2 PLATO'S ADVICE

1 "The worship of Stefan George had assumed the proportions of a cult . . . I owe to George the most profound and influential experience of my personal education. . . ." Rudolf Rahn, *Ruheloses Leben*, Diederichs Verlag, Dusseldorf, 1949, p. 36. Count Claus von Stauffenberg who made an attempt on Hitler's life on July 20th 1944 was also a follower of George's; *see* Walter Goerlitz, *History of the German General Staff 1657–1945*, Praeger, New York, 1961, p. 432. George refused the Presidency of the German Academy of the Third Reich. He left Germany in August 1933 and died in Switzerland in the same year.

2 E. M. Butler, *The Tyranny of Greece over Germany*, Beacon Press, Boston, Mass., 1958, p. 324, where she states: "Even Goethe has suffered from this critic's [Gundolf] monstrous adoration; and George who has not the fourth part of the vitality of Goethe will certainly suffer at least four times as much."

3 *See* Lionel Kochan, *Russia and the Weimar Republic*, Bowes & Bowes, 1954, pp. 127–128. Sir Austen Chamberlain denied any such intention to Streseman.

4 Memorandum written by Dr Paul Lips. For the part played by the Catholic Centre Party *see* Terence Prittie, *Germans Against Hitler*, Hutchinson, 1964, p. 71. Monsignor Kaas assisted at the negotiations of the Concordat signed between Germany and the Vatican in July 1933. He also helped to establish contact between the German Resistance and the Vatican; *see ibid.*, p. 90.

5 Information supplied to the author.

6 Benito Mussolini, *Memoirs 1942–3*, Weidenfeld & Nicolson, 1949, p. 282.

7 David Roxan, and Kenneth Wanstall, *The Jackdaw of Linz*, Cassell, 1964, pp. 109–110.

8 Adolf Hitler, *Table Talk (1941–1944)*, English translation, with Introduction by Professor H. R. Trevor-Roper, Weidenfeld & Nicolson, 1953, p. 688.

3 THE PERFECT CENTRE

1 All quotations unless otherwise indicated are from Dr Wolf to the author.

2 Signora Maria Comberti, a prominent Florentine Quaker, is the secretary of "Amici dei Friends". She is also the cofounder of the "Movimento per la Nonviolenza" in Perugia.

3 Miss Hutton to the author.

4 Information supplied to the author.

4 SALUS REPUBLICAE

1 Dollmann, *op cit.*, p. 220. *See also* Wilhelm Hoettl, *The Secret Front*, Weidenfeld &

Nicolson, 1953, p. 231. I am indebted to Dr Eugen Haas, a former secretary at the German Embassy in Rome and Fasano for additional information.

2 Berenson, *op cit.*, p. 124.

3 Charles F. Delzell, *Mussolini's Enemies, the Italian, Anti-Fascist Resistance*, Princeton University Press, N.Y., 1961, p. 239, quoting Pietro Badoglio *Italy in the Second World War*, Oxford University Press, 1948, pp. 61–62.

4 T. L. Gardini, *Towards a New Italy*, with preface by H. G. Wells, Drummond, 1943, p. 67.

5 Delzell, *op cit.*, pp. 30–32 and pp. 158–160. The Rossellis were assassinated in June 1937.

6 A full and authoritative account had been given by Professor Carlo Frankovich, a notable Resister, in his book *La Resistenza a Firenze*, La Nuova Italia, Florence, 1961.

7 *Ibid.*, p. 26.

8 Berenson, *op cit.*, p. 134.

9 Raffaele Guariglia, *La Diplomatie Difficile*, Librairie Plon, Paris, 1955, pp. 346–347.

10 *Ibid.*, p. 347 and p. 288.

11 *Ibid.*, p. 348.

12 Rahn, *op cit.*, p. 228. Guariglia, a far from friendly witness, admitted that Dr Rahn did all he could to improve Italo-German relations in the few days available to him before the Armistice; *see* Guariglia *op cit.*, p. 348.

13 Rahn, *op cit.*, p. 239. Also information supplied to the author. There have Leen conflicting opinions about Rudolf Rahn's attitude towards the Nazis. Elizabeth Wiskemann, *op cit.*, p. 330, described him as "a relatively mild Nazi who succeeded in taking his job seriously. He occasionally protested to Sauckel about the drain of Italian labour to Germany and he occasionally protested over German looting of Italian works of art. But he was not much less futile than Mackensen and he could not stem the tide of the New Order which lashed across Italy." F. W. Deakin, *The Brutal Friendship*, Weidenfeld & Nicolson, 1962, p. 514, gives a fuller estimate: "He was a ductile Rhinelander, determined under a genial manner, full of ideas and imagination, a shrewd politician with a sharp legal mind." (*See also* p. 619, footnote 81, where Deakin gives Ribbentrop's estimate of Rahn. According to Dr Wolf, the Ambassador was fully acquainted with his work in Florence "which without Dr Rahn would have been impossible". From the incomplete research which I have been able to make in various archive sources, it appears that Dr Rahn may have over-estimated his chances and possibilities in making the Nazis amenable to his policy in Italy. He showed

commendable courage and intelligence in his attempts to frustrate Sauckel's raids on Italian labour and in the "solution" of the Jewish Question in Italy.

14 *See* Mario Roatta, *Otto Milioni di Baionette*, Mondadori, Milan, 1946, pp. 286, 289, 291. Deakin, *op. cit.*, p. 513 (footnote g) confirms Roatta's ignorance of the Lisbon negotiations. According to Kesselring (*Memoirs*, Kimber, 1953, p. 171), "Roatta's struggles for military requirements, if dexterous, as far as I could see were above board. I liked working with him because he was the only person who now and then assumed responsibility for something. Even today I am not at all clear in my mind whether the general condemnation of Roatta as an enemy and a traitor was justified." Roatia was indicted as a war criminal by the Yugoslav Government and brought to trial in November 1944. He escaped and vanished on March 3rd 1945.

15 Deakin, *op. cit.*, pp. 529–530.

16 For Guariglia's version, *op. cit.*, p. 359. Rahn alters this in some particulars, *op. cit.*, p. 229.

5 FUGITIVE FROM THE WINNING SIDE

1 Fascist Party Secretary, head of the provincial *Fasci*, responsible to the Party Secretary, at this time, Alessandro Pavolini. On the role of the *Federale*, *see* H. Finer, *Mussolini's Italy*, Frank Cass, 1964, pp. 355–357.

2 Dr Wolf to the author.

3 Berenson, *op. cit.*, p. 135.

4 Miss Mariano to author. *See also* Sylvia Sprigge, *Berenson, A Biography*, Allen & Unwin, 1960, p. 251, where she wrote: "For the Berensons all now depended on Dr Gerhard Wolf, the German Consul. By then the German army had descended in force into Tuscany, and Berenson was already in hiding two miles away as the crow flies from 'I Tatti'".

5 Marchesa Gilberta Serlupi to the author.

6 Berenson, *op. cit.*, p. 138.

7 *Ibid.*, p. 53

8 Frankovich, *op. cit.*, p. 64; *see also* Iris Origo, *War in the Val D'Oreia*, Cape, 1947, p. 83.

9 Marchese Blasco Lanza d'Ajeta, head of Ciano's secretariate, who was one of Badoglio's emissaries in Lisbon (Deakin, *op. cit.*, p. 502). He was also Sumner Welles's cousin according to Wiskemann, *op. cit.*, p. 202.

10 Origo, *op. cit.*, p. 106, where she notes that hostages had been taken as reprisals to protect Fascists arrested in southern Italy—"But if so, it is difficult to understand why most of the people arrested have been let out, after only a week or ten days in prison." Marchesa Origo

was not as yet aware of Consul Wolf's efforts to secure these releases. Later she herself turned to him for assistance.

6 THE CYPRESSES

1 Origo, *op. cit.*, p. 96.

2 Information supplied to the author.

3 Letters to Dr Rahn, December 11th, 14th 1943.

4 Some 1500 Carabinieri officers and men were disarmed and deported to Germany after the occupation of Rome in September 1943. *See* Delzell, *op. cit.*, p. 275.

The Consul was protesting about the treatment meted out to the Carabinieri as late as June 1944. In a letter (June 17th 1944) sent to him by a Captain J. Hoppe, the latter stated: "Unfortunately, the problem of the Carabinieri, which was so clearly recognised by you, has taken the course we had predicted but could not longer prevent". Captain Hoppe was writing on behalf of Lt.-Col. Jandl. Regarding Jandle, *see* Deakin, *op. cit.*, p. 607 *et passim.*

7 CARITÀ

1 Frankovich, *op. cit.*, pp. 87–89.

2 *Ibid.*, p. 87.

3 Dr Wolf to E. F. Moellhausen, October 21st 1943. The Consul exaggerated the Corsinis' "pro-German" attitude.

4 According to the former Italian chief of Police Dollmann and Kappler had "a cordial reciprocal aversion" to each other. *See* Carmine Senise, *Quando ero capo della polizia 1940–1943*, Ruffolo, Rome, 1946, p. 272.

5 Information supplied to the author.

6 Letter to Dr Rahn, November 8th 1943.

7 Letter to Dr Rahn, November 17th 1943.

8 Some 400 Allied prisoners of war were rescued by the Partito d'Azione's commission to which Cav. Pretini belonged, among them one hundred British soldiers and officers; Frankovich, *op. cit.*, p. 91; also Origo, *op. cit.*, p. 13, states that some 70,000 Allied prisoners were at large in Italy on September 8th 1943, of whom nearly half escaped.

9 Cav. Pretini made his testimony available to the author.

10 Frankovich, *op. cit.*, p. 98. Padre Ildefonso's lay name was Epaminonda Troia.

11 Information supplied to the author.

12 Dr Wolf's memorandum to Dr Rahn, May 11th 1944.

13 *Una Lotta Nel Suo Corso*, edited by Contini Bonacossi and C. L. Ragghianti, Neri Poza, Venice, 1954, p. 330. Professor Ciampini continued to listen to the Allied radio and transmit the news, as well as aiding Jews

through the Convent of San Marco.

8 BERENSON AND OTHERS

1 Dr Rahn's intervention on behalf of the Jewish population in Tunis where he served as political adviser to the Wehrmacht (end of 1942 to May 1943) may be worth noting. According to one testimony in the records of the Quaderni del Centro di Documentazione Ebraica Contemporanea, Milan, "Through the intervention of Rahn, the Tunisian Jews were exempted from being placed under the jurisdiction of the Gestapo. Whilst the women, children, old people and the disabled were left in peace, the men capable of work were incorporated into special detachments which were directly dependent on the Wehrmacht and were assigned to various army detachments."

Dr Ernst Heinitz, one of the Jewish representatives in Florence during the Consul's tenure, stated that his close co-operation with Dr Wolf in dealing with individual cases would have been "impossible" but for Dr Rahn's assistance.

Another interesting sidelight on Rahn's attitude to "the Jewish problem" is given by Baron Hasso von Etzdorf. On his arrival as Consul-General in Genoa early in 1945, he was told by Rahn that he was opposed to Hitler's anti-semitic policy and that he (Etzdorf) should do everything to oppose it. Rahn himself knew that this would lead to "constant friction with the S.S." but he accepted this.

2 According to Philip Friedman, *Their Brothers' Keepers*, Crown Publishers, New York, 1957, p. 72, Mussolini had declared in 1924 that antisemitism was "an alien weed that cannot strike roots in Italy". A year after Hitler's accession to power, Mussolini said: "Thirty centuries enable us to face with sovereign pity some of the theories now popular beyond the Alps and supported by men whose ancestors ignored the art of writing."

3 *See* Renzo de Felice, *Storia degli ebrei italiani sotto il fascismo*, Einaudi, Turin, 1961, p. 512.

4 Dr Rahn to the author. Mussolini's "sovereign pity" however melted under pressure from the Nazis when antisemitic measures were introduced in Italy in October 1938.

5 According to Friedmann, *op. cit.*, p. 74, some 40,000 Jewish lives were saved in Italy, although 15,000 persons perished. The much-maligned General Mario Roatta declared that "he would not dishonour the Italian colours by trafficking in the lives of innocent Jews". (*Ibid.*, p. 75.)

There was little love lost between Preziosi and Buffarini whom the former accused of being "the friend of Jews and Freemasons" (Deakin, *op. cit.*, p. 620). Colonel Jandl who reported on the Duce's activities wrote: "One group centres round the sly Minister of the Interior, Buffarini, who looks like a Jewish cattle-dealer . . ." (*ibid.*, pp. 622–623). Despite all the intrigues to get rid of Buffarini, he was dismissed only in February 1945. According to Dr Eugen Haas, one of the secretaries at the German Embassy in Fasano, Preziosi's name brought "bad luck" each time it was mentioned. On one such occasion Dr Haas counted as many as "twelve punctures in the tyres of Embassy cars". Preziosi nevertheless continued to fulminate against the "traitors" of Salo over Munich Radio, until he was rewarded with the post of Minister of State. (Deakin, p. 623).

6 Berenson, *op. cit.*, p. 138.

7 Frankovich, *op. cit.*, p. 110.

8 Berenson, *op. cit.*, p. 139.

9 Text of this letter dated June 18th 1944 is quoted on p. 18.

10 Military Plenipotentiary (*see* Deakin, *op. cit.*, pp. 618–619).

11 Information supplied to the author by Dr Heinitz, later Rector of the Free University of Berlin (1962–1963); Prorector (1964–1965).

12 "There was little else they could give. We did not ask nor require such kindness," Monsignore Meneghello told the author when the latter visited him in October 1960. There is much corroborative evidence on the Catholic Church's assistance to the Jews (Berenson, Origo and others), but for a more general picture, *see The Catholic Church and Persecuted Jewry, 1939–45: A Survey of Contemporary Press Reports*, Wiener Library Bulletin, No. 1, Vol. XVIII, January, 1964, written by Olga Abrahams. *See also* Guenter Lewy, *The Catholic Church and Nazi Germany*, Weidenfeld & Nicolson, 1964.

13 Origo, *op. cit.*, p. 132. *See also* Berenson, *op. cit.*, p. 218, where he states: "The other day a parish priest of the diocese was arrested for harbouring a Jew. The Cardinal of Florence intervened, declaring that he himself was the culprit and requesting to be jailed in place of the priest; which, of course, resulted in the liberation of the prisoner."

14 Cardinal Dalla Costa to the author, October 1960. The Cardinal died on December 22nd 1961.

15 Affidavit, dated January 1st 1946, signed by the Superior, Sister M. Agatha.

16 Affidavit signed by Franz von Hoesslin, Geneva, May 7th 1946.

## 9 SHOP-WINDOW ON THE WORLD

1 Deakin *op. cit.*, p. 512. The main defensive plans had been drawn up by Rommel and Jodl and discussed between Roatta, Rommel and Jodl at Bologna on August 15th 1943.

2 *Ibid.*, pp. 560–561. Neither Rahn nor Kesselring were in favour of the "neo-Fascist experiment". Rahn, however, had been over-ruled by both Hitler and Mussolini. According to Kesselring *op. cit.*, p. 190: "I gradually came to the conclusion that the conduct of the war in Italy would have been easier and more effective without the intermediary of an unpopular government—this being really the only question on which there was any basic difference of opinion between the German embassy and the military."

3 Nuremberg Trial Documents, Supplementary volume B, pp. 1675–6. Quoted by Deakin *op. cit.*, p. 619 (footnote h).

4 Rahn, *op. cit.*, p. 261.

5 G. Dolfin, *Con Mussolini nella tragedia (Diario del Capo della Segreteria Particolare del Duce 1943–4)*, p. 50. For Mussolini's tribute to Rahn *see* Deakin, *op. cit.*, p. 595.

6 Rahn to the author.

7 Frankovich, *op. cit.*, p. 102.

8 Dr Wolf's report, January 30th 1944.

9 Frankovich, *op. cit.*, pp. 102–103.

10 Kesselring, *op. cit.*, p. 224.

11 Aimone, Duke of Spoleto (1900–1948), nephew of the Italian King, became Duke of Aosta in 1942 on the death of his brother Amedeo in Eritrea. He was offered the "crown" of Croatia by Pavelic, the Croatian Quisling, but never took up residence in his "kingdom". Captain, and later Admiral, in the Italian Navy, he escaped to the King's Italy in September 1943. According to a *Manchester Guardian* report of September 29th 1943, he arrived at an advanced Mediterranean base aboard a private yacht escorted by an Italian destroyer. He said: "I must stress how happy I am to be cut off from the Germans. We look now to the Allies that the covenants of our agreement and our interests may be protected."

12 Professor Karl Gebhard (1898–1948), hanged for experiments in gas gangrene, July 2nd 1948. Professor H. R. Trevor-Roper, *The Last Days of Hitler*, Macmillan, pp. 74–75, states that Gebhard was universally regarded as Himmler's evil genius, concealing his intrigues behind the innocent cloak of medicine.

13 Farinacci, former Fascist Party secretary. *See Deakin, op. cit.*, p. 422, footnote b. Berenson, *op. cit.*, pp. 247–248, makes the interesting observation in his diary entry of February 25th

1944: "It seems that the Nazi authorities have ordered the present Duchess of Aosta to quit Florence and to go where she wished, provided it was safe from the Allied occupation. She protested that she did not want to leave. They have allowed her to remain for the present, warning her, however, that at the next summons she might have no more than one hour to get ready in.

"Why? The only explanation that occurs to me—the explanation offered by the person who reported this piece of news—is that the Nazis want to keep firm hold on the baby the Duchess had some months ago. Consequently, in case of victory they would not countenance the resurrected regime of Mussolini and his republic, but restore the monarchy in the person of this infant of the Aosta branch. They could then rule Italy through men of straw who acted as regents. In that case the dowager Duchess of Aosta—author, I believe, of many of our woes—would at last be able to sing *Nunc Dimittis*. She would have seen the ambitions of a lifetime, the plotting of many decades, brought safe to port and crowned with success."

L. Villari, *The Liberation of Italy*, 1943–47, Nelson, Appelton, Wisconsin, 1959, p. 130, claims that the dowager Duchess of Aosta refused to meet British generals at her villa at Capodimonte on the outskirts of Naples because of the ill-treatment alleged to have been accorded to her son Amedeo, the Duke of Aosta, defender of Italian East Africa, as he lay dying in a Kenya hospital. This account should probably be treated with some reserve. According to a Swiss report quoted by Reuter (*see Evening Standard*, December 22nd 1944) "a new monarchist party has been founded in German-occupied Italy by Piero Narini, former Governor of Milan Province. This party does not support the Savoy-Carignano line, of which Victor Emmanuel is the head, but the Savoy-Aosta line." This was surprising since the two duchesses and their children had been taken in July 1944 first to a castle in Turin and later removed to Dachau.

14 According to Senise, *op. cit.*, p. 275, who met the two duchesses and their children in Dachau, they had not deserted Florence nor "its people in time of its need...." They were "like rays of sunshine in the dark days of autumn...." Dachau was liberated by French forces on May 1st 1945.

15 There was no sinister implication in this demand. The Consul asked for the 10,000 lire in order to replace a bicycle which had been stolen from one of the musicians playing with

the Florence Municipal Orchestra!

16 Stefan George, *Poems*, rendered into English by Carol North Valhope and Ernst Morwitz, Pantheon, New York, 1943, p. 193.

10 YOUR MAJESTY

1 Dollmann, *op. cit.*, p. 214. Hitler's hatred for the Bavarian Royal House dated from November 9th 1923, when his so-called *Munich Putsch* came to an abrupt end. Some three thousand *Kampfbund* rowdies and officer cadets marched to the Odeonsplatz with Hitler and Ludendorff at their head but were dispersed by the police. Hitler, Ludendorff and others were tried. Ludendorff was acquitted, but Hitler was sentenced to five years imprisonment of which he served only nine months in the fortress of Landsberg, where he dictated much of *Mein Kampf*. *See* Alan Bullock, *Hitler, A Study in Tyranny*, Odhams, 1952, pp. 85–101.

2 Dr Wolf's memorandum dated January 17th 1944 to First Secretary Bock.

3 For Zenone Benini's account see his *Virgilia a Verona*, Garzanti, 1949. According to Senise, *op. cit.*, p. 206, both Benini and Polverelli, the Minister of Popular Culture, had declared their fidelity to the King. This did not prevent Polverelli from voting against the Grandi motion at the meeting of the Grand Council, July 24th 1943.

4 Deakin, *op. cit.*, p. 637, footnote f. Dollmann, *op. cit.*, p. 181, however, claimed that Dr Rahn urged Mussolini to kill his son-in-law!

5 Dr Rahn to the author.

6 Sir Ivone Kirkpatrick: *Mussolini, Study of a Demagogue*, Odhams, London, 1964, pp. 575–576.

7 Dolfin, *op. cit.*, p. 230.

8 Dr Wolf wrote: "In a private letter to the Ambassador on February 1st, I enquired about the Marchese Emilio Pucci. I then reminded Fräulein Neugebauer (the Ambassador's secretary) by telephone and by letter, but I am still without a reply."

9 Dr Rahn has no recollection of the Pucci incident (information to the author), nor was Marchese Pucci aware of the Consul's efforts on his behalf (communication to the author). Later, in October 1944, the Consul's wife saw Edda Ciano and Pucci driving around Lausanne in a white sports car. Today, Marchese Pucci is one of Florence's leading dress designers and a Liberal (right-wing) member of parliament. *See also* Roman Dombrowski, *Mussolini; Twilight and Fall*, Heinemann, 1956, pp. 124–125 for Pucci's account.

10 *See* Origo, *op. cit.*, pp. 192–193, where she describes Professor Heydenreich as "a gentle, cultivated human being", and his efforts to preserve Florence's art treasures.

11 Dr Wolf to the author.

12 *L'Osservatore Romano*, February 14th 1944, quoted by P. Duclos, *Le Vatican et La Seconde Guerre Mondiale*, Pedone, Paris, 1955, p. 146. General Sir Terence Airey, discussing war damage in Italy in a private communication to the author, stated: "I think that Cassino was the one Allied lapse in this respect although one can understand the pressure to destroy it when one recalls the misery of the troops on that mountainside throughout the winter. It (the Abbey) seemed to look threateningly from its black windows across all the exposed allied positions on the open hillside and one ran for shelter when one found oneself suddenly exposed to its view. It stood in the centre of immensely strong German positions and the fire seemed to come from all round it and it must have seemed to the troops to have been the source of all their miseries and the colossal casualties". General Sir Terence Airey was chief of intelligence at Allied Headquarters in Italy at this time.

13 Kesselring, *op. cit.*, p. 309.

14 Origo, *op. cit.*, pp. 137–138.

15 According to Dr Rahn his meetings with Sauckel belonged to "some of the most painful and sad experiences of my political life". (Rahn, *op. cit.*, p. 196.) Graziani was also opposed to Sauckel's demands, which depleted his own army reserves: Deakin, *op. cit.*, p. 699.

16 *Il Ponte*, September 1954, p. 1473, in an article by Professor Carlo Frankovich, "La Stampa a Firenze dall' armistizio alla liberazione".

11 THE HOUSE OF SORROW

1 E. Dollmann, *Roma Nazista*, Longanesi, 1951, pp. 282–283.

2 Dr Wolf's memorandum to the Ambassador, May 11th 1944.

3 Affidavit signed by Signor Danilo de Micheli, Florence, January 8th 1946.

4 Former S.S. General Karl Wolff to the author, July 1961.

5 Avv. Boniforti to the author.

6 Berenson, *op. cit.*, p. 263.

7 First Lt. Benjamin C. McCartney, *Return to Florence*, The National Geographic Magazine, Vol. LXXXVII, No. 3, March 1945, p. 257.

8 Berenson, *op. cit.*, p. 268.

9 Resistance pamphlet reproduced by N. P. Comnène: *Firenze, "Città Aperta"*, Vallecchi, Firenze, 1945, facsimile opposite p. 57.

10 *Berenson, op. cit.*, p. 274.

11 *See The Prince and Other Pieces from the Italian of Nicolò*

*Machiavelli: with an introduction by Henry Morley*, Routledge, 1888, pp. 158–164.

12 Comnène, *op. cit.*, pp. 29–30.

13 *Ibid.*, p. 31.

14 *Ibid.*, p. 14.

15 The distinguished member of the Fascist Party to whom Dr Wolf referred was Mirko Giobbi, the editor of *La Nazione*. *See* Dr Wolf's letter to Rahn quoted on p. 146.

16 H. G. Wells, *Crux Ansata: An Indictment of the Catholic Church*, Penguin Books, 1943.

17 Kesselring, *op. cit.*, p. 225, states: "Partisan bands began to be a nuisance in and on both sides of the Appenines for the first time in April 1944, being most active in the region of Florence, where, as their presence jeopardised our supplies, military counter-measures were required." Further he asserts (*ibid.*, p. 228) that "the proportion of casualties on the German side alone exceeded the total Partisan losses".

18 *Ibid.*, p. 299.

19 Admiral Canaris, head of the Abwehr, German military intelligence, implicated in the plot against Hitler, July 1944. He made contact with the Consul through his righthand man General Oster and Dr von Dohnanyi.

12 THE GENTLE PROFESSOR

1 Berenson, *op. cit.*, p. 235.

2 Dr Wolf's letter to the Ambassador, May 27th 1944.

3 Berenson, *op. cit.*, p. 265. Origo, *op. cit.*, p. 166, calls Gentile's assassination, "A mean and despicable crime, worthy of those committed on the other side, and an instance of the blind party hatred by which this unhappy country is torn". *See also* Frankovich, *op. cit.*, p. 187, *seq.* on details of murder and reactions. For Gentile's influence on Fascist ideology *see* Dante L. Germino, *The Italian Fascist Party in Power*, Minnesota Press, 1959, p. 134.

4 Dr Wolf to Professor Prinzing, April 22nd 1944.

5 Gaetano Casoni, *Diario fiorentino*, Firenze, 1946, pp. 169–170. Villari, *op. cit.*, p. 119, (footnote), on the other hand claims that the assassination was "suggested" by the B.B.C. and Bari radio. According to this version Gentile was killed on his way from the Prefecture where he had gone to plead for some anti-Fascist professors who had recently been arrested. In fact, the professors were arrested *after* Gentile's murder.

6 Berenson, *op. cit.*, p. 265.

7 Professor Bandinelli's affidavit, Rome, December 18th 1945.

8 Orazio Barbieri, *Ponte sull 'Arno*, Reuniti, Rome, 1958, pp. 161–162. For the Action Party's disavowal of any responsibility or approval of Gentile's murder

*see* Frankovich, *op. cit.*, Appendix I, pp. 295–296.

13 POSTSCRIPT

1 *See* Graziani's report at the Klessheim conference between Hitler and Mussolini on April 22nd 1944, where he stated: "Although 100,000 men had come in, there were still many slackers. For that reason the death penalty had had to be introduced, not only for deserters, but also for those who sought to avoid service." Deakin, *op. cit.*, p. 683. S.S. General Karl Wolff added that "in the valleys infested by the partisans, good results had been achieved by deporting the entire male population". *Ibid.*, p. 684.

2 The Consul was trying to make out as good a case as he could. He was still aware that the entire Coletti family was anti-Fascist.

3 Frankovich, *op. cit.*, p. 194.

4 The clandestine paper *Il Popolo*, July 18th 1944, quoted by Frankovich, *op. cit.*, p. 195.

5 Deakin, *op. cit.*, p. 622, quoting Colonel Jandl's report, December 1943.

6 Dr Rahn to the author.

7 Deakin, *op. cit.*, pp. 660–661.

8 *Ibid.*, p. 661, footnote d.

9 Dr Wolf to the author.

10 Dr Wolf's report May 11th 1944.

11 Origo, *op. cit.*, p. 179.

12 Dr Kiel to the author.

13 Dr Wolf's memorandum, May 9th 1944.

14 THE ORDER OF HUMANITY

1 *The British Year Book of International Law*, 1945, Oxford University Press, pp. 260–261.

2 *See* Kesselring, *op. cit.*, p. 203 and p. 309. According to Delzell, *op. cit.*, p. 385: "The Germans made no effort to fight for Rome, despite orders from Hitler to defend the city until the last German had left it and to blow up the bridges across the Tiber. Marshal Kesselring saw no valid military reason for trying to retain possession of the city and decided as early as May 16th not to blow up the bridges. Because there had been very few German combat troops in the city since the previous autumn, he faced no great danger in evacuating the few who were there." Nevertheless Kesselring made great play with the loss of 10,000 of his troops to the Americans, in later statements to the Consul and Dr Rahn.

3 General Alexander (Earl Alexander of Tunis), Allied Commander-in-Chief, Italy, *London Gazette*, *op cit.*, p. 2929, (footnote) stated: "The German offer to declare Rome an open city belongs rather to a history of propaganda than to a military history. The offer was broadcast at a time when Allied troops were already on the outskirts of the city following hard on the

heels of the enemy retreating through it. In the circumstances the enemy undertaking "to carry out no troop movements in Rome" was both belated and insincere. The most significant point about this announcement is that it showed the Germans had not expected Rome to fall so soon."

4 Berenson, *op. cit.*, p. 287.

5 Frankovich, *op. cit.*, p. 156.

6 *Ibid.*, p. 222.

7 Information supplied to the author by Enzo Enriques Agnoletti.

8 *Ibid.*

9 Frankovich, *op. cit.*, p. 236.

10 Berenson, *op. cit.*, p. 291.

11 *Ibid.*, p. 281.

12 F. Hartt, *Florentine Art Under Fire*, Princeton University Press, 1949, p. 20. Dr Hartt, now Chairman of the Department of Art of the University of Pennsylvania, received the honorary citizenship of the City of Florence on February 25th 1946 for his efforts to recover and restore Florentine art and monuments during and after the war.

13 *Ibid.*, p. 21.

14 Berenson, *op. cit.*, pp. 299–300.

15 Secret memorandum, June 21st 1944. The directive was circulated on June 23rd down to divisional level of the 14th Army commanded by General of Artillery Joachim Lemelsen who was responsible for the overall defences of Florence. On July 5th Kesselring's Chief of Staff reiterated the order that "the character of the open city" was to be preserved and the 9th Battalion of military police entered the city to enforce the order.

16 Berenson, *op. cit.*, p. 313.

17 *Ibid.*, p. 347.

18 Casoni, *op. cit.*, p. 36 and pp. 65–73.

19 Hartt, *op. cit.*, p. 21.

20 Dr Rahn obtained this concession from Hitler during one of his many excursions to Führer Headquarters in November 1943, probably on or around November 22nd, ten days after he had obtained Hitler's "unofficial" declaration of Florence's open city status. (*See* Chapter 9.) On the later date, Hitler agreed that the Cassino art treasures which included the abbey's famous library, manuscripts and incunabula, together with the collection of the Naples National Museum which had also been stored at Cassino, should be handed over to the Vatican for safe-keeping. On his return to Fasano, Rahn was informed by Eugen Haas, one of the Embassy's secretaries, that he had received an urgent call from Barracu, an Italian under-secretary of State, telling him that the Herman Goering S.S. Division had removed these works of art to Spoleto, with the intention of moving them to

Germany. Rahn then expressed his anger and immediately contacted Hitler by telephone who confirmed that the Cassino art treasures should be handed to the Vatican. A few days later, Dr Haas attended the handing over ceremony with General Mälzer, the German commandant of Rome. Mälzer remarked jokingly: "Thus Napoleon took away the art treasures from Rome: Mälzer returns them!" Some forty or fifty lorries arrived with the Cassino and Naples art treasures in the courtyard of the Castello Sant' Angelo which were ceremoniously handed over to Vatican representatives, in the presence of the Abbot of Monte Cassino. The whole proceedings were filmed and broadcast, and a little later an exhibition of these art treasures was shown in the Palazzo Venezia. Dr Rahn believed (erroneously) that this handing over ceremony occurred "two days before the great bombing attacks on Monte Cassino", but since the monastery was bombed and reduced to ruins on February 15th 1944, this was clearly impossible. The more likely date of December 10th 1943 is given by Fred Majdalany, *Cassino, A Portrait of a Battle*, Longmans, 1952, p. 52, where he quotes from Miss Scrivener's diary. And Alberto Giovanetti, *Roma Città Aperta*, Ancora, Milan, 1962. Rahn himself received scant recognition for his efforts to preserve the Cassino treasures. Kesselring, *op. cit.*, p. 308, claimed that these were handed over to the Vatican at his orders.

21 Berenson's diary entry of July 6th 1944 reads: "Soon after last midnight, two officers sent by Marshal Kesselring woke the Cardinal-Archbishop of Florence with an imperatively urgent request. It was to get into a car and rush to Rome, there to get a promise of the Allies that they would not occupy Florence, or even pass through it, but treat it as an open city as by the Germans defined."

22 E. Dollmann, *Call Me Coward*, Kimber, 1952, pp. 62–63.

23 Kesselring's letter to the Cardinal is quoted by Comnène, *op. cit.*, pp. 71–72.

24 Frankovich, *op. cit.*, p. 236 and pp. 239–240.

25 Berenson, *op. cit.*, p. 308.

## 15 THE JEWEL OF EUROPE

1 Berenson, *op. cit.*, p. 313.

2 Kesselring, *op. cit.*, pp. 207-209.

3 Delzell, *op. cit.*, p. 401.

4 Frankovich, *op. cit.*, pp. 236–237.

5 Casoni, *op. cit.*, p. 102 seq.

6 *Ibid.*, pp. 129–130.

7 In an affidavit signed by Avv. Giancarlo Zoli, Florence, January 7th 1946, he stated that

Consul Wolf was well known in anti-fascist circles as "a moderate man and an adversary of the excesses of the Nazi regime". Further, "I know for certain that Consul Wolf made every effort in my favour when I was arrested and detained as a hostage".

8 Frankovich, *op. cit.*, pp. 173–174, and pp. 242–243. Barbara Barclay Carter, *Italy Speaks*, Gollancz, 1947, p. 113, mentions the three Englishwomen rescued in this operation.

9 Affidavit signed by Dr Ernst Heinitz, January 3rd 1946.

10 Kesselring, *op. cit.*, p. 308, claimed that this villa was "excluded from the defence zone at my direct order".

11 Berenson, *op. cit.*, pp. 319–320.

12 "We had an extraordinary fear of Dollmann. He himself later asserted that he had prevented Carità's cruelties." (Dr Heinitz in a communication to the author.) Dr Wolf stated that Dollmann "was helpful in minor matters" but made no reference to his efforts to control Carità. *See* p. 128.

13 Frankovich, *op. cit.*, pp. 244–246.

14 Dr Kiel to the author.

15 Hartt, *op. cit.*, pp. 33–34.

16 *Ibid.*, p. 34.

17 Dr Wolf only knew of *one* missing Cranach (reported to him after the war). The two panels were recovered from an Austrian gaol, shortly after the end of the war, together with most of the paintings from Montagnana, a number of which are still missing. (Hartt, *op. cit.*, p. 104 seq.).

18 Information supplied to the author by General Sir Oliver Leese. According to Clement Attlee (then Deputy Prime Minister, now Earl Attlee): "I think that if Alexander had been allowed to go on in Italy, he would have joined hands with the Yugoslavs and moved across Czechoslovakia and perhaps right over Germany before the Russians got there." (Francis Williams, *A Prime Minister Remembers*, Heinemann, 1961, p. 51.)

19 Ernest Percy Schramm, *OKW War Diary*, Bernard and Graefe Verlag, Frankfurt-on-Main, 1961, Vol. IV, first "half volume", pp. 533–536.

20 Deakin, *op. cit.*, p. 711.

16 *STATUE DE SAXE*

1 Supplement to the *London Gazette*, p. 2939. The Allied and German order of battle at the end of August was substantially the same before Florence. *See ibid.*, p. 2960. The Germans fielded twenty-five divisions, supported by two Italian Republican Divisions, the Allies had twenty Divisions. *See also* Delzell, *op. cit.*, p. 408.

2 Hartt, *op. cit.*, p. 58 and p. 61.

3 General Frido von Senger und Etterlin, *Neither Fear nor Hope*, translated from the German by George Malcolm, Macdonald, 1963, pp. 265–269.

4 Dr Rahn cabled Kaltenbrunner, head of the Berlin Gestapo, stating that he knew Adam Trott zu Solz, one of the Resisters arrested after the July Plot, "personally" and that he was convinced of his "innocence". This was an act of considerable courage on Rahn's part. (Information supplied to the author by Frau Dr Trott zu Solz, July 1961.)

5 Princess Antonia was subjected to "vile treatment at the hands of the Nazi torturers. James Donohoe, *Hitler's Conservative Opponents in Bavaria, 1930–1945*, Brill, Leiden, 1961, p. 144.

6 Information supplied to the author.

7 Casoni, *op. cit.*, p. 167.

8 Information given by Dr Hanna Kiel. The Consul has only an indefinite recollection of the events described on pp. 205–206.

9 Hitler's orders to Kesselring given on July 19th 1944 that the Florentine bridges should not be destroyed, still stood (*see* Schramm's OKW Diary, *op. cit.*

10 Carlo Steinhäuslin, *Che Cosa Ho Fatto Per Firenze*, p. 1 and appendix note 1. This private diary covers the period between July 27th 1944 and August 24th 1944, and provides an invaluable record of the days preceding and following the liberation of Florence.

11 Comnène, *op. cit.*, p. 45, Casoni, *op. cit.*, p. 208.

12 Steinhäuslin, *op. cit.*, p. 5. Also Nicky Mariano, "A Month with the Paratroopers in the Front Line", diary entry for July 29th 1944. (For the Italian version of this diary *see Il Ponte*, No. 9, September 1954.)

13 Frankovich, *op. cit.*, p. 359 (appendix notes).

14 *Ibid.*, pp. 251–252.

15 Comnène, *op. cit.*, p. 45. For the visit of the two German majors to Comnène, *ibid.*, pp. 43–44.

16 Information supplied to the author.

17 Casoni, *op. cit.*, p. 158.

18 Hartt, *op. cit.*, pp. 67–68.

19 Baroness Theo Fraunberg, the wife of Crown Prince Rupprecht's adjutant, reported this information to Mrs Wolf. The Partisans in question were probably the "Fiamma Verde", belonging to the Christian Democratic Party, with pro-Monarchist leanings.

20 Affidavit signed by Alessandro de Taberelli, January 1946. The Consul first met him in Bolzano in September 1943 where the young law student was hiding from the German authorities.

17 OPERATION *FEUERZAUBER*

1 Winston S. Churchill, *The Second World War: Triumph and Tragedy*, Vol. VI, Cassel, 1954, p. 94, "considerable efforts were made by both sides to destroy as little as possible".

2 Supplement to the *London Gazette*, p. 2945.

3 *Ibid.*, p. 2960. Also *Manchester Guardian* leader, August 12th 1944 stated: "Although helped by the mountains and by the narrowness of the front, Kesselring's defence in Italy will not go unpraised by military historians."

4 Hartt, *op. cit.*, p. 34. *See also* chapter 15, appendix note 17.

5 *Ibid.*, pp. 58–59.

6 Casoni, *op. cit.*, p. 191.

7 Steinhäuslin diary, *op. cit.*, p. 4.

8 Hartt, *op. cit.*, p. 40, quoting from a report by Professor Ugo Procacci, Superintendent of the Pitti, now Superintendent of all Florentine and provincial art galleries.

9 Comnène, *op. cit.*, p. 51. Frankovich, *op. cit.*, p. 262 gives the figure of 150,000 persons.

10 Nicky Mariano's diary, *op. cit*. It should be noted, however, that the order to evacuate the two sides of the Lungarni had been given by the German command twenty-four hours *before* General Alexander's "Special Message" had been thrown on Florence. The Message had been broadcast by the B.B.C. on July 29th and disseminated by the R.A.F. on Sunday. The message emanated from the Psychological Warfare Branch at AFHQ, which coordinated the joint directives of the Office of War Information (American) and the Psychological Warfare Executive (British) with the propaganda plans of the Supreme Allied Commander General Eisenhower. Psychological warfare functions at AFHQ were at first charged to Civil Affairs Section, but were transferred to Information, News, and Censorship Section on 5th January 1943.

11 General Alexander's "Special Message" reads:

"The Allied armies are approaching Florence. The liberation of the city is at hand. You, the citizens of Florence, must stand united to prevent your city from destruction and to defeat our common enemies: the Germans and the Fascists.

These instructions come from the Headquarters of General Alexander, the commander-in-chief of all Allied troops in Italy. They are as much in your interests as in the interests of the Allies.

Do all you can to prevent the destruction of your city.

Prevent the enemy from exploding mines which have been placed under bridges, public buildings, plants and other city utilities.

Protect the central telephone and telegraph exchanges and other centres of communication.

Safeguard in your own interest your public services such as water supplies, electrical power supplies and gasometers.

Protect the rail communications, installations and all public transport facilities such as the tramways.

Hide your food stocks from the enemy.

Note where the enemy has placed his mines and booby traps. Indicate their positions to advance allied patrols by saying 'main' and pointing to their positions.

Remove all obstacles, barricades and other obstructions from the streets.

Allow the unimpeded progress of all military vehicles along the streets and through squares.

It is vital for Allied troops to cross Florence without delay in order to complete the destruction of German forces on their retreat northwards.

Citizens of Florence! This is not the time for public demonstrations. Follow these instructions and go about your daily business.

Florence is yours! You have the means to save the city. It is our job to destroy the enemy.

Citizens of Florence, these are your instructions. The future of Florence is in your hands!"

This "message" merely succeeded in promoting the very thing it feared. Partisan forces could hardly have been expected to fight a pitched battle inside the city without reducing it to shambles. Moreover the Germans who were aware of this, forbade not only "demonstrations" but threatened to shoot anyone found in the streets.

12 Casoni, *op. cit.*, p. 206.

13 Steinhäuslin diary, *op. cit.*, p. 5.

14 Comnène, *op. cit.*, p. 49.

15 Casoni, *op. cit.*, p. 208.

16 Hartt, *op. cit.*, p. 40.

17 Casoni, *op. cit.*, p. 210.

18 *See* chapter 9, pp. 93–94. Dr Rahn's meeting with Kesselring is based on notes provided to the author.

19 Schramm, *op. cit.*

20 AOK 14th German Army's war diary, National Archives, Washington D.C. Microcopy T-312, Rolls 476–496.

21 Kurt Bruggisser, *Vorgeschichte der Florentiner Brueckensprengung vom 4 August 1944*, *Neue Zürcher Zeitung*, January 23rd 1945.

22 Kesselring, *op. cit.*, pp. 209–210.

18 THE LAST DEFENDER

1 Comnène, *op. cit.*, p. 55.

2 Hartt, *op. cit.*, pp. 40–41.

3 *Ibid.*, p. 41.

4 Barbieri, *op. cit.*, p. 288.
5 Hartt, *op. cit.*, pp. 16–19. The report was broadcast by the B.B.C. Home and Overseas Services on July 31st 1944.
6 Steinhäuslin diary, *op. cit.*, pp. 8–10.
7 Barbieri, *op. cit.*, pp. 279–281.
8 *Ibid.*, p. 278.
9 Hartt, *op. cit.*, p. 42, quoting Professor Procacci's report.
10 Steinhäuslin diary, p. 11.
11 Casoni, *op. cit.*, p. 220.
12 Schramm, *op. cit.*, p. 536. No confirmation, however, can be found in Allied military records that any shells were directed at the bridges over the Arno. Steinhäuslin's diary, *op. cit.*, p. 15, confirms this. Hartt, *op. cit.*, p. 49, referring to the later period of the Allied liberation of the city also states that: "Not an Allied shell fell in Florence".
13 Steinhäuslin diary, *op. cit.*, p. 13. "Since there was neither men nor equipment to move the statues the arrangements of which Professor Poggi was informed seemed bitterly ironical," according to Professor Procacci. (Information supplied to the author.)
14 Hartt, *op. cit.*, p. 43.

19 REQUIEM FOR A BRIDGE

1 Gladys Hutton, *Il Ponte*, *op. cit.*, p. 1412, in an article "Dieci Anni Dopo".
2 Miss Elliot later heard Nazi propaganda claim that the R.A.F. destroyed the Florentine bridges!
3 Hartt, *op. cit.*, pp. 43–44.
4 Professor Piero Calamandrei, *Il Ponte*, *op. cit.*, p. 1312.
5 *The National Geographic Magazine*, *op. cit.*, p. 277.
6 Information supplied to the author. Attempts were made by Partisans to save the Ponte della Vittoria and the alla Carraia. (*See* Barbieri, *op. cit.*, p. 304.) *See also* Enzo Enriques Agnoletti, *Perché i ponti di Firenze non furono difesi?*, *Il Ponte*, I (1945), pp. 58–63, and Frankovich, *op. cit.*, Appendix V, pp. 309–312. The Allied broadsheet, *Italia Combatte*, of August 1st 1944, urged Partisans north of the city to stay behind the German lines.
7 Kesselring, *op. cit.*, p. 309. In a manifesto entitled *A Crime* circulated by the Germans, General Alexander was accused of refusing to treat Florence as an open city. Giovanni Favilli, *Il Ponte* 9, September 1945, p. 1357, "Diario familiare di Firenze assediata".
8 Hartt, *op. cit.*, p. 46.
9 Information to the author.
10 Hitler's anger must have been very short-lived, because barely three weeks later, just before the liberation of Paris, he ordered General Speidel to destroy all the Paris bridges and other important installations "even if artistic monuments are

destroyed thereby". *See* William Shirer, *The Rise and Fall of the Third Reich*, footnote, p. 1085. Speidel did not obey this order.

11 Information supplied to the author. Sir Terence did say, however, that General Alexander was concerned to preserve the bridges both for military and aesthetic reasons. "He badly needed all the bridges intact," Sir Terence observed. "In cases like this one must forego the military advantages. If the Allies had acted on the principle which prompted Kesselring to blow them (the bridges) up behind him they would have long before bombed the bridges, together with all the other less important ones in Italy, as part of their 'interdiction' programme, but they did not for obvious reasons, and Kesselring should have spared them too."

12 AOK 14th's Army's war diary. *See* chapter 17, note 20 above.

13 Comnène, *op. cit.*, p. 59.

14 Hartt, *op. cit.*, pp. 45–46.

15 *The Times* special correspondent, August 5th 1944.

16 *New York Times*, August 5th 1944.

17 Supplement to the *London Gazette*, *op. cit.*, p. 2939. General Alexander also made the interesting observation that: "As I have already explained (*ibid.*, p. 2916, footnote), it had been found by experience that the destruction of bridges caused very much more embarrassment to the enemy than the previous policy of attacking marshalling yards." Kesselring may have also shared this "experience" since he was fully aware that the Ponte Santa Trinita was capable of bearing heavier traffic than the narrow Ponte Vecchio.

18 Information supplied to the author.

19 *Sunday Times*, March 12th 1961. This passage is omitted from *The Alexander Memoirs, 1940–1945*, edited by John North, Cassell, 1962, p. 135. (Note: the passage is taken from the serialisation of the above which appeared in the *Sunday Times*.)

20 Calamandrei, *op. cit.*, *Il Ponte*, 1954, pp. 1312–1315.

21 Information supplied to the author by Dr Gizdulich.

22 Berenson, *op. cit.*, p. 345.

20 ALBA E SERENA

1 Berenson, *op. cit.*, p. 362.

2 Hartt, *op. cit.*, p. 49.

3 The *Manchester Guardian*'s special correspondent, August 9th 1944.

4 *Daily Express*, August 14th 1944.

5 Frankovich, *op. cit.*, p. 284.

6 Delzell, *op. cit.*, p. 410. *See also* C. R. S. Harris, *Allied Military Administration of Italy*

1943–1945, HMSO, 1957, p. 187 *seq.*
7 M. McCarthy, *op. cit.*, p. 23.
8 Frankovich, *op. cit.*, pp. 287–288.
9 Delzell, *op. cit.*, p. 410.
10 Frankovich, *op. cit.*, p. 291.
11 *Ibid.*, p. 278.
12 Hartt, *op. cit.*, p. 79. This information was given to him by Colonel Michie, the American Civil Affairs Officer, Florence, having passed into General Clark's Fifth Army zone of operations after August 18th 1944.
13 Calamandrei, *Il Ponte*, September 1954, *op. cit.*, p. 1315.
14 Hartt, *op. cit.*, pp. 68–69.
15 *Ibid.*, p. 99.
16 Consul Wolf's personal file was among the captured German Foreign Office material consulted by the author.
17 Shortly before the end of the war, General Wilhelm Harster, head of the Gestapo in Italy, informed Ambassador Rahn: "But for you, your Excellency, Consul Wolf would have been in a concentration camp long ago." This tribute did not appear on the Consul's personal file.
18 Barbara Barclay Carter, *op. cit.*, p. 124.
19 una lotta nel suo corso, *op. cit.*, p. 258 *seq.*
20 Information supplied by Avv. Boniforti. Frankovich, *op. cit.*, p. 337, states that Carità was killed before he could draw his revolver.
21 Deakin, *op. cit.*, p. 798. Also Rodolfo Graziani, *Ho Difeso La Patria*, Garzanti, Rome, 1948, p. 493.
22 Dr Rahn to the author. Deakin in his version suggests that the gift of the pistol may have been an invitation to Graziani to commit suicide "as Cavallero had done". For Marshal Cavallero's suicide *see* Deakin, *op. cit.*, pp. 536–537.
23 The Archbishop of Genoa, Giuseppe Siri, in a personal letter to von Etzdorf, December 9th 1947, expressed his appreciation and admiration for the great assistance which the former Consul-General gave in saving the city from destruction. *See also* Pietro Secchia and Filippo Frassati, *La Resistenza e gli alleati*, Feltrinelli, Milan, 1962, p. 403.
24 Kesselring, *op. cit.*, pp. 288–289.
25 Deakin, *op. cit.*, p. 802.
26 Information supplied by Dr Wolf to the author.
27 Cardinal Ildefonso Schuster, Archbishop of Milan, *My Last Meeting with Mussolini*, account given in *Mussolini: Memoirs*, *op. cit.*, pp. 258–259.
28 Raffaele Cadrona, *La riscossa*, Rizzoli, Milan, 1948, p. 252.
29 Schuster, *Mussolini: Memoirs*, *op. cit.*, p. 260.
30 Comnène, *op. cit.*, p. 74. In

a later statement (May 28th 1947) the Cardinal joined the name of Dr Rudolf Rahn who, he said, had assisted the Consul in all his endeavours, particularly in their efforts to have Florence declared an open city.

31 Maestro Vittorio Gui in a letter to Dr Hanna Kiel, attested by the Swiss Consul, Carlo Steinhäuslin, January 15th 1946. Further, Maestro Gui said: "It seems strange that the authorities should not have been more exactly informed about this *real gentleman* (Maestro Gui's italics) while so many persons who are really guilty have managed to clear themselves."

Berenson's affidavit dated January 16th 1946 is also of some interest. In this he stated: "I, the undersigned, Bernard Berenson, citizen of the United States of America, member of the American Academy of Arts and Letters, resident in Florence, declare that during the German occupation of Florence, when as an enemy alien of Jewish extraction, I ran considerable risks, I owed my safety largely to Consul Gerhard Wolf's humane attitude towards me. This was all the meritorious on his part as we had never met or had any previous communications. (Berenson refers to Consul Wolf's efforts on his behalf prior to their meeting on November 7th 1943, described in Chapter 8.) Moreover the safety of my art treasures and library, both known to all students of art history as among the most remarkable of private collections, was equally due to Consul Wolf's efforts in turning off the agents of Goering and Co. from their pursuit.

I can affirm likewise that what Consul Wolf did for me he did for many others, indeed for all others whom he could help to save from the Gestapo and the Fascist secret police."

32 Miss Hutton to the author.

33 Signor Jean-Léon Steinhäuslin to the author. On this occasion Cardinal Elia Dalla Costa and N. P. Comnène also received the freedom of the city. The award to Bernard Berenson came some months later. Friedrich Kriegbaum had been given the award posthumously, shortly after his death in an air-raid of September 1943.

34 Professor La Pira to the author.

35 Report in *The Times*, March 17th 1958. The preparatory work of reconstructing the Ponte Santa Trinita had taken some ten years (*see Comunitä, op. cit.*). Stones taken from the original quarries in the Boboli Gardens used by Ammannati were excavated and painstakingly shaped by hand. The four statues of the Seasons, large

sections of which were found scattered over the Lungarni and in the Arno, were also reconstructed. Only the head of Primavera was missing. Rumours abounded that an American Negro had taken it during the fighting in the city: others claimed that an Australian or New Zealand soldier had carted it away in his knapsack. The Parker Pen Company of America offered three thousand dollars for its recovery. Seventeen years later divers recovered Primavera's head near the Ponte Vecchio. (*See* McCarthy, *op. cit.*, pp. 52–55). According to *The Times* report of October 7th 1961, "Professor Raffaello Ramat, in charge of fine arts, said a first examination of the head and comparison with photographs of the original indicates that it was that of the statue. A plaster cast is being made to see whether the head fits the rest of the statue."

The reconstructed bridge was opened in March 1958 in the presence of the then Prime Minister of Italy, Adone Zoli, by the mother of the Resistance heroine, a Red Cross sister, attached to the "G.L." division of the Action Party, killed on August 21st 1944 (Frankovich, *op. cit.*, pp. 289–290). The reconstructed Ponte Santa Trinita was blessed by Cardinal-Archbishop Elia dalla Costa. The Consul himself was in Porto Alegre, Brazil, completing his tour of duty as Consul-General in that city before his retirement.

# INDEX